Madame Alexander

2009
Collector's Dolls
Price Guide
#34

Linda
Crowsey

COLLECTOR BOOKS
A Division of Schroeder Publishing Co., Inc.

On the front cover:
Left — Cissette Queen, 10", 1963, #765, $650.00.
Center — Cissette, 10", 1958, rare outfit, $650.00.
Right — Cissette FAO Schwarz Special, 10", 1958, #836, $950.00.

Cover design by Beth Summers
Book design by Allan Ramsey

COLLECTOR BOOKS
P.O. Box 3009
Paducah, Kentucky 42002-3009

www.collectorbooks.com

Copyright © 2009 Linda Crowsey

The current values in this book should be used only as a guide. They are
not intended to set prices, which vary from one section of the country to
another. Auction prices as well as dealer prices vary greatly and are affected
by condition as well as demand. Neither the author nor the publisher assumes
responsibility for any losses that might be incurred as a result of consulting
this guide.

Searching for a Publisher?

We are always looking for people knowledgeable within their fields. If you feel
that there is a real need for a book on your collectible subject and have a large
comprehensive collection, contact Collector Books.

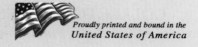

Proudly printed and bound in the
United States of America

Dedication

I dedicate *Madame Alexander 2009 Collector's Doll Price Guide #34* to my six grandchildren. Timothy, Megan, Katherine, Miranda, Jack, and Daniel have brought much joy to my life. Our family sometimes has to change family celebrations because of doll events and conventions. I appreciate their love and patience. They love to see and hear about the dolls and events. I love you very much!

My grandchildren
Left to right: Jack, Megan holding Daniel, Miranda holding a picture of Timothy who is in the Air Force, and Katherine.

Madame Alexander Doll Club

For membership information, write to:
Madame Alexander Doll Club (M.A.D.C.)
P.O. Box 2739
New York, NY 10027-9998
www.madc.org

Photo Credits

Gary Green, Susan Huey, Shirley Kronkowski, Ann McCurdy, Christine McWilliams, Gayle Morton, Terri Queen, Helen Thomas, Ben Thomas, Mike Way.

The Madame Alexander Doll Company

Madame Beatrice Alexander Behrman and her husband Phillip Behrman founded the Madame Alexander Company in 1923 and began manufacturing dolls in New York City. Beatrice's father, Maurice Alexander owned the first doll hospital in New York City where he repaired broken dolls as well as sold new ones. He also sold fine porcelain pieces. Madame grew up seeing the happiness that dolls brought to children. During WWI when dolls were hard to obtain from Europe Madame began making cloth dolls. The operation soon grew to a point where a factory space was needed. Madame Alexander used only the best materials and became known for making the finest of dolls. Madame Alexander made wonderful composition dolls and began making hard plastic dolls in 1948. Some of the most highly prized dolls today were made during these years as well as during the 1950s. The golden era of the 1950s produced the Glamour Girls, Beaux Arts, Coronations Set, Me and My Shadow Series, Bible Characters, and many more. Cissy, Wendy, Cissette, and Lissy dolls were designed during the 1950s and are timeless as they comprise a large part of the dolls in the line today.

The Alexander Company under the leadership of President Gale Jarvis continues to bring new dolls into the line and win awards for their dolls. The 2008 line includes Raggedy Ann and Andy, Holly Hobbie, Madeline, Eloise, Fancy Nancy, Strawberry Shortcake, Dr. Seuss dolls, Ugly Betty, Desperate Housewives, as well as introducing Tiny Betty in a variety of designs back to the line.

The Alexander Company is located at 615 W. 131st Street, New York City. This location includes the doll hospital, showroom, doll store, and the Heritage Gallery where a huge variety of vintage Alexanders are on display. Collectors may contact the company for tours and also for birthday parties that can be held on the premises. I can highly recommend visiting the Alexander Company. The Alexander staff makes certain that each collector has a memorable time. It is absolutely the ultimate place for Alexander Collectors to see and learn about new as well as vintage Alexanders.

Linda Crowsey pictured in a window box with a wrist tag at the Alexander Doll Company office in New York City. Dolls are packaged in similar window boxes.

4

What Is a Price Guide?

Price guides must be based upon values for a perfect doll, since all collectors need accurate prices for insurance purposes. Insurance companies and postal services must have a way to determine the value of a damaged or stolen doll. Collectors must also have a way to appraise and insure their collections. A price guide, while not the final word, is a starting point to determine the value of a doll. The prices listed are for perfect dolls. Imperfect dolls will bring considerably less than exceptional dolls, which collectors call "tissue mint." Original boxes are important because the information on the box helps determine the age and manufacturer of the doll. The prices quoted are for dolls without their boxes, prior to 1972. Prices for dolls from 1973 to present are for dolls with their original boxes. Prices of these dolls would be adjusted lower if they are missing their boxes. Boxes can be a fire hazard. It is possible to fold most boxes and store them inside a larger box and place the boxes in an airy, dry room. Collectors will pay a higher price for a doll in its original box. Beware of storing dolls for a long time in their boxes — clothing, wigs, and vinyl can fade or change colors. Also, vinyl dolls tend to become greasy or sticky when stored in their boxes.

The Wendy on the right is a straight leg walker, #442, 1955. She is an all original and "tissue mint" doll. The Wendy on the left has the wrong hairdo and shoes, and is the incorrect doll for the outfit. Her dress is faded and badly shelf worn. Wendy (right) is worth $800.00 while Wendy (left) is worth $100.00.

Perfect Dolls
❦ Complete outfit on correct doll
❦ Beautiful face color
❦ Clothes and doll in excellent condition
❦ Has all accessories, such as hats, etc.
❦ Clothes not laundered or ironed
❦ Hair in original set

Less Than Perfect Dolls
❦ Re-dressed or has part of original clothes
❦ Washed, cleaned, ironed clothes
❦ Stains, soil, faded, shelf dust, holes in fabric
❦ Faded face color
❦ Tag cut or missing
❦ Hair mussed or dirty

Exceptional Dolls
❦ Extremely rare doll
❦ Has wrist tag or original box
❦ Autographed by Madame Alexander
❦ Unique outfit or doll
❦ "Tissue mint" condition
❦ Has wardrobe or trunk
❦ Matched set of same year
(such as "Little Women")

There is no guarantee that any doll, antique or modern, will appreciate in price year after year. However, prices remain high on exceptional dolls, and always will.

Mold Marks

Mold marks can be the same for an extended period of time. For example, 14" Mary Ann dolls will be marked "1965" which is the first year the doll was made. From then to now, all Mary Ann dolls will be marked "1965." Another example is the 21" Jacqueline, first introduced in 1961. This doll has been used for the Portraits since 1965 and, up to now, still bears the 1961 date mark on the head. Determining the exact year can be difficult for that reason.

Doll Names

The dolls named after real people are listed with last name first (example: Bliss, Betty Taylor). Make-believe doll names will be listed with first name first (example: Tommy Snooks).

Abbreviations

h.p. – hard plastic
compo. – composition
FAD – factory altered dress
SLNW – straight leg non-walker
SLW – straight leg walker
BKW – bend knee walker
BK – bend knee
U.F.D.C. – United Federation of Doll Clubs
M.A.D.C. – Madame Alexander Doll Club
C.U. – Collectors United

Photo Captions

Listings highlighted in dark green correspond to a photo shown in the respective section.

Box Numbers

Order/box numbers for the 8" dolls with "0" prefix (example: 0742) were used in 1973 only. It must be noted the box numbers found with doll's name are from the Madame Alexander catalogs, but many dolls were placed in wrong boxes by the stores from which they were sold.

Auction Prices

Auction prices have little or no effect on general pricing for Madame Alexander dolls. Dolls often sell at auction for exorbitant prices. It is as simple as two or more people wanting the same item — the bidders just get carried away! Another reason is the rarity or the pristine condition of a doll. This type of doll is extremely difficult to find and warrants the high auction price.

The final word is Madame Alexander dolls have always been collectible and should continue to be. They should endure in time and value. Wise collectors purchase dolls that they really like rather than purchasing dolls that are rumored to go up in value. Then, even if the doll's value doesn't go up, the collector has a beautiful doll that he or she loves. I hope you will continue to build the collections you desire, be they of older dolls or the wonderful current dolls that become available each year.

8" Alexander-Kins, Wendy Ann, Wendy, or Wendy-Kin

1953 – 1976:
Has "Alex" on back of doll.

1953:
First year of production, straight leg, non-walker. Only year Quiz-Kins were produced with two buttons on their backs for the heads to nod "yes" or "no."

1954:
Straight leg walker.

1955:
Straight leg walker with no painted lashes under the eye.

1956 – 1965:
Bend knee walker.

1965 – 1972:
Bend knee, does not walk.

1973 – 1976:
Straight leg, non-walker with "Alex" on back of doll.

1977 – Present:
Has "Alexander" on back.

The Many Faces of Madame Alexander Dolls

Wendy Ann (composition)

Tiny and Little Betty

Princess Elizabeth

Maggie

Margaret (O'Brien)

Cissy

Elise (1950s – 1960s)

Lissy (1950s)

Cissette

Mary-Bel

Jacqueline

Mary Ann

Elise (1960s – 1980s)

Polly and Leslie

Nancy Drew

Wendy Ann – new 1988 face

Maggie Mixup (1960 – 1961)

Wendy Ann (1953 – 1965)

Active Miss — 18" h.p., 1954 only (Violet/Cissy)..$850.00
Adams, Abigail — 1976 – 1978, Presidents' Ladies/First Ladies Series, First Set (Mary Ann) ..$125.00
Adams, Louisa — 1976 – 1978, Presidents' Ladies/First Ladies Series, First Set (Louisa).......$100.00
Addams Family — #31130, 1997 – 1998, set of four dolls (8", 10") and Thing $200.00
    #31110, 1997 – 1998, 10" Gomez and Morticia...$115.00
    #31120, 1997 – 1998, 8" Wednesday and Pugsley...$110.00
Adorable Silk Victorian — 8", #26875, 2001, white dress $80.00
Africa — 8" h.p., #766, 1966 – 1971, BK (Wendy Ann) straight leg, #523 – 583, 1988 – 1992 ...$210.00
African Bride — 10", #28600, 2001, includes broom...$75.00
African Safari — 8", #33501, Caucasian, 2002, #33500, African-American, 2002, tan costume with lion ..$65.00
Agatha — 18" h.p. (Cissy)
    1954 only, Me and My Shadow Series, rose taffeta dress, excellent face color.................$1,900.00 up
    8" h.p. (Wendy Ann), #00308, 1953 – 1954, black top and floral gown ....$1,900.00 up
    10" Portrette, #1171, 1968 only, red velvet (Cissette)..$350.00
    21" Portrait, #2171, 1967, red gown (Jacqueline) $625.00
        #2297, 1974, rose gown with full length cape (Jacqueline) $425.00
        #2291, 1975, blue with white sequin trim (Jacqueline).....................................$350.00
        #2294, 1976, blue with white rickrack trim (Jacqueline)..................................$250.00
        #2230, 1979, 1980, lavender; #2230, 1981, turquoise blue (Jacqueline) $225.00
        #2230, 1981, turquoise blue (Jacqueline) $225.00
Age of Innocence — 10", #28400, 2001, dark blue vintage gown $100.00
Agnes — cloth/felt, 1930s...$750.00
Aladdin — 8" h.p., #482, 1993; #140482, 1994 only, Storybook Series.................................$50.00
Alaska — 8", #302, 1990 – 1992, Americana Series (Maggie smile face) $50.00
Albania — 8", straight leg, #526, 1987 only (Wendy Ann)...$55.00
Alcott, Louisa May — 14", #1529, 1989 – 1990, Classic Series (Mary Ann) $75.00
    8" h.p., #409, 1992 only, Storyland Series (Wendy Ann) $85.00
    8" h.p., #36760, 2003, long brown dress with black trim, book $85.00
    10", #47030, 2007, Cissette, ltd. to 500, blue plaid long dress..$135.00
Alegria — 10" h.p., #20118, 1996 Cirque du Soleil, silver outfit..$75.00
Alex — 16" plastic/vinyl
    Fashion Doll Editor-in-Chief, 2000, #25570, brown skirt, white sweater, camel coat.............$70.00
    Millennium Ball, 2000, #25580, ball gown with beading $125.00
    Museum Gala, 2000, #27280, gray sweater, beaded taffeta skirt...$100.00
    Runway Review, 2000 – 2002, #27275, black evening dress $70.00
    Magazine Launch, 2000, #27285, beaded jet black suit $70.00
    Alexandra Fairchild Ford, 2000, #26930, pink chiffon and taffeta dress $85.00
    Lunch at 2, 2000, #27290, gray crepe dress $75.00
    Woman of the Year, 2001 – 2002, #30640, stunning gold gown $125.00
    Tides, #30630, 2001 – 2002, BK, redhead $60.00
    Tides, #30620, 2001 – 2002, BK, blonde...$60.00
    Tides, #30625, 2001 – 2002, BK, brunette $60.00
    Book Tour, #31625, 2001 ....$125.00
    Mardi Gras, #31155, 2001 – 2002..$160.00
    Cyber Launch, #31215, 2001 ....$80.00
    Sunset Grille, #31165, 2001 – 2002..$75.00
    Milano, #31221, 2001 ....$80.00
    New Year's Eve, #28455, 2001 – 2002 ....$135.00
    Music Video Awards, #31220, 2001...$80.00
    Santa Baby, #30635, 2001, red dress, coat with Christmas room.......................................$225.00
    Paris, 2001 African-American Fashion Doll Grand Entrance, #31170, 2001 – 2002,
        stunning orange gown with lavender accents..$170.00
    La Concorde, #31175, 2001..$90.00
    Crocus, long gown, #33260, 2002 ....$90.00
    Newport, #33255, 2002 ....$80.00
    Breakfast at the Breakers, brunette, #33246; blonde, #33245; blonde, #33247, p.j's, robe........$75.00

Graphic Impact, #33605, 2002, two-piece black checked dress (Jadde) $80.00

VIP, #33265, 2002 (Paris), limited to 1,000 ....$80.00

Backstage Pass, #33270, 2002 (Paris) $85.00

Cherry Blossom, #33275, 2002 (Jadde) $80.00

Sedona, #33205, 2002 (Alex) $80.00

Houston Blues, #32181, 2002 (Alex) $85.00

Denver Days, #33210, 2002 (Alex) $85.00

Arabesque, #33215, 2002 (Alex), black silk and velvet gown $115.00

Twilight, #33225, 2002 (Alex), blue formal silk ball gown $115.00

Blue Maxe Jadde Lee, 2003, #36530, blue dress, limited to 750 ....$90.00

Sold Out Show Paris Williams, 2003, #36535, long lacy dress, limited to 750 ....$180.00

Back to the Basic Alexandra Fairchild Ford, #36250, black dress, hat, limited to 750 ....$80.00

Cheongsam Jadde Lee, 2003, #36520, pink short kimono, limited to 500 ....$110.00

Spotlight Paris Williams, #36235, black and white ball gown, limited to 500 ....$125.00

Dancing Til Dawn Alexandra Fairchild Ford, 2003, #37995, long ball gown $125.00

Bordeaux Alex, 2003, #36190, long wine gown, limited to 750 ....$110.00

Breathtaking Jadde, 2003, #36525, tan gown trimmed in faux fur, limited to 750 ....$125.00

Dots Alex, #36225, 2003, black dress with big dots at hem, limited to 750 ....$100.00

Bouquet Alex, 2003, #36210, pink sequin gown, limited to 750 ....$150.00

Dinner for Two Paris, 2003, #36545, black pants, cream suede jacket, limited to 750 ....$100.00

Firecracker Alex, 2003, #36195, red skirt, black top, limited to 750 ....$135.00

Red Label Alex, 2003, #36200, two outfits with red coat, limited to 750 ....$175.00

Fuchsia Jadde, 2003, #36740, fuchsia and black gown, limited to 750 ....$140.00

Camellia Paris, 2003, #36730, pink ball gown, limited to 750 ....$120.00

Betrayal Alex, 2003, #36755, long black gown and cape, limited to 750 ....$125.00

Greed Paris, 2003, #36715, ball gown, tiara, and candlestick, limited to 750 ....$125.00

Desire Jadde, 2003, #36720, red ball gown, dagger, limited to 750 ....$125.00

Red Carpet Alex, 2003, #36390, black sequin gown, limited to 750 ....$125.00

Amanda Fairchild, 2003, #36220, ball gown, limited to 500 ....$135.00

Strike a Pose, 2004, six hair colors, body suits $70.00

Alexandra Fairchild Ford, denim bathing suit, 2004 ....$60.00

Straight Cuts Jadde Lee, 16", #40185, 2005, silk top, skirt, architect's bag $85.00

Flirting with the Fifties Amanda Fairchild Ford, #40205, 2005, white hat, sheath dress $100.00

Elan's "It" Girl Suzette Morgan, #40225, 2005, jacket, pants, portfolio $85.00

Set for Style Alexandra Fairchild Ford, #40180, 2005, suit with dress coat $100.00

Fashion Fix Paris Williams, #40195, 2005, blue sweater dress with fringe $100.00

Power Play Sophia Cruz, #40190, 2005, white and red suit dress $100.00

Miami Modern Alexandra Fairchild Ford, #42285, 2006, pants, white coat, scarf $100.00

Looks and Luxury Amanda Fairchild, #42310, 2006, brown dress $100.00

Elegant Sunset Sofia Cruz, #42300, 2006, orange long gown $120.00

Flawless Finish Jadde Lee, #42290, 2006, silk dress, floral coat $110.00

World Class Suzette Morgan, #42305, 2006, pink print dress $110.00

Cocktail Chic Sienna Evans, #42295, 2006, black dress $110.00

True Romance Alexandra Fairchild Ford, bride gown $125.00

Sequins & Fur Holiday Rockette 1987, #47740, 2007, red bodysuit dance costume $110.00

Diamond Nights Suzette, #45870, navy blue long ball gown, fur stole $150.00

Beauty of the Moment Sofia Cruz, #45795, cocktail dress with black lace jacket $120.00

Rising Star Jadde Lee, #45800, 2007, green halter gown $110.00

Unmatched Elegance Amanda Fairchild, #47120, 2007, black dress with white collar $130.00

Spring Is Blooming Sienna Evans, #45810, 2007, pink dress with roses $120.00

Travel with Style Alexander Fairchild Ford, #45790, 2007, black pants, long coat $120.00

Always a Lady Paris Williams, 16", #45805, 2007, striped dress, straw hat $120.00

Flity 30s Glamour Suzette Morgan, 16", #48910, 2008, white long gown $150.00

40s New York Fashion Plate Amanda Fairchild, 16", #48915, 2008, checked skirt, brown $150.00

Hopelessly Fabulous 50s Sienna Evans, 16", #48920, 2008, pink halter dress, fur stole $150.00

Captivating Swashbuckler Shadow, 16", #48395, 2008, black pants, red coat, parrot $300.00

Alexander-kin, 8", SLW, #452, 1954. Known as "Plane Trip." Polished cotton dress with felt jacket and hat. $475.00 up.

Alexander-Kins — 7½" – 8" h.p., must have excellent face color (also referred to as Wendy, Wendy Ann, or Wendy-Kin). If doll is not listed here, see regular listing for name. (Add more for mint or mint in box dolls. Special hairdos are higher priced.)

Straight leg non-walker, 1953 (Add more for Quiz-Kins.)

Coat/hat (dress)	$650.00 up
Cotton dress, organdy or cotton pinafore, hat, green	$550.00 up
Dresser, doll, wardrobe, mint	$3,200.00 up
Easter doll	$950.00 up
Felt jackets, pleated skirt dresses	$550.00 up
Garden Party long gown	$1,400.00 up
Jumper, one-piece bodysuit	$375.00
Nude, perfect doll (excellent face color)	$375.00
Organdy dress, cotton or organdy pinafore, hat	$575.00 up
Satin dress, organdy or cotton pinafore, hat or taffeta dress, organdy pinafore	$650.00
Sleeveless satin dress, organdy or cotton pinafore	$450.00
Robe, nightgown or p.j.'s	$300.00
Wendy Gift Set, window box, extra clothes	$2,800.00 up

Straight leg walker, 1954 – 1955, must have good face color.
(Add more for mint or mint in box dolls.)

Basic doll in box, panties, shoes, socks	$525.00
Coat, hat (dress)	**$475.00 up**
Cotton or taffeta dress, pinafore, hat	$475.00 up
Cotton school dress	$375.00 up
Day in Country	$975.00 up
Garden Party, long gown	$1,400.00 up
Jumper dress with blouse effect, any material	$475.00 up
Maypole Dance	$600.00
Nightgown, robe, or p.j.'s	$300.00
Organdy party dress, hat	$550.00 up
Riding Habit	$375.00 up
Sailor dress	$950.00 up
Sleeveless organdy dress or mint swimsuits	$375.00 each
Taffeta/satin/nylon party dress/hat	$575.00 up

Bend knee walker, 1956 – 1965, must have good face color.
(Add more for mint or mint in box dolls.)
"Alexander-Kin" dropped in 1963 and "Wendy Ann" used through 1965.

Nude (excellent face color)	$175.00
Basic doll in box, panties, shoes, and socks (mint in box)	$475.00
Car coat set	$1,700.00
Cherry Twin	$1,600.00 up
Coat, hat, dress	$450.00 up
Cotton dress, cotton pinafore, hat	$450.00
Cotton, taffeta, or satin dress, organdy pinafore, hat	$475.00 up
Easter Egg, doll, 1965, 1966 only	$1,500.00 up
Felt jacket, pleated skirt, dress, cap or hat	$425.00 up
First Dancing Dress (gown)	$800.00 up
Flower girl	$900.00 up
French braid, cotton dress, 1965	$650.00
June Wedding	$900.00 up
Long party dress	**$800.00 up**
Nightgown, robe	$275.00

Neiman-Marcus (clothes must be on correct doll with correct hairdo)

Doll in case with all clothes	$1,400.00 up
Name of store printed on dress material	$700.00
Two-piece playsuit, navy with red trim	$650.00 up
Robe, navy (no doll)	$100.00

Alexander-kin, BKW, #376, 1957. Variation of first long party dress. $800.00 up.

Red coat, lined with blue stripe (no doll) $125.00
Nude, perfect doll with excellent face color, bend knee, non-walker $85.00
Organdy dress, hat, 1965 .... $475.00 up
Organdy dress, organdy pinafore, hat .... $500.00 up
Riding habit, boy or girl $350.00
Riding habit, checked pants, girl, 1965, boy, 1965 .... $375.00
Sewing Kit, doll, 1965, 1966 only .... $950.00 up
Skater .... $750.00 up
Sundress **$375.00**
Swimsuits, beach outfits $325.00
Taffeta or nylon party dress, hat .... $475.00 up
Tennis $450.00

Alexander Rag Time Dolls — cloth, 1938 – 1939 only .... $850.00 up
Algeria — 8" straight leg, #528, 1987 – 1988 only (Maggie) $50.00
Alice — 18" h.p., 1951 only, saran wig to waist (Maggie) $750.00
Alice and Her Party Kit — 1965 only, included case, wardrobe, wigs (Mary Ann) $700.00
Alice (in Wonderland) — 16" cloth, 1930 flat face, eyes painted to side $875.00
    1933 formed mask face $650.00
    7" compo., 1930s (Tiny Betty) $425.00
    9" compo., 1930s (Little Betty) $425.00
    11" – 14" compo., 1936 – 1940 (Wendy Ann) .... $425.00 – 525.00
    13" compo., 1930s, has swivel waist (Wendy Ann) $425.00
    14½" – 18" compo., 1948 – 1949 (Margaret) .... $450.00 – 850.00
    21" compo., 1948 – 1949 (Margaret, Wendy Ann) $950.00
    14" h.p., 1950 (Maggie) $750.00
    17" – 23" h.p., 1949 – 1950 (Maggie and Margaret) ..... $600.00 – 950.00
    15", 18", 23" h.p., 1951 – 1952 (Maggie and Margaret) .. $450.00 – 950.00
    14" h.p. with trousseau, 1951 – 1952 (Maggie) .... $1,600.00 up
    15" h.p., 1951 – 1952 (Maggie and Margaret) .... **$650.00 up**
    17" h.p., 1949 – 1950 (Maggie and Margaret) .... $700.00 up
    23" h.p., 1942 – 1952 (Maggie and Margaret) .... $850.00 up
    29" cloth/vinyl, 1952 (Barbara Jane) .... $700.00 up
    8" h.p., #465 – #590, 1955 – 1956 (Wendy Ann) .... $800.00 up
    8", #494, Storyland Series, blue/white eyelet pinafore, 1990 – 1992 ... $65.00
        #492, 1993, #140492, 1994 blue/white with red trim ... $65.00
    8" h.p., 1972 – 1976, Disney crest colors (Disneyland, Disney World) ... $300.00
    8" h.p., blue with lace trim, organdy pinafore, 1995 .... $65.00
    8" h.p., #13000, 1997 – 1998, Alice with calendar, blue party dress,
        gold crown, #13001, 1999 – 2000 .... $65.00
    12", Prom Party Set, 1963 (Lissy) .... $1,100.00 up
    14" plastic/vinyl, #1452 to 1974, #1552, 1966 – 1992,
        Literature & Classic Series (Mary Ann) $70.00
    14" plastic/vinyl, #87001, 1996 Storyland Friends $80.00
    14" h.p., #25905 (Margaret), 2000 – 2001, blue with white dot dress, organdy pinafore ... $110.00
    18", #16001, 1996 Rag Doll Series (cloth doll) .... not available for sale
    8", #30665, 2001 – 2005, includes plush rabbit, eyelet pinafore, blue dress ... $50.00
    5", #36295, 2004, vinyl, with rabbit $25.00
    8", #33545, 2005, Wendy-Kin Wood with white rabbit $260.00
    8", #42425, 2006 – 2008, blue dress, white pinafore $50.00
All-American Wendy — 8", #35600, 2003, patriotic outfit, bear $65.00
All-American Beauty — 10", #45710, Cissette, 2007, 1940s pin-up outfit, red shorts, blue top .. $100.00
Allison — 18" cloth/vinyl, 1990 – 1991 .... $60.00
All My Love — 8", #40945, 2006, white dress, red heart box $65.00
    8", #42425, 2006, blue dress, eyelet trimmed pinafore $50.00
All Star — 8" h.p., #346 – 346-1, Americana Series, 1993 white or black, 1994 white only ... $50.00
All Wrapped Up Christmas — 8", #45345, 2006, red and gold dress $60.00

Alexander-kin, BKW, 1965. Wendy in a school dress. $375.00.

Alice in Wonderland, 15", 1951 – 1952. Mint and all original. Close-up of a mint Maggie face. $650.00 up.

Aloha — 8", #38870, 2004 – 2005, Latin doll, grass skirt, surfboard.................................$85.00
Alpine Boy and Girl — 1992 (see Christmas Shoppe under Special Events/Exclusives)
Altar Boy — 8" h.p., #311, 1991 only, Americana Series $55.00
Amanda — 8" h.p., #489, 1961 only, Americana Series, burnt orange,
    lace trim (Wendy Ann) .... $2,000.00 up
American Babies — 16" – 18" cloth, 1930s ....$150.00 – 375.00
American Beauty — 10" Portrette, #1142, 1991 – 1992, all pink $65.00
American Farm Couple — 8", 1997, #22160, 1930s rural America............................$100.00
American Flag Wendy — 8", 2001, Caucasian, African-American................................$60.00
American Girl — 7" – 8" compo., 1938 (Tiny Betty)..$385.00
    9" – 11" compo., 1937 (Little Betty, Wendy Ann) ....$325.00 – 550.00
    8" h.p., #388, #788, 1962 – 1963, became "McGuffey Ana" in 1964 – 1965 (Wendy Ann).....$350.00
American Indian — 9" compo., 1938 – 1939 (Little Betty) $375.00
American Legend, An — 10", #12510, 1999, with hardcover book with doll (Cissette) $200.00
    #17330, 1999 – 2002, hardcover book, no slipcase $40.00
    #12520, 1999 – 2002, deluxe book, slipcase $55.00
American Parade — 8", #36465, 2003, black and red checked dress, with bear on tricycle $75.00
American Sweetheart — 8", #39110, 2004, red skirt..$50.00
American Tots — 16" – 21" cloth, dressed in child's fashions ....$275.00 – 550.00
American Women's Volunteer Service (A.W.V.S.) — 14" compo., 1942 (Wendy Ann).. $850.00 up
Amish Boy — 8" h.p., BK, #727, 1966 – 1969, Americana Series (Wendy Ann) $375.00
Amish Girl — 8" h.p., BK, #726, 1966 – 1969, Americana Series (Wendy Ann) $375.00
Amy — **(see Little Women)**
Amy Goes to Paris Trunk Set — 8", #14635, 1996 ....$200.00
Amy the Bride — 10", #14622, 1996, ivory lace dress..$85.00
Anastasia — 10" Portrette, #1125, 1988 – 1989 (Cissette) $65.00
    14" (see M.A.D.C. under Special Events/Exclusives)
    8" h.p., 2003 – 2004, #35695, white dress, blue bodice, gold locket...............$75.00
Anatolia — 8" straight leg, #524, 1987 only..$60.00
Angel — 8", in pink, blue, off-white gowns (Wendy and Maggie) .... $950.00 up
    Baby Angel — 8" h.p., #480, 1955, multi-layered chiffon wings (Wendy Ann)................. $975.00 up
    Guardian Angel — 8", #480, 1954 only (Wendy Ann) .... $800.00 up
    Guardian Angel — 8", #618, 1961 (Maggie smile face)............................. $800.00 up
    Guardian Angel — 10", #10602, 1995, first in series, all pink with white wings...................$100.00
    Pristine Angel — 10", #10604, 1995, second in series, white with gold trim...........................$100.00
    Angel of Bliss — 10", #32155, 2000, long pink dress, white wings..........................$100.00
Angel and 8" Music Box Créche — 8", #19530, 1997 – 2000, Nativity set $185.00
Angel Face — (see Shirley's Doll House under Special Events/Exclusives)
Angel Harmony Tree Topper — 8", #39465, 2005, gold wings $100.00
Angelique Innocence Angel — 10", #35855, 2003, white gown, wings...........................$135.00
Angel Tree Topper — (see Tree Topper)
Anglund, Joan Walsh — Joy, 10", #28805..$35.00
Anna and the King of Siam — 8", 1996, #14656, sold as set................................$125.00
Anna Ballerina — 18" compo., 1940, Pavlova (Wendy Ann) .... $950.00 up
Annabelle — 14" – 15" h.p., 1951 – 1952 only, Kate Smith's stories of Annabelle (Maggie) $700.00
    14" – 15" trousseau/trunk, 1952 only, FAO Schwarz (Maggie) .... $1,500.00 up
    18" – 23" h.p., 1951 – 1952 (Maggie) .... $750.00 up
Annabelle at Christmas — (see Belk & Leggett under Special Events/Exclusives)
Anna Karenina — 21" Portrait, #2265, 1991 (Jacqueline)................................$275.00
    10", #21900 (Cissette) bustle dress, 1998 – 1999 ....$90.00
    10", #21910 (Cissette) trunk set, doll, three outfits, 1998 – 1999........................$185.00
Anne of Green Gables — 14", #1530, 1989 – 1990 only (Mary Ann)..........................$95.00
    14", #1579, 1992 – 1994, Goes to School, with trunk/wardrobe (Louisa/Jennifer)................$150.00
    14", #1570 in 1993 only, #261501 in 1995, Arrives at Station $85.00
    14", 1993, Becomes the Teacher $85.00
    8" h.p., 1994 – 1995, #260417, At the Station (Wendy Ann), 1994, #260418 ....$85.00

8" h.p., #26423, 1995, concert dress..$95.00
8" h.p., #26421, 1995, trunk playset...$225.00
8" h.p., #13830, 1998 – 1999, floral dress, drawstring bag, straw hat...............$75.00
8" h.p., #36115, 2003 – 2004, brown print dress, straw hat.............................$75.00
Ann Estelle — 8", #17600, 1999 – 2001, Mary Engelbreit sailor outfit $70.00
Annie Laurie — 14" compo., 1937 (Wendy Ann) .... $675.00 up
    17" compo., 1937 (Wendy Ann) $925.00
Annie the Artist — 20", #35001, 1996, artist outfit, crayons ....not available for sale
Antiqua — 8", #45215, 2006, African-American, blue skirt, hat $55.00
Antique Chaos the Bear and Wendy — 8", #36420, 2003 – 2004, 5" bear $90.00
Anniversary Bouquet — 8", #36625 (Wendy), 2003 ....**$85.00**
Antoinette — 21" compo., 1946, extra make-up, must be mint (Wendy Ann) .... $2,300.00 up
Antoinette, Marie — 21", 1987 – 1988 only, multi-floral with pink front insert $350.00
Antony, Mark — 12", #1310, 1980 – 1985, Portraits of History (Nancy Drew) $55.00
Ants Go Marching, The — 8", #39920, 2005 – 2006, with two ants $70.00
Apple a Day, An — 8", #38530, 2004 – 2005, doctor outfit with chart, etc $75.00
Apple Annie of Broadway — 8" h.p., 1953 – 1954 (Wendy Ann) .... $1,100.00 up
Apple of Madame's Eye — 8", #41980, 2006, apple dress, basket of apples.............$90.00
Apple Picking — 8", #33025, 2002 (Maggie), denim dress, basket of apples $60.00
Apple Pie — 14", #1542, 1991 only, Doll Classics (Mary Ann).........................$65.00
Apple Tree — 8", #13290, 2000 – 2001, dressed as a tree trunk with leaves and apples $75.00
April — 14", #1533, 1990 – 1991, Doll Classics (Mary Ann and Jennifer)..............$70.00
April in Paris — 8", #42530, 2006, pink outfit, beret $70.00
April Showers Bring May Flowers — 8", #13480, 1998 – 1999, pink taffeta and lace, parasol $80.00
Aristocrats — 8", #45915, 2007, purple fur, plush cats $90.00
Aquarius — 8", #21310, 1998, orange and gold mermaid costume $80.00
Argentine Boy — 8" h.p., BKW and BK, #772, 1965 only (Wendy Ann) $375.00
Argentine Girl — 8" h.p., BK, #0771-571, 1965 – 1972 (Wendy Ann)....................$125.00
    BKW, #771 (Wendy Ann) $140.00
    8" h.p., straight legs, #571, 1973 – 1976, marked "Alex" $55.00
    8" h.p., straight legs, #571, 1976 – 1986 (1985 – 1986 white face).................$50.00
Argyle Twist Total Moves Wendy — 8", 2004, #38800 ....$75.00
Ariel — 9", #37810, 2005 – 2007, vinyl, mermaid outfit, ball gown...................$35.00
Aries — 8", #21330, 1998, gray furry ram outfit....................................$85.00
Armenia — 8", #507, 1989 – 1990 (Wendy Ann), #46320, 2007, red veil.................$60.00
Arriving in America — 8" h.p., #326, 1992 – 1993 only, Americana Series (Wendy Ann).........$60.00
Artie — 12" plastic/vinyl, 1962, sold through FAO Schwarz (Smarty) $275.00
Artiste Wendy — 8", #31250, 1998 – 1999, pink smock and black beret $70.00
Asakusa Ichimaru — 10", #42090, 2006, Japanese kimono $125.00
Ashley — 8", #628, 1990 only, Scarlett Series, tan jacket, hat $125.00
    8" h.p., #633, 1991 – 1992 only, Scarlett Series, as Confederate officer............$125.00
Ashley Rose — 14", #34335, 2002 – 2003, African-American, print dress $80.00
Astor — 9" early vinyl toddler, 1953 only, gold organdy dress and bonnet.............$150.00
Astrological Month Dolls — 14" – 17" compo., 1938 (Wendy) $525.00
A-Tisket-A-Tasket — 8", #34315, 2002 – 2003, pink dress, white pinafore, basket $70.00
Aunt Agatha — 8" h.p., #434, 1957 (Wendy Ann), checked taffeta gown.........................$1,400.00 up
Aunt Betsy — cloth/felt, 1930s..$900.00
Auntie Em — 8" h.p., #14515, 1995 only, Wizard of Oz Series, 2006, #39910............$60.00
Aunt March — 8", #14621, 1996 ....$70.00
Aunt Pitty Pat — 14" – 17" compo., 1939 (Wendy Ann), from *Gone with the Wind* .... $1,500.00 up
    8" h.p., #435, 1957 (Wendy Ann), from Gone with the Wind .... **$1,600.00 up**
    8" h.p., straight leg, #636, 1991 – 1992, Scarlett Series $85.00
    8" h.p., #33465, 2002, blue dress, black lace trim $85.00
Austen, Jane — 10", #41560, 2007, Cissette, long white dress $140.00
Australia — 8" only (Wendy Ann) $55.00
    8" h.p., #35965, 2003 – 2005, kangaroo skirt, binoculars, plush kangaroo................$85.00

Anniversary Bouquet, 8", #36625, 2003 (Wendy). $85.00.

Ashley, 8", #633, 1991 – 1992 (Wendy). Confederate officer uniform, Scarlett Series. $125.00.

Aunt Pitty Pat, 8", #435, BKW, 1957 (Wendy). Taffeta overdress over a checked taffeta skirt. A very hard find doll. $1,600.00 up.

Austria Boy* — 8" h.p., 1974 – 1989 (Wendy Ann), straight legs, #599 – #533, 1973 – 1975, marked "Alex" $60.00
  #599, 1976 – 1989, marked "Alexander $55.00
Austria Girl* — 8" h.p., 1974 – 1993 (Wendy Ann) straight legs, #598, 1973 – 1975, marked "Alex" $60.00
  #598 – #532, 1976 – 1990, marked "Alexander," 1994 only, #110539 (Maggie) $55.00
Autumn — 14", 1993, Changing Seasons doll with four outfits $85.00
  5" porcelain, #25860, 2000, brown dress and jacket, black hat $50.00
Autumn Afternoon — 8", 45850, 2007, print dress $80.00
Autumn in N.Y. — (see First Modern Doll Club under Special Events/Exclusives)
Autumn Leaves — 14", 1994, Classic Dolls $75.00
  8", #42840, 2006, brown dress, Chaos bear $85.00
Avril, Jane — 10" (see Marshall Fields under Special Events/Exclusives)
Baa Baa Black Sheep — 8", #34020, 2002 – 2003, black polka dot outfit, white hat...............$75.00
Babbie — cloth with long thin legs, inspired by Katharine Hepburn ....$1,000.00 up
  16" cloth child doll, 1934 – 1936...$800.00
  14" h.p. (Maggie) ....$800.00 up
Babette —10" Portrette, #1117, 1988 – 1989, short black dress (Cissette) $55.00
Babs — 20" h.p., 1949 (Maggie) $850.00
Babsie Baby — compo./cloth, moving tongue $550.00
Babsie Skater (roller) — 15", 1941 (Princess Elizabeth)..$850.00
Babs Skater — 18" compo. (Margaret) ....$1,300.00 up
  15" – 18" h.p., 1948 – 1950 (Margaret) ....$1,200.00 up
  21" h.p. ....$1,500.00 up
Baby Betty — 10" – 12" compo.,1935 – 1936 ....$300.00
Baby Brother and Sister — 20" cloth/vinyl, 1977 – 1979 (Mary Mine)...........................$125.00 ea.
  14", 1979 – 1982, reintroduced 1989 only..$65.00 ea.
Baby Clown — (see clown)
Baby Ellen — 14", 1965 – 1972 (black Sweet Tears) $125.00
Baby Genius — 11" all cloth, 1930s...$425.00
  11" – 12" compo./cloth, 1930s – 1940s ....$275.00 up
  16" compo./cloth, 1930s – 1940s..$275.00
  22" compo./cloth, 1940s..$475.00
  15", 18" h.p. head, vinyl limbs, 1949 – 1950 (some get sticky or turn dark).............$100.00 – 225.00
  21" h.p. head, vinyl limbs, 1952 – 1955...$350.00
  8" h.p./vinyl, 1956 – 1962 (see Little Genius)
Baby in Louis Vuitton — trunk/wardrobe or wicker basket with legs, any year .... $900.00 up
Baby Jane — 16" compo., 1935...$950.00 up
Baby Lynn — 20" cloth/vinyl, 1973 – 1976..$125.00
  14" cloth/vinyl, 1973 – 1976..$100.00
Baby Madison — 14", #29750, 1999, vinyl, with layette $75.00
Baby McGuffey — 22" – 24" compo., 1937 ....$325.00
  20" cloth/vinyl, 1971 – 1976...$125.00
  14" cloth/vinyl, 1972 – 1978...$100.00
Baby Precious — 14" cloth/vinyl, 1975 only...$125.00
  21" cloth/vinyl, 1974 – 1976...$150.00
Baby's Breath Flower Girl — 8", #42500, 2006, white dress with flowers...........................$75.00
Baby Shaver — 12" cloth h.p., 1941 – 1943, yellow floss wig, round painted eyes (Little Shaver).. $650.00 up
Baby Sister — 18", #30300, cloth, 2001 –2002, pink checked dress $50.00
Baby Snoopy Huggums — 8", #26440, 2002, Snoopy booties..$50.00
Bad Little Girl — 116" cloth, 1966 only, blue dress, eyes and mouth turned down, looking sad$250.00
Baker, Josephine — 10", #45960, 2007, Cissette, banana skirt, blue robe $130.00
Bali — 8" h.p., #533, 1993 only $55.00
Ballerina — (Also see individual dolls – Leslie, Margaret, etc.)
  9" compo., 1935 – 1941 (Little Betty) $375.00

*Formerly Tyrolean Boy and Tyrolean Girl

11" – 13", 1930s (Betty) $400.00
11" – 14" compo., 1936 – 1938 (Wendy Ann)...$450.00
17" compo., 1938 – 1941 (Wendy Ann) ....$700.00 up
21" compo., 1947, "Debra" ("Deborah") Portrait ballerina in mint condition
   (Wendy Ann) ....$8,500.00 up
   (Also see Enchanted Doll House under Special Events/Exclusives)
   (Also see M.A.D.C. under Special Events/Exclusives)
SLNW, 8" h.p., #354, 1953 – 1954, lavender, yellow, pink, or blue (Wendy Ann) .... $750.00 up
SLW, #454, 1955, lavender, yellow, pink, or white.................................$675.00 up
BKW, #564, 1954 – 1960, golden yellow ....$575.00 up
   #454, 1955, white ....$475.00 up
   #564, 1956, rose $675.00
   #564 – 631, 1956, yellow...$650.00
   #364, 1957, blue...$400.00
   #544, 1958, pink...$375.00
   #420, 1959, gold, #420, 1961, lavender..$700.00
   #640, 1964, pink...$350.00

Ballerina, 8", BKW, #730, 1965. Mint in box. Hard to find yellow ballerina. $350.00.

BK, #620 – 730, 1965 – 1972, yellow (BKW #730 1965 only) $350.00
   #440 – 730, 1962 – 1972, blue $250.00
   #440 – 730, 1962 – 1972, pink $175.00
   8" straight leg, #0730, #530, #430, 1973 – 1992 (1985 – 1987 white face).........$55.00
SLNW, #330, 1990 – 1991 (black or white dolls, 1991), Americana Series,
   white/gold outfit (Wendy Ann)..$60.00
   #331 – 331-1, 1992, black or white doll in pink/silver outfit (Wendy Ann) $60.00
   #331, 1993, white doll only, pink/silver outfit....................................$60.00
   #100331, 1994 – 1995, white doll, pink tutu.......................................$60.00
   #13900, 1998, lace tutu over pink tulle $60.00
   #17640, 1999 – 2000, blue Ballet Recital, wears silver crown.............$60.00
   #17660, 2000 – 2001, pink Ballet Class $55.00
   #17650, 1999 – 2000, lilac Ballet Recital, lilac and silver $65.00
   #17690, 1999 – 2000, pink Ballet Recital, pink knit outfit..................$65.00
   #25030, 2000, Irish Dream, green bodice, white tutu with shamrocks...................$70.00
   #26810, 2000, pink petal, light pink costume $60.00
   #35075, 8", Twirling Confetti Ballerina, 2004 – 2005, lavender tutu $50.00
   #35635, 8", The Red Shoes, 2004, white tutu, red shoes.....................$70.00
   #38560, 8", Plié Total Moves Wendy, 2004 – 2005, pink tutu..............$80.00
   #38620, 8", Land of Sweets Ballerina, 2004, gold tutu $85.00
   #38855, 8", 2004 – 2005, Caucasian, Ballet Lessons, with dog, bear, and cat $80.00
   #38856, 8", 2004 – 2005, African-American, Ballet Lessons, with dog, bear, and cat........$80.00
   #39100, 8", Tutu Cute, 2004 – 2006, white tutu, pastel top $75.00
   #38857, 8", 2004 – 2005, Asian, Ballet Lessons, with dog, bear, and cat $80.00
   #38875, Enchanted Garden Ballernia, 2005, pink petal costume.....................$70.00
   #40175, Encore Performance, 2005 – 2006, blue and white costume $75.00
   #40285, Polka Dot Plié, 2005 – 2006, pink costume.............................$65.00
   #45485, Marzipan Ballerina, 8", 2006, pink, green tutu $75.00
   #42635, 8", 2006, pink tutu, hippo, ostrich $80.00
   #42345, 8", 2007, Tiny Lilac Dancer $70.00
   #45995, 8", 2007 – 2008, Springtime Confection $50.00
   #45820, 8", 2007, Garden Recital Ballerina $75.00
   #42350, 8", 2007, Peach Pirouette $70.00
   #42085, 8", 2007 – 2008, Pink Shimmer Ballerina.............................$70.00
   #47925, 8", 2008, blue tutu, roses in hair, 2008, #47930, 8", lilac tutu $75.00
Autumn Ballerina, #30445, 5", 2002, porcelain, white tutu $55.00
Spring Ballerina, #30435, 5", 2002, porcelain, pink tutu $55.00
Summer Ballerina, #30440, 5" porcelain, 2002, green ballet costume...................$55.00
Winter Ballerina, #30450, 5" porcelain, 2002, white ballet costume $55.00

10" – 11" h.p., #813, 1957 – 1960, must have excellent face color (Cissette)......................$385.00 up

12", 1964 only (Janie) $275.00

12", 1989 – 1990, "Muffin" (Janie) $70.00

12", 1990 – 1992 only, Romance Collection (Nancy Drew) $60.00

12", 1993 only, lavender (Lissy) $135.00

14", 1963 only (Melinda) $275.00

15" – 18" h.p., 1950 – 1952, must have good face color (Margaret).....................$625.00 – 900.00

16½" h.p., 1957 – 1964, jointed ankles, knees, and elbows, must have good face color (Elise).. $450.00 up

    1957, yellow, rare $900.00

    1958, white $450.00

    1959, gold $475.00

    1960, pink, 1962, blue...$425.00

    1961, upswept hairdo, pink $500.00

    1963 – 1964 only, small flowers in 1963; large flowers in 1964 (Mary-Bel) (18" also Elise).. $400.00 up

16" plastic/vinyl, #38350, Principal Ballerina, 2004, white/gold tutu $150.00

16" plastic/vinyl, #38355, Dance Under the Stars, 2004, blue tutu $150.00

17" plastic/vinyl, 1967 – 1989, discontinued costume (Elise) $95.00

17" plastic/vinyl, 1990 – 1991, "Firebird" and "Swan Lake" (Elise) $100.00

17", 1966 – 1971 only (Leslie – black doll) $450.00

16", #22700, 2000 only, Classic Ballerina $125.00

16", #40410, 2005, Standing Ovation Ballerina, pink and green $175.00

16", #38350, 2005, Principal Ballernia, eyelet and organdy $175.00

16", #42355, 2006, Ballet Imperial, white and red ballet outfit...................................$200.00

Bandstand Swing Set — 8", girl, boy, #39610, 2004 – 2005, poodle skirt $135.00

Barbara Jane — 29" cloth/vinyl, 1952 only, mint $500.00

Barbara Lee — 8", 1955, name given by FAO Schwarz $650.00

Barton, Clara — 10", #1130, 1989 only, Portrette, wears nurse's outfit (Cissette) $100.00

    10", #42070, 2006, green vintage dress and hat..$130.00

Baseball Boy — 8", #16313, 1997, red and white baseball outfit $50.00

Baseball Girl — 8", #16300, baseball outfit with ball glove...................................$50.00

Bathing Beauty Coca-Cola — 10", red vintage bathing suit, life preserver $125.00

Beary Best Friends — 8" with 2½" bear, #32160, 2000, white dress $65.00

    8", #32161, 2002, with 3½" bear, 100th Anniversary Edition $75.00

Beast — 12", #1317, 1992 only, Romance Series (Nancy Drew)...............................$85.00

    8", #140487, Storyland Series – 1994, Fairy Tales Series – 1995 ....$70.00

Beat the Summer Heat — 8", #48085, 2008, pink sundress, popsicle $55.00

Beatrice — 18", 2005, vinyl baby dolls, assorted outfits $80.00

Beau Brummel — cloth, 1930s $800.00

Beauty — 12", #1316, 1992 only, Romance Series (Nancy Drew)...........................$85.00

    8", #140486, Storyland Series – 1994, Fairy Tales Series – 1995 ....$70.00

Beauty Queen — 10" h.p., 1961 only (Cissette) $400.00

Beaux Arts Dolls — 18" h.p., 1953 only (Margaret, Maggie) ....$2,750.00 up

Beddy-Bye Brenda — (Brooke's sister) (see FAO Schwarz under Special Events/Exclusives)

Beddy-Bye Brooke — (see FAO Schwarz under Special Events/Exclusives)

Bee My Friend — 8", #38125, 2004 – 2005, dress with bees on it $80.00

Bee Keeper Wendy — 8", #46015, 2007, checked dress, beehive purse $80.00

Being Just Like Mommy — (see Wendy Loves)

Belgium — 8" h.p., BK, #762, 1972 only (Wendy Ann) $95.00

    8" straight legs, #0762, #562, 1973 – 1975, marked "Alex".....................................$55.00

    8" straight legs, #562, 1976 – 1988, marked "Alexander" $50.00

    7" compo., 1935 – 1938 (Tiny Betty) $325.00

    9" compo., 1936 only (Little Betty)..$325.00

Belle — 14", #18402, 1996 Dickens, red jacket, long skirt $100.00

    9", #36375, 2004 – 2007, vinyl, yellow dress $35.00

    16", #49040, 2008, Disney, ltd to 300, yellow long dress $150.00

Belle Brummel — cloth, 1930s $800.00

Belle of the Ball — 10", #1120, 1989 only, Portrette, deep rose gown (Cissette) $80.00
Belle's Enchanted Christmas — 10", #34945, 2002, red satin ball gown with plastic Angelique $125.00
Belle Enchantress — 10", #48335, 2008, couture blue and black gown $110.00
Belle Watling — 10", 1992 only, Scarlett Series (Cissette) $125.00
   21", #16277, 1995 only, red outfit with fur trim (Jacqueline) $325.00
   10", #30820, 2001, gold satin dress, brown trim $95.00
Bellows' Anne — 14" plastic/vinyl, #1568, 1987 only, Fine Arts Series $75.00
Bernhardt, Sarah — 21", #2249, 1987 only, dressed in all burgundy $275.00
Berries and Cream — 8", #28475, 2001 – 2002, pink stripe dress, hat $75.00
Bessy Bell — 14" plastic/vinyl, #1565, 1988 only, Classic Series (Mary Ann) $65.00
Bessy Brooks — 8", #487, 1988 – 1991, Storybook Series (Wendy Ann) $60.00
Best Friend — 8", #26090, 2000, blue silk dress with smocking $80.00
   8", #26085, 2000 – 2001, pink silk dress with smocking $80.00
Best Friends — 8", #36895, 2003 – 2004, doll, 18" Chaos bear, toy box $125.00
Best Man — 8" h.p., #461, 1955 only (Wendy Ann) $875.00
Better Not Pout — 8", #48115, 2008, red jacket and hat $70.00
Betty — 14" compo., 1935 – 1942 ....$425.00
   12" compo., 1936 – 1937 only $350.00
   16" – 18" compo., 1935 – 1942 ....$425.00
   19" – 21" compo., 1938 – 1941 ....$550.00
   14½" – 17½" h.p., 1951 only, made for Sears (Maggie) $575.00
   30" plastic/vinyl, 1960 only $400.00
Betty Bag — 23" all cloth, holds clothes back of head $225.00
Betty Blue — 8" straight leg, #420, 1987 – 1988 only, Storybook Series (Maggie) $55.00
Betty Boop — 10", #17500 (Cissette), red dress, 1999 – 2001 ....$125.00
   21", #25125, 2000, doll with two outfits $225.00
   10", #26450, 2000 – 2001, Razzle Dazzle, long white dress, hat $110.00
Betty, Little — 9" compo., 1935 – 1943 ....$350.00 up
Betty, Tiny — 7" compo., 1934 – 1943 ....$350.00 up
Bible Character Dolls — 8" h.p., 1954 only (Wendy Ann) (Mary of Bethany, David, Martha,
   Ruth, Timothy, Rhoda, Queen Esther, and Joseph), very rare dolls ....$7,500.00 up, ea.
   1995 (see Delilah, Joseph, Queen Esther, and Samson)
Big Sister Wendy — 8", #36550, 2003 – 2004, blue dress, stuffed doll, book $90.00
Bike Riding Wendy — 8", #41580, 2006, pink checked outfit, bike $90.00
Bill/Billy — 8" h.p., #320, #567, #420, 1955 – 1963, has boy's clothes and hairstyle
   (Wendy Ann) ....$450.00 up
   #577, #464, #466, #421, #442, #488, #388, 1953 – 1957, as groom ....$450.00 up
Billy-in-the-Box — 8" jester, 1996, Alexander signature box $85.00
Binah — 8", #39450, 2004 – 2005 (Wendy), with mouse $80.00
   5", #39440, 2004 – 2005, petite, red skirt $25.00
   9", #39435, 2004 – 2005, vinyl, with mouse $35.00
   12", #39160, posable cloth doll, 2006 ....$25.00
   6", #39445, 2004, cloth, red skirt $10.00
Binnie — 18" plastic/vinyl toddler, 1964 only $350.00
Binnie Walker — 15" – 18" h.p., 1954 – 1955 only (Cissy) ....$250.00 – 425.00
   15", 1955 only, in trunk with wardrobe $750.00
   15", 1955 only, h.p. skater ....$700.00 up
   18", toddler, plastic/vinyl, 1964 only ....$350.00 up
   25", 1955 only, in formals ....$550.00 up
   25" h.p., 1954 – 1955 only, dresses ....$400.00 up
Birds, The — 10", #14800, green dress, fur coat, pictured 1998 catalog, 2005 ....$130.00
   10", #40720, 2006, dress, fur coat with birds attached $130.00
Birthday Celebration — 8", #45515 blonde, #45516 brunette, pink dress,
   Alexander bag and mini doll, 2007 – 2008 ....$85.00
Birthday Dolls — 7" compo., 1937 – 1939 (Tiny Betty) ....$375.00 up
Bitsey — 11" – 12" compo., 1942 – 1946 ....$225.00

Bible Character, Mary of Bethany, 8", SLW (Wendy). Polished cotton dress and overskirt. A very rare doll. $7,500.00 up.

Birthday Doll, Tiny Betty, 7". All composition and all original. $375.00 up.

11" – 16", with h.p. head, 1949 – 1951 ....$250.00

19" – 26", 1949 – 1951 ....$150.00 – 375.00

12" cloth/vinyl, 1965 – 1966 only $150.00

Bitsey, Little — 9" all vinyl, 1967 – 1968 only $125.00

11" – 16" ....$75.00 – 250.00

Black and White Ball — 10", #38735, 2004, white gown, black flowers................$125.00

Black Forest — 8", #512, 1989 – 1990 (Wendy Ann) $55.00

Blast Off 2000 — 8", #17830, 2000 only (Maggie), silver and gold costume $70.00

Bless the Night Tree Topper — 8", #38710, 2004 – 2005, wine and beige angel costume $100.00

Bliss, Betty Taylor — 1979 – 1981, second set Presidents' Ladies/First Ladies Series
(Mary Ann) $100.00

Bloomer, Amelia — 10", blue striped dress, straw hat, 2007 – 2008, #47695...........$120.00

Blooming Rose — 8", #28470, 2001 – 2002, pink stripe dress, hat.....................$80.00

Blue Bird Shadow Wendy — 8", #37135, African-American or Caucasian, 2004,
white dress, straw hat $85.00

Blue Boy — 16" cloth, 1930s..$650.00

7" compo., 1936 – 1938 (Tiny Betty) $350.00

9" compo., 1938 – 1941 (Little Betty) $375.00

12" plastic/vinyl, #1340, 1972 – 1983, Portrait Children (Nancy Drew)...............$55.00

1985 – 1987, dressed in blue velvet $60.00

8", #22130, 1997 – 1998, blue satin outfit $60.00

Blue Danube — 18" h.p., 1953 only, pink floral gown (#2001B – blue floral gown)
(Maggie) ....$1,800.00 up

18" h.p., 1954 only, Me and My Shadow Series, blue taffeta dress (Margaret)............. $1,900.00 up

Blue Edwardian Lady — 5" porcelain, #27025, long blue gown, 2000 ....$65.00

Blue Fairie — 10", #1166, 1993; #201166, 1994, Portrette, character
from Pinocchio (Cissette) $100.00

Blue Fairy — 8", #32135, 2000, blue gown, wings.......................................$75.00

10", #31760, 2003 – 2004 and 10" wooden Pinocchio, long blue ball gown...........$175.00

Blue Gingham Chloe — 14" vinyl, #25350, 2001 ....$70.00

Blue Hat Doll — 8", #25310, 2000, Maud Humphrey design $60.00

Blue Mist Angel — 10", #25290, 2000 – 2001, Caucasian doll, blue costume $100.00

10", #25291, 2000 – 2001, African-American doll, blue costume $100.00

Blue Moon — 14", #1560, 1991 – 1992 only, Classic Series (Louisa) $75.00

Blue Skies Angel — 8", #37900, 2003 – 2004, blue and white dress....................$85.00

Blue Zircon — 10", #1153, 1992 only, Birthday Collection, gold/blue flapper..........$110.00

Bobby — 8" h.p., #347, 1957 only (Wendy Ann) $575.00

8" h.p., #361, #320, 1960 only (Maggie Mixup)..$625.00

Bobby Q. — cloth, 1940 – 1942 ....$750.00

Bobo Clown — 8", #320, 1991 – 1992, Americana Series (Wendy Ann).................$65.00

Bohemia — 8", #508, 1989 – 1991 (Wendy Ann) $50.00

Bolivia — 8" h.p., BK and BKW, #786, 1963 – 1966 (Wendy Ann) $350.00

Bonnet Top Wendy — 8", #14487, 1995, Toy Shelf Series, yarn braids and large bonnet $50.00

Bonnie (Baby) — 16" – 19" vinyl, 1954 – 1955, 24" – 30"........................$125.00 – 250.00

Bonnie Blue — 14", #1305, 1989 only, Jubilee II (Mary Ann)..........................$125.00

8" h.p., #629, #630, 1990 – 1992 (Wendy Ann)...$90.00

8", #16649, 1995, side-saddle riding outfit..$100.00

8", #42280, 2006 – 2007, blue party dress, white lace collar................................$80.00

Bonnie Goes to London — 8", #640, 1993, Scarlett Series, #160640 – 1994...........$110.00

Bonnie Toddler — 18" cloth/h.p. head/vinyl limbs, 1950 – 1951.......................$175.00

19" all vinyl, 1954 – 1955, 23" – 24" $225.00

Bon Voyage — 8" and 10" (see I. Magnin under Special Events/Exclusives)

Bon Voyage Paris Wendy Trunk Set — 8", #39730, 2005 – 2006, six outfits,
bear and mini doll $275.00

Boone, Daniel — 8" h.p., #315, 1991 only, Americana Series, has no knife (Wendy Ann) $55.00

Bo Peep, Little — 7" compo., 1937 – 1941, Storybook Series (Tiny Betty) $375.00

9" – 11" compo., 1936 – 1940 (Little Betty, Wendy Ann) $350.00
7½" h.p., SLW, #489, 1955 only (Wendy Ann) $650.00
8" h.p., BKW, #383, 1962 – 1964 (Wendy Ann) $300.00
8" h.p., BK, #783, 1965 – 1972 (Wendy Ann) $125.00
8" h.p., straight leg, #0783 – 483, 1973 – 1975, marked "Alex" (Wendy Ann) $75.00
8" h.p., 1976 – 1986, #483 – #486, marked "Alexander" (Wendy Ann) $60.00
14", #1563, 1988 – 1989, Classic Series (Mary Ann) $75.00
14", #1567, 1992 – 1993 only, candy stripe pink dress (Mary Ann) $90.00
12" porcelain, #009, 1990 – 1992 ....$110.00
10" Portrette Series, 1994 ....$80.00
8" (see Dolly Dears under Special Events/Exclusives)
8", #25960, 2000 – 2003, long blue dress and hat with staff $75.00
8", #42570, 2006 – 2007, pink dress, staff and sheep $80.00
Born to Ride — 10", #40695, 2005, black leather coat, boots $130.00
Boston Tea Party — 8", #45480, 2006 – 2007, blue coat, tea box $85.00
Bow, Clara — 10", #45950, 2007, Cissette, white flapper dress $110.00
Bowl-O-Rama — 8", #39720, 2005, pants outfit, bowling bag and ball $75.00
Boys Choir of Harlem — 8", #20170, 1997 – 1998, maroon blazer, Kufi hat..........$75.00 each
Brazil — 7" compo., 1937 – 1943 (Tiny Betty) $375.00
9" compo., 1938 – 1940 (Little Betty) $375.00
8" h.p., BKW, #773, 1965 – 1972 (Wendy Ann) $125.00
BK, #773..$100.00
8" h.p., straight leg, #0773, #573, 1973 – 1975, marked "Alex" (Wendy Ann) $60.00
#573, #547, #530, 1985 – 1987 ....$55.00
8" straight leg, #11564, 1996 International, carnival costume $55.00
Breakfast in Bed — 8", #34040, 2003, white dress, tray with coffee, glasses $65.00
Brenda Starr — 12" h.p., 1964 only (became "Yolanda" in 1965) $350.00
Bride $375.00
Street dresses or raincoat/hat/dress $375.00
Ball gown..$450.00
Beach outfit $275.00
Briar Rose — (see M.A.D.C. under Special Events/Exclusives)
10", #14101, 1995, Brothers Grimm Series, blue floral with apron (Cissette) $85.00
8", #42540, 2006, blue skirt, red shawl $65.00
Brick Piggy — 12", #10010, 1997, denim overalls, maize felt cap $75.00
Bride — Tiny Betty: 7" compo., 1935 – 1939 ....$375.00
9" – 11" compo., 1936 – 1941 (Little Betty)...$350.00
Wendy Ann: 13", 14", 15" compo., 1935 – 1941 (Wendy Ann) ....$300.00 – 550.00
17" – 18" compo., 1935 – 1943 (Wendy Ann) $475.00
21" – 22" compo., 1942 – 1943 (Wendy Ann) ....$650.00 up
In trunk/trousseau (Wendy Ann) ....$1,650.00 up
21" compo., 1945 – 1947, Royal Wedding/Portrait (Wendy Ann) ....$2,400.00 up
Margaret, Maggie: Hard plastic
15" h.p., 1951 – 1955 (Margaret) ....$675.00 up
17" h.p., 1950, in pink (Margaret) ....$900.00 up
18" h.p., tagged "Prin. Elizabeth" (Margaret)..$750.00
18" h.p., 1949 – 1955 (Maggie, Margaret) ....$750.00 up
21" h.p., 1949 – 1953 (Margaret, Maggie) ....$1,200.00 up
18" – 21", pink bride, 1953 (Margaret) ....$1,200.00 up
23" h.p., 1949, 1952 – 1955 (Margaret) ....$850.00 up
25" h.p., 1955 only (Margaret) ....$875.00 up
Elise: 16½" h.p., 1957 – 1964, jointed ankles, elbows, and knees, must have good face
color, 1957, nylon tulle, chapel length veil ....$475.00 up
1958, wreath pattern on hem of skirt...$650.00
1959, tulle puffed sleeves, long veil (pink) $850.00
1960, satin gown, lace bodice with sequins and beads.....................................$475.00

1961, short bouffant hair, tulle with puff sleeves $475.00
1962, lace pattern bodice and trim on tulle skirt...$450.00
1963, tulle, rows of lace on bodice $475.00
1964, lace bodice and sleeves, lace on skirt, chapel length veil, #1740 ....$425.00
2000, 16", Classic Bride, white lace and tulle gown...$125.00

Cissy: 20" h.p., 1955 – 1958
1955 only, Dreams Come True Series, brocade gown with floor length veil............ $1,900.00 up
1956 only, tulle gown, tulle cap and chapel length veil, Fashion Parade Series....... $1,200.00 up
1957 only, Models Formal Gowns Series, nylon tulle with double train of satin........ $950.00 up
1958 only, Dolls to Remember Series, lace circles near hem (wreath pattern), #2280.... $1,500.00 up
1959 only, tulle over white satin...$900.00
1962 only, #2170, elaborate lace gown over tulle .... $3,100.00 up

Cissette: 10" h.p., 1957 – 1963, must have good face color
1957, tulle gown, short veil or lace and tulle cap veil...$375.00
1958, lace wreath pattern, matches Elise and Cissy...$575.00
1959 – 1960, tulle gown, puff sleeves...$450.00
1961, tulle, rhinestones on collar and veil..$475.00
1962, lace bodice and trim on skirt, long veil...$425.00
1963, tulle, rows of lace on bodice and at hem (matches Elise from the same year)........$475.00
In trunk/trousseau, various years.. $950.00 up
#1136, 1990 – 1991, Portrette..$75.00
#14103, 1995, 1920s style...$100.00
#22470, 10" Empire Bride, 1998, lace gown, straw bonnet $100.00
#22460, 10" Rococo Bride, 1998, peach gown, lace train $100.00
#22480, 10" Victorian Bride, 1998, blue satin gown $100.00
#26880, 10", Contemporary Bride, blonde, 2000 ....$90.00
#26881 (brunette), 2000 ....$90.00
#32990 (blonde), 2002, white gown, pink trim, limited to 1,000.....................................$100.00
#33325 (blonde), #33326 (brunette), Down the Aisle, 2002 – 2003 ....$90.00
#33327, African-American, 2002 – 2003, Down the Aisle...$90.00
#38750, 10", 2004, My Special Day, blonde, white dress, lace trim...................................$100.00
#38751, 10", 2004, My Special Day, brunette, white dress, lace trim $100.00
#38752, 10", 2004, My Special Day, African-American, white dress, lace trim $100.00
#40355, 10", 2005, blonde, Lasting Memories Bride, #40356, 2005, brunette $90.00
#40357, 10", 2005, African-American, Lasting Memories Bride...$90.00
#42480, 10", 2006, brunette, Visions of Love, 2006, #42475, blonde $100.00
#42485, 10", 2006, Visions of Love Bride $100.00
#42490, 10", 2006, African-American $100.00
#46290, 10", 2007, Cosmopolitan Bride, rhinestone necklace, bouquet..........................$120.00

Lissy: 12" h.p., 1956 – 1959
1956, jointed knees and elbows, tulle, tulle cap veil, #1247... $650.00 up
1957, same as 1956 except long veil...$675.00
1958 – 1959, dotted net, tulle veil .... $850.00 up
1991 – 1992 only, porcelain (version of 14" head) $140.00

Jacqueline: 21" Portrait
#2151, 1965, full lace, wide lace edge on veil (Jacqueline) $950.00
#2192, 1969, full lace overskirt and plain veil $750.00

Alexander-Kin (Wendy Ann): 8" h.p. or plastic/vinyl
8" h.p., #315, 1953 only, Quiz-Kin...$700.00
8" h.p., 1954 .... $650.00 up
SLW, BKW, #735 in 1955, #615 in 1956, #410 in 1957, #582 in 1958 .... $400.00 up
BKW, #482, 1959, pink.. $1,100.00 up
BKW, #735, 1960 ....$425.00
BKW, #480, 1961 ....$400.00
BKW, #760 (#630 in 1965), 1963 – 1965 ....$350.00
BK, #470 in 1966, #735 in 1967 – 1972 ....$175.00

Bride, 8", SLNW, 1953 (Wendy). All original and mint with wrist tag. MADC Convention blue ribbon winner. $700.00.

Cloe-up of bride.

Straight legs, #0735-435, 1973 – 1975, marked "Alex"..$80.00

Straight legs, #435, 1976 – 1994, marked "Alexander"..$70.00

#337, white doll; #336-1, black doll, 1991 – 1992 ....$65.00

#337, 1993, white only..$60.00

#435, 1985 – 1987 ....$55.00

Collectors United (see under Special Events/Exclusives)

#10395, 1995, Special Occasions Series, African-American $65.00

#10392, 1995, Special Occasions Series, three hair colors $60.00

#17016, 1996 white lace and satin gown...$60.00

#21030, 1997 – 1998, white gown, comes with cake top, #21033 – African-American.....$90.00

#21171, 1999, blonde or brunette, satin ribbon at hem $60.00

#25015 (blonde), #25016 (brunette), 2000...$60.00

#25017, 2000, African-American $65.00

#30650 (blonde), #30652 (brunette), 2001 – 2002, white dress, sequin trim $65.00

#30651, African-American, 2001 – 2002, Memories of a Lifetime................................$65.00

#36275, blonde, 2003 – 2004, Rosette Dreams, white dress, pink roses............................$65.00

#36276, brunette, 2003 – 2004, Rosette Dreams...$65.00

#36277, African-American, 2003 – 2004, Rosette Dreams...$65.00

#39065, 8", 2005 – 2006, blonde, Honeymoon Sweet Dreams....................................$80.00

#39066, 8", 2005 – 2006, brunette, Honeymoon Sweet Dreams $80.00

#39067, 8", 2005 – 2006, African-American, Honeymoon Sweet Dreams $80.00

#46295, 8", blonde, To Have and to Hold, 2007, #46296, burnette $80.00

#46297, 8", African American, To Have and to Hold, 2007...$80.00

Mary Ann, Jennifer, Louisa: 14" plastic/vinyl

#1465 (#1565 in 1974, #1565 in 1977, #1570 in 1976), 1973 – 1977 (Mary Ann) $85.00

#1589 in 1987 – 1988; #1534 in 1990, Classic Series (Mary Ann, Jennifer).....................$85.00

#1566, reintroduced 1992 only, ecru gown (Louisa, Jennifer) $85.00

Elise, Leslie, Polly: 17" plastic/vinyl or 21" porcelain

1966 – 1988 (Elise) $110.00

1966 – 1971 (Leslie) $250.00

1965 – 1970 (Polly)...$225.00

Porcelain, 1989 – 1990, satin and lace look like bustle $150.00

Porcelain, Portrait Series, 1993 – 1994...$150.00

Bridesmaid — 9" compo., 1937 – 1939 (Little Betty) $350.00

11" – 14" compo., 1938 – 1942 (Wendy Ann)..$325.00 – 475.00

15" – 18" compo., 1939 – 1944 (Wendy Ann)..$375.00 – 600.00

20" – 22" compo., 1941 – 1947, Portrait (Wendy Ann) ....$1,800.00 up

21½" compo., 1938 – 1941 (Princess Elizabeth) ....$950.00 up

15" – 17" h.p., 1950 – 1952 (Margaret, Maggie) ....$400.00 – 600.00

15" h.p., 1952 (Maggie) $650.00

18" h.p., 1952 (Maggie) ....$750.00 up

21" h.p., 1950 – 1953, side part mohair wig, deep pink or lavender gown (Margaret)......$850.00 up

19" rigid vinyl, in pink, 1952 – 1953 (Margaret)..$600.00 up

15" h.p., 1955 only (Cissy, Binnie)..$475.00

18" h.p., 1955 only (Cissy, Binnie)..$525.00

25" h.p., 1955 only (Cissy, Binnie) ....$475.00 up

20" h.p., 1956 only, Fashion Parade Series, blue nylon tulle and net (Cissy).................$1,500.00 up

10" h.p., 1957 – 1963 (Cissette)..$475.00

12" h.p., 1956 – 1959 (Lissy) ....$800.00 up

16½" h.p., 1957 – 1959 (Elise) ....$475.00 up

8" h.p., SLNW, 1953, pink, blue, or yellow (Wendy Ann) ....$900.00 up

8" h.p., SLW, #478, 1955 (Wendy Ann)..$800.00 up

BKW, #621, 1956 ....$750.00 up

BKW, #408, #583, #445, 1957 – 1959 ....$700.00 up

8", 2000, Little Gardenia, #26855 (Wendy), white tulle and satin $65.00

8", 2000, Little Pearl, #26800 (Wendy), lace bodice $75.00

17" plastic/vinyl (Elise) 1966 – 1987 ....$125.00

17" plastic/vinyl, 1966 – 1971 (Leslie) $325.00

Brigitta — 11" and 14" (see Sound of Music)

British Mod — 8", #46625, 2007, flag dress, purse $60.00

Brooke — (see FAO Schwarz under Special Events/Exclusives)

Bubbles the Clown — 8" h.p., #342, 1993 – 1994, Americana Series $90.00

Buck Rabbit — cloth/felt, 1930s ....$700.00 up

Bud — 16" – 19", 1952 only, cloth/vinyl (Rosebud head) ....$175.00 – 250.00

19" and 25", 1952 – 1953 only ....$175.00 – 350.00

Bulgaria — 8", #557, 1986 – 1987, white face (Wendy Ann) $55.00

Bumble Bee — 8" h.p., #323, 1992 – 1993 only, Americana Series $60.00

Bunny — 18" plastic/vinyl, 1962 only, mint..$275.00

Bunny Tails — 8", #28200, 2000 – 2003, yellow dress, bunny pinafore, basket of eggs $70.00

Burma — 7" compo., 1939 – 1943 (Tiny Betty)..$350.00

Butch — 11" – 12" compo./cloth, 1942 – 1946 ....$175.00

14" – 16" compo./cloth, 1949 – 1951 ....$185.00

14" cloth, vinyl head and limbs, 1950 only $175.00

12" cloth/vinyl, 1965 – 1966 only $125.00

Butch, Little — 9" all vinyl, 1967 – 1968 only $125.00

Butch McGuffey — 22" compo./cloth, 1940 – 1941 ....$275.00

Butterfly Queen — 8", #25670, 2000 – 2001 (Wendy), lavender costume $70.00

C is for Cookie — 8", #41820, 2006, with Cookie Monster, cookies $80.00

C.U. — (see Collectors United under Special Events/Exclusives)

Cafe Rose and Ivory Cocktail Dress — 10", #22200 – white, #22203 – black, 1997 – 1998 ....$90.00

Caitlin — 5", #27405, 2003, Petite, checked sundress...................................$20.00

Cake Topper — 6", Caucasian, 2002, bride and groom, #33570 ....$80.00

6", #33571, 2002, African-American bride and groom $80.00

Calamity Jane — 8" h.p., Americana Series, 1994 only (Wendy Ann)...............$65.00

Calendar Girls — 5", #33070 – 33130, Jan. – Dec., 2002 – 2004, set of 12 ....$320.00, $20.00 each

Calendar Girls Prepack — 5", #33065, 2002, 12 dolls, Jan. – Dec.................$20.00 each

Calla Lilly — 10", #22390, 1998 (Cissette), white gown, hand beaded jewels $165.00

Cameo Lady — (see Collectors United/C. U. under Special Events/Exclusives)

Camille — 21" compo., 1938 – 1939 (Wendy Ann) ....$3,500.00 up

Camomille Tea Wendy — 8", #46275, 2007, yellow print, teacup.................$85.00

Canada — 8" h.p., BK, #760, 1968 – 1972 (Wendy Ann) $90.00

Straight legs, #0706, 1973 – 1975, marked "Alex" $55.00

Straight legs, #560 (#534 in 1986), 1976 – 1988 (white face 1985 – 1987),

marked "Alexander" $55.00

Straight legs, #24130, 1999, hockey skater.......................................$60.00

Cancer — 8", #21360, 1998, red crab costume $75.00

Candy Cane Rockette — 8", #48905, 2008, striped tutu $65.00

Candy Kid — 11" – 15" compo., 1938 – 1941 (Wendy Ann), red/white striped dress.....$275.00 – 450.00

8" h.p., #27060, 2000, Peter Pan series, red coat, black pants...............$70.00

Candy Land Game — Princess Lolly, 8", #25250, 2000, yellow costume $75.00

Capricorn — 8", #21300, 1998 (Maggie), fuchsia snakeskin body.................$70.00

Captain Hook — 8" h.p., #478, 1992 – 1993 only, Storyland Series (Peter Pan)

(Wendy Ann) $90.00

8" h.p., #27060, 2000 – 2001, Peter Pan series, red coat, black pants.................$85.00

8", #46385, 2007, red coat, plush crocodile, sword $90.00

Caraboose — 10", #48370, 2008, elaborate black and gold long ballet costume $135.00

Careen — (see Carreen)

Carhop Takes Your Order — 8", #17710, 2000, black checked dress $70.00

Caribbean, The — 8", #46315, 2007, pirate costume, pirate...........................$75.00

Carmen — Dressed like Carmen Miranda, but not marked or meant as such.

7" compo., 1938 – 1943 (Tiny Betty) $375.00

9" – 11" compo., 1938 – 1943, boy and girl (see also "Rumbera/Rumbero")

(Little Betty) ....$325.00 ea.

11" compo., 1937 – 1939, has sleep eyes (Little Betty) $375.00

14" compo., 1937 – 1940 (Wendy Ann) $450.00

17" compo., 1939 – 1942 (Wendy Ann) $650.00

21" compo., 1939 – 1942, extra make-up, mint (Wendy Ann) .... $1,400.00 up

21" compo., 1939 – 1942, Portrait with extra make-up .... $1,900.00 up

14" plastic/vinyl, #1410, 1983 – 1986, Opera Series (Mary Ann) $75.00

10" h.p., #1154, 1993 only, Portrette Series (Miranda), yellow/red...........$75.00

16", #28395, 2001, red Spanish dress, black lace $175.00

Carmen Miranda Lucy — 10", #25760, 2000, white dress with ruffles.................$150.00

Carnavale Doll — (see FAO Schwarz under Special Events/Exclusives)

Carnival in Rio — 21" porcelain, 1989 – 1990.................................$350.00

Carnival in Venice — 21" porcelain, 1990 – 1991 ....$375.00

Caroline — 15" vinyl, 1961 – 1962 only, in dresses, pants, jacket............$375.00

In riding habit $400.00

In case/wardrobe.. $900.00 up

8", 1993 (see Belk & Leggett under Special Events/Exclusives)

8", 1994 (see Neiman-Marcus under Special Events/Exclusives)

Caroling with Minnie and Mickey — 8", #42610, 2006 – 2007, Minnie, Mickey.................$120.00

Carousel Melody — 8", #42140, 2006, with carousel horse $120.00

Carol of the Bells Rockette 1987 Cissette — 10", #49190, 2008, gold and white tutu $110.00

Carreen/Careen — 14" – 17" compo., #1593, 1937 – 1938 (Wendy Ann) ....$750.00 up

14" plastic/vinyl, 1992 – 1993 only (Louisa/Jennifer) $110.00

8", plaid, two large ruffles at hem, #160646, 1994 only........................$85.00

8", #15190, 1999 (Wendy), blue dress, straw hat $85.00

Carrot Kate — 14", #25506, 1995, Ribbons & Bows Series, vegetable print dress

(Mary Ann)...$100.00

Carrot Top — 21" cloth, 1967 only..$125.00

Casablanca — 16", #48460, tan suit, straw hat $135.00

Casey Jones — 8" h.p., 1991 – 1992 only, Americana Series $60.00

Casper's Friend Wendy — 8" (Maggie), #15210, 1999, red costume, broom...........$70.00

Catch a Falling Star — 8", #33060, 2002, white dress..........................$65.00

Catch a Tiger — 8", #48190, 2008, long dress, plush tiger $80.00

Caterpillar — 8" h.p., #14594, 1995 – 1996, has eight legs, Alice in Wonderland Series..........$100.00

8", #46515, 2008, caterpillar costume, mushroom, hookah........................$65.00

Cat in the Hat, The — 8", #46420, 2007, Maggie, two plush things................$75.00

Cat on a Hot Tin Roof — 10", #20011, "Maggie," white chiffon dress $125.00

Celebrating America — 8", #38515, 2004, patch quilt dress, vintage $85.00

Celtic Bride — 10", #28595, 2001, white gown, gold trim, red rose headpiece

and bouquet..$100.00

Celtic Dancer — 8", #40120, 2005, green sweater...............................$50.00

Century of Fashion — 14" and 18" h.p., 1954 (Margaret, Maggie, and Cissy)............. $2,000.00 up

Champs-Elysées — 21" h.p., black lace over pink, rhinestone on cheek ....$6,500.00 up

Change of Season — 8", #40120, 2005 – 2006, green sweater $50.00

Changing Seasons — (Spring, Summer, Autumn, Winter) 14", 1993 – 1994 ....$85.00 ea.

Chanukah Celebration — 8", #27330, 2001 – 2002, blue dress, brunette $80.00

Charity — 8" h.p., #485, 1961 only, Americana Series, blue cotton dress

(Wendy Ann) ....$1,900.00 up

Charlene — 18" cloth/vinyl, 1991 – 1992 only $90.00

Charlie Brown — 10", #26425, 2001 – 2003, Peanuts Gang, includes Snoopy

and ball glove $40.00

10", #33710, 2002 – 2004 Charlie Brown Christmas, tree, Snoopy, blanket $50.00

10", #36055, 2003 – 2004 Trick or Treat, with Snoopy and doghouse $60.00

10", #38805, Happy Birthday, 2004, with cake and Snoopy $65.00

Charlotte's Web — 8", #41955, 2006 – 2008, yellow dress, spider, goose, pig............$85.00

Trunk set, 8", #45455, 2006 – 2008, pig, goose, sheep, rat, spider, trunk $130.00

Out for a stroll with Wilbur, 8", #48500, 2008, with pig, doll, blanket, pram $95.00

Chatterbox — 24" plastic/vinyl talker, 1961 only..$250.00

Cheerleader — 8", #324, 1990 – 1991 only, Americana Series (Wendy Ann)..............................$60.00

    8" h.p., #324, #324-1, 1992 – 1993 only, Americana Series, black or white doll,
        royal blue/gold outfit..$60.00

Chef Alex — 8", #31260, 1998 (Maggie), chef attire...$65.00

Cheri — 18" h.p., 1954 only, Me and My Shadow Series, white satin gown,
    pink opera coat (Margaret) .... $1,800.00 up

Cherry Blossom — 14", #25504, 1995, Ribbons & Bows Series, cherry print dress
    (Mary Ann) $100.00

Cherry Girl — 8", #17590, 1999 – 2001, Mary Engelbreit, comes with basket and card..........$80.00

Cherry Parfait — 8", #42175, 2006, red skirt with cherry parfait..$80.00

Cherry Twins — 8" h.p., #388E, 1957 only (Wendy Ann).............................$1,600.00 up, ea.

    8", BK, #17700, 1999, pair, remake of 1957 set...$130.00

Cherub — 12" vinyl, 1960 – 1961...$250.00

    18" h.p. head, cloth and vinyl, 1950s..$350.00

    26", 1950s...$375.00

Cherub Babies — cloth, 1930s... $450.00 up

Cheshire Cat — 8", #13070, 1997 – 1999 Storyland Series,
    pink velvet cat suit...$65.00

Chicken Little — 8", #39905, 2005 – 2006, green dress..$50.00

Child at Heart Shop — (see Special Events/Exclusives)

Children's Prayer — 8", #28385, 2001 – 2002, pink gown, bonnet $70.00

Child's Angel — 8", #14701, 1996, gold wings, harp, halo..$70.00

Chile — 8" h.p., #528, 1992 only (Maggie)...$55.00

Chili in Santa Fe — 8", #46140, 2007, western outfit, chiminea, chiliristro.............................$85.00

China — 7" compo., 1936 – 1940 (Tiny Betty) $350.00

    9" compo., 1935 – 1938 (Little Betty) $300.00

    8" h.p., BK, #772, 1972 (Wendy Ann)..$90.00

    8" (Maggie) $125.00

        Straight legs, #0772 – #572, 1973 – 1975, marked "Alex".......................................$60.00

        Straight legs, #572, 1976 – 1986, marked "Alexander" (Wendy Ann) $55.00

        #572, 1987 – 1989 (Maggie)...$55.00

    8", #11550, 1995 only, three painted lashes at edges of eyes (Wendy Ann) $55.00

    8", #11561, 1996 International, Little Empress costume $70.00

    8", #26280, 2000 – 2001 (Wendy), red silk costume with panda bear $60.00

Chinese New Year — 8", #21040, 1997 – 1998, two dolls..$120.00

    8", #21050, 1997 – 1998, three dolls, dragon $165.00

    8", #42250, 2006, red silk Chinese pants outfit, dog...$80.00

Chloe — Blue gingham, 14", #25350, 2000, dress and hat; pink, #25345...............................$60.00

Christening Baby — 11" – 13" cloth/vinyl, 1951 – 1954..$100.00

    16" – 19"..$175.00

Christmas Angels — (see Tree Topper)

Christmas at Grandma's — 8", #27445, 2000 – 2002, red coat and hat, black trim $75.00

Christmas Ballerina — 8", white tulle, red bodice, green leaves, 2003 – 2004.........................$75.00

Christmas Bear with Lenox Ornament — 8", Wendy, Lenox bear, #38535,
    2004 – 2005 ....$95.00

Christmas Candy — 14", #1544, 1993 only, Classic Series $85.00

Christmas Cardinals — 8", #38850, 2004 – 2005, cardinals on pinafore $75.00

Christmas Carol — (see Saks Fifth Avenue under Special Events/Exclusives)

Christmas Caroler — 8", #19650, 1997, red velvet cape, print skirt $75.00

Christmas Caroling — 10", #1149, 1992 – 1993 only, Portrette, burnt orange/gold dress $85.00

Christmas Classic — 8", #49895, 2008, red dress, gingerbread house $90.00

Christmas Cookie — 14", #1565, 1992 (also see 'Lil Christmas Cookie) (Louisa/Jennifer) $85.00

Christmas Eve — 14" plastic/vinyl, #241594, 1994 only (Mary Ann).....................................$85.00

    8", #10364, 1995, Christmas Series...$70.00

Christmas Fun — 8", 2008, #49900, green coat, snow man..$85.00
Christmas Holly — 8", #19680, 1998 – 1999, print dress, red coat $70.00
Christmas Is Coming — 8", #42375, 2006 – 2007, with tree, ornaments.....................$95.00
Christmas Pudding — 8", #45510, 2006 – 2007, Maggie, pudding cake....................$75.00
Christmas Shoppe — (see Special Events/Exclusives)
Christmas Song — 10", #33455, 2002, long red dress, limited to 1,000 ....$125.00
Christmas Stocking — Dancing Wendy, 20" stocking, #28530, 2001....................$50.00
    Skating Maggie, 20" stocking, #31255, 2001..$50.00
Christmas Stocking Stuffers — 8", #38890, 2004 – 2005, stocking with toys.........$85.00
Christmas Story, A — 8", #47710, 2007 – 2008, BB gun, leg lamp $95.00
Christmas Tea with Ornament — 8", #38540, 2004 – 2005, with teapot ornament $90.00
Christmas Tree Topper — (see Spiegel's under Special Events/Exclusives; also Tree Topper)
Christopher Robin — 8", #31890, 2003 – 2004, yellow top, blue pants, 4½" Pooh bear............$85.00
    12", #47455, 2008, checked jacket, straw hat, Pooh Bear......................................**$115.00**
Chrysanthemum Garden Ball — 10", #31245, 2001, green and pink ball gown....................$100.00
Churchill, Lady — 18" h.p., #2020C, 1953 only, Beaux Arts Series, pink gown
    with full opera coat (Margaret)... $2,300.00 up
Churchill, Sir Winston — 18" h.p., 1953 only, hat (Margaret) .... $1,250.00 up
Cinderella — (see also Topsy-Turvy for two-headed version)
    7" – 8" compo., 1935 – 1944 (Tiny Betty)...$375.00
    9" compo., 1936 – 1941 (Little Betty)..$375.00
    13" compo., 1935 – 1937 (Wendy Ann)..$375.00
    14" compo., 1939 only, Sears exclusive (Princess Elizabeth) $500.00
    15" compo., 1935 – 1937 (Betty)...$450.00
    16" – 18" compo., 1935 – 1939 (Princess Elizabeth) .... $550.00 up
    8" h.p., #402, 1955 only (Wendy Ann)..$900.00
    8" h.p., #498, 1990 – 1991, Storyland Series (Wendy Ann) $60.00
    8", #476, 1992 – 1993, blue ball gown, #140476, 1994 Storyland Series $70.00
    8", #475, 1992 only, "Poor" outfit in blue with black stripes.....................$65.00
    8" h.p., #14540, 1995 – 1996, pink net gown with roses, Brothers Grimm
        Series, #13400, 1997 – 2000..$70.00
    8" h.p., #13410, 1997 – 1999, calico skirt with broom and pumpkin..................$60.00
    8" h.p., #13490, 1999 – 2001, Cinderella's wedding, white gown....................$80.00
    8", At the Ball, #30670, 2002 – 2003, white dress, long blue cape..................$80.00
    8", #35625, 2004 – 2006, Stroke of Midnight, blue ball gown......................$80.00
    8", #46375, 2007 – 2008, blue ball gown, tiara..$85.00
    8", #46380, 2007 – 2008, poor outfit, green dress, broom.........................$50.00
    5", #36320, vinyl, petite, 2004 – 2005, pink gown $25.00
    12" h.p., 1966 only, Literature Series (Classic Lissy) .... $950.00 up
    12" h.p., 1966, "Poor" outfit...$675.00
    1966, in window box with both outfits .... $1,900.00 up
    14" h.p., 1950 – 1951, ball gown (Margaret)................................... $900.00 up
    14" h.p., 1950 – 1951, "Poor" outfit (Margaret) .... $750.00 up
    14" h.p., #25940, 2000, pink, lace-trimmed long gown $100.00
    18" h.p., 1950 – 1951 (Margaret)... $800.00 up
    21", #45501, 1995, pink and blue, Madame's Portfolio Series.....................$300.00
    14" plastic/vinyl (#1440 to 1974; #1504 to 1991; #1541 in 1992) 1967 – 1992,
        "Poor" outfit (can be green, blue, gray, or brown) (Mary Ann) $70.00
    14", #140 on box, 1969 only, FAO Schwarz, all blue satin/gold trim, mint (Mary Ann).........$400.00
    14" plastic/vinyl, #1445, #1446, #1546, #1548, 1970 – 1983, Classic Series,
        dressed in pink (Mary Ann)...$80.00
    #1548, #1549, 1984 – 1986, blue ball gown, two styles (Mary Ann) $100.00
    14", #1546, #1547, 1987 – 1991, Classic Series, white or blue ballgown
        (Mary Ann, Jennifer), #1549, 1992 only (Jennifer) $90.00
    14", 1994, has two outfits (see Disney Annual Showcase of Dolls under
        Special Events/Exclusives)

Christopher Robin, 12", #47455, 2008 (Lissy). With Pooh Bear. $115.00.

Cissette, 10", #900, 1959. Basic doll in chemise, mint in box. $350.00 up.

Cissette, 10", 1959. Very elaborate gold ballgown. $550.00 up.

14", 1996, #87002, white gown, gold crown (Mary Ann)..$100.00
14", #25940, 2001 (Margaret), long pink ball gown $125.00
10", #1137, 1990 – 1991, Portrette, dressed in all pink (Cissette) $90.00
10", #34950, 2002 – 2004, blue ball gown with three mice, long white gloves $150.00
9", #36240, 2004 – 2007, vinyl, blue satin gown..$35.00
10", #45970, 2007, Cissette, pink ballet outfit $95.00
10", #45990, 2007, Cissette, Roaring 20s Cinderella pink and silver outfit, poor oufit............$130.00
16", #48655, 2008, ltd to 300, blue satin long dress $150.00

Cinderella's Carriage — #13460, 1999 – 2000, white metal carriage................................$135.00
Cinderella's Footmouse — 8", #13470, 1999 – 2000, painted face $85.00
Cinderella's Prince — 8", #35630, 2003 – 2005, white hat, blue pants......................$75.00
Cinderella's Wicked Stepmother — 8", #38625, 2005, red and black dress....................$75.00
Cissette — 10" – 11" h.p., 1957 – 1963, high heel feet, jointed elbows
    and knees, must have good face color, in various street dresses..................................$450.00 up
    Basic Cissette in various chemises, mint in box..**$350.00 up**
    Rare or fancy outfits, mint in box ....$600.00 up
    In formals, ball gowns ....**$550.00 up**
    Coats and hats..$350.00
    1961 only, beauty queen with trophy..$375.00
    Special gift set, three wigs ....$950.00 up
    Doll only, clean with good face color $150.00
    1957, Queen, trunk, trousseau ....$1,200.00 up
    Slacks or pants outfits..$375.00
Cissette Barcelona — 10", Spanish costume, black lace, 1999 ....$100.00
Cissette Lingerie Trunk — 10", #40700, 2005, doll, armoire, trunk with
    padded bench, and lingerie..$150.00
Cissette Shadow Yardley — 10", #36605, blonde, blue dress, perfume bottle $140.00
Cissette Christmas Trunk Set — 10", #49905, 2008, two outfits $250.00

Dating Cissette Dolls

Eyelids: 1975, beige; 1958, pale pink; 1959 – 1963, beige

Clothes: 1957 – 1958, darts in bodice; 1959 – 1963, no darts except ball gowns

Fingernails: 1962 – 1963, polished

Eyebrows: 1957 – 1963, single stroked

Body and legs: 1957 – 1963, head strung with hook and rubber band, legs jointed with plastic socket

Feet: 1957 – 1963, high heels

Wigs: 1957 – 1958, three rows of stitching; 1959 – 1963, zigzag stitches except 1961 – 1962 with fancy hairdos, then three rows; 1963, few have rooted hair in cap, glued to head or removable wigs

Tags: 1957 – 1962, turquoise; 1963, dark blue

Portrette: 1968 – 1973, two or three stroke eyebrows, blue eyelids, no earrings, strung head with hook, high heels

Jacqueline: 1961 – 1962, two or three stroke eyebrows, side seam brunette wig, small curl on forehead, blue eyelids, eyeliner, painted lashes to sides of eyes, polished nails, head strung, socket jointed hips with side seams, high heels

Sleeping Beauty: 1959 only, three stroke eyebrows, pink eyelids, no earrings, mouth painted wider, no knee joints, flat feet, jointed with metal hooks

Sound of Music: 1971 – 1973 (Brigitta, Liesl, Louisa), two stroke eyebrows, the rest same as Portrettes

Tinker Bell: 1969 only, two stroke eyebrows, blue eyelids, painted lashes to side of eyes, no earrings, hair rooted into wig cap, head and legs strung with metal hooks

Margot: 1961, same as Jacqueline, except has three stroke eyebrows and elaborate hairdos

Cissy — 20" h.p. (also 21"), 1955 – 1959, jointed elbows and knees, high heel feet,
    must have good face color, in various street dresses ....$750.00 up
    Dress and full-length coat ....**$800.00 up**
    In ball gowns ....**$1,000.00 up**

Trunk, wardrobe .... $1,400.00 up
Pants set .... $750.00 up
1950s magazine ads using doll (add $10.00 if framed) .... $30.00 up
21", reintroduced in the following 1996 MA Couture Collection:
    #67303, aquamarine evening column and coat $300.00
    #67302, cafe rose and ivory cocktail dress $325.00
    #67306, cafe rose and ivory cocktail dress, African-American $450.00
    #67301, coral and leopard travel ensemble $350.00
    #67601, ebony and ivory houndstooth suit $600.00
    #67603, ebony and ivory houndstooth suit, African-American $675.00
    #67304, onyx velvet lace gala gown and coat $350.00
    #67602, pearl embroidered lace bridal gown $600.00
    #86003, limited edition red sequin gown $350.00
21", 1997 MA Couture Collection
    #22210, daisy resort ensemble, limited to 2,500 .... $425.00
    #22230, tea rose cocktail ensemble $350.00
    #22220, calla lily evening ensemble $425.00
    #22290, gardenia gala ball gown $400.00
    #22250, Cissy's secret armoire trunk set (1997 – 1998) $1,100.00
21", 1998 MA Couture, each limited to 1,500
    #22300, Cissy Paris, gold houndstooth outfit, sable, feathered hat $575.00
    #22330, Cissy Barcelona, coral charmeuse with black lace $550.00
    #22333, Cissy Barcelona, African-American $675.00
    #22320, Cissy Milan, long fur coat and fur-trimmed hat $575.00
    #22310, Cissy Venice, brocade gown, blue taffeta cape $525.00
    #22340, Cissy Budapest, blue dress and coat trimmed with fur $550.00
21", 1999, Cissy Designer Originals (see Madame Alexander Doll Company
    under Special Events/Exclusives)
21", 2000, #25555, Rome Cissy $450.00
    #26980, New York Cissy $425.00
    #25585, Vienna Cissy $450.00
    #25560, Cairo Cissy $450.00
    #25565, Shanghai Cissy $350.00
    #26865, Hollywood Cissy $400.00
    #26866, Hollywood Cissy, African-American $500.00
    #27005, Romantic Dreams Cissy $400.00
    #28450, Peacock Rose Cissy, limited to 600 .... $825.00
    #27370, Yardley Cissy, blue dress, blonde $525.00
21", 2001, all limited to 500 pieces
    #28415, Society Stroll Cissy (Caucasian) $400.00
    #28415, Society Stroll Cissy (African-American) $550.00
    #28441, Royal Reception Cissy $500.00
    #28430, Black and White Ball Cissy $450.00
    #28420, A Day in the Life of Cissy, trunk set $500.00
    #28435, Haute Couture, black suit, hat with feathers $425.00
    #28440, On the Avenue Yardley Cissy, green suit, plush dog $450.00
    #31235, Promise of Spring Cissy $600.00
21", Cissy Amethyst, #32070, 2001, limited to 350 .... $425.00
21", Manhattan Gothic, #31965, 2001, limited to 100 .... $1,200.00
21", Madame Du Pompadour Cissy, #31520, 2001, limited to 100 ...... $1,700.00
21", Prima Donna Cissy, #31970, 2001, limited to 100 .... $1,200.00
21", #33175, 2002, Maimey Cissy, blue dress, white sweater, limited to 350 .... $450.00
    #33165, 2002, Blue Bird Cissy, embroidered skirt with birds $450.00
    #33166, 2002, Blue Bird Cissy, African-American, limited to 150 ..... $500.00
Renaissance Garden Cissy, 21", #33200, 2002, evening gown, embroidered skirt,
    limited to 350 .... $500.00

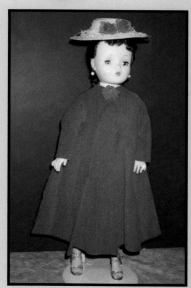

Cissy, 21", 1950s. Red velvet coat and straw hat. $800.00.

Cissy, 21", #2095, 1955. Ballgown of sheer organdy trimmed in lace and red rosebuds. Straw hat and red satin bag. $1,000.00.

Cissy, 21", 1958, mint. $1,000.00.

Cissy, 21", #2043, 1956. Black velvet torso gown trimmed with pink roses. $1,000.00.

Taffeta Romance Cissy, 21", #33160, 2002, pink ball gown, black trim, limited to 350 ....$375.00

Dance the Night Away Cissy, 21", #33160, 2002, black fitted long gown, black gloves and purse, limited to 350 ....$450.00

Cissy's European Holiday Trunk set, 21", #33190, 2002, trunk, two dresses, ball gown, wigs, etc., limited to 350 ....$425.00

Equestrian Cissy, 21", #33965, 2002, black hat, jodhpurs, brocade vest, limited to 200..........$475.00

Baby Doe Cissy, 21", #33960, 2002, blue plaid bustle dress, umbrella, limited to 200 ....$650.00

Pompadour Cissy, 21", #34400, 2002, vintage eighteenth century design, green jacket, straw hat...$850.00

Sitting Pretty Yardley Cissy, 21", #33185, 2002, slacks set, chair, pillows..................................$375.00

80th Anniversary Cissy, 21", #34980, 2002, black top and crochet long skirt, limited to 200 .$525.00

Fifties Swing Cissy, 21", #36090, 2003, black dress and hat with flowers, limited to 350 ....$500.00

Sixties Go-Go Cissy, 21", #36095, 2003, red, white, and black short dress, limited to 350 .....$400.00

Seventies Strut Cissy, 21", #36100, 2003, hot pants, long black coat, limited to 250 ....$450.00

Seventies Strut Cissy, 21", #36101, 2003, African-American, limited to 350.........................$500.00

Eighties Elegance Cissy, 21", #36105, 2003, ball gown, red shawl, limited to 350 ....$475.00

Dressed to the Nines Cissy, 21", #36110, 2003, black cocktail dress, limited to 350 ....$500.00

Center Stage Cissy, 21", 2000, #36255, 2003, pink ruffle dress, limited to 350 ....$450.00

Pocahontas, 21", 2003, #36080, English Court costume, limited to 200 ....$450.00

Cocktails, 21", 2003, #36070, copper cocktail dress, black hat, limited to 200 ....$500.00

Pompadour Cissy Summer, 21", #36745, 2003, gold court gown, limited to 200 ....$525.00

In Her Honor, 21", #36140, 2003, long blue gown, pink cape, limited to 350 ....$475.00

Lavensque Yardley Cissy, 21", #36085, 2003, black suit, table, cup, bowl $450.00

English Waltz Cissy, 21", #36065, 2003, lacy white ball gown, limited to 350 ....$475.00

Curtain Call Cissy, 21", #36060, 2003, blue ballet outfit, limited to 350 ....$300.00

Cissy Boutique, 21", #38010, 2003, black dress, accessories, limited to 250 ....$450.00

Dorothy Cissy, 21", #36355, 2003, flat chested torso, Toto in basket $275.00

Pompadour Cissy "Fall" and Louis XV, 21", #38300, 2004, lavish court costumes, three dogs...$1,200.00

Smokin', 21", #38305, 2004, silk plaid long skirt over pants, 1950s style, limited to 200........$375.00

Sweet Life Cissy, The, 21", #38320, 2004, green silk sheath dress, straw hat $350.00

Opulent Shimmer Boutique Cissy, 21", #38375, 2004, blue hair, long sequin sparkle dress ...$400.00

Object of Desire Cissy, 21", #38330, 2004, long red gown with bustle, black hat $375.00

Cissy and the City, 21", #38325, 2004, pants, long green trench coat, plush dog....................$400.00

Life in the Limelight Cissy, 21", #38345, 2004, long gold silk dress.....................................$400.00

Life in the Limelight Cissy, 21", #38348, 2004, African-American $450.00

Romancing the Railway Cissy, 21", #38315, 2004, suit, trunk with extra clothes....................$375.00

Extravagance Cissy by Mel Odom, 21", #39840, 2005, green jacket over floral silk dress $400.00

Gold and the Beautiful Cissy, The, 21", #39870, 2005, gold beaded dress with fur stole $400.00

Luxe be a Lady Cissy, Latin, 21", #39876, 2005, velvet gown with a train $400.00

Luxe Be a Lady, African-American, 21", #39876, 2005, velvet gown with a train...................$400.00

Closet Full of Couture Cissy, 21", #39895, 2005, gray silk suit plus chiffon dress..................$400.00

On the A-List Cissy, 21", #39890, 2005, green bolero jacket and skirt.....................................$400.00

Cissy Takes Manhatten, 21", #39865, long red coat over skirt and sweater $400.00

Smart Style Cissy, 21", #42770, 2005, black jacket, blue taffetta dress $400.00

Couture Noir Cissy, 21", #45370, 2006, long black dress with ruffles $500.00

Nouveau Dynamite Cissy, 21", 2006, #42720, African-American, green dress $450.00

Scene Stealer Cissy, 21", #42705, 2006, navy silk dress..$400.00

Bewitching Salem Cissy, 21", #45610, 2006, black silk...$350.00

Charmed Life Cissy, A, 21", 2006, #42710, flat foot Cissy, plaid dress, also suede skirt and sweater set...$500.00

Cissy in Twilight, 21", 2006, #42695, blue silk gown $550.00

Heiress Elegance Cissy, 21", 2006, #42700, blue skirt, organza jacket, brocade coat.............$600.00

Belle Fleur Cissy, 21", #45605, 2006, black silk gown $450.00

Velvet Deco Dreams Cissy, 21", #47045, 2007, brown velvet long kimono...........................$600.00

Southwestern Style Cissy, 21", #46595, 2007, suede vest, purple leather skirt $500.00

Captivating Swashbuckler Cissy, 21", #46095, 2007, long striped jacket, black hat, plush parrot...$600.00

Vanity Affair Cissy, 21", #46590, 2007, brown brocade cocktail dress, fur jacket $500.00
Simply Irresistible Cissy, 21", #46600, 2007, fuchsia taffeta beaded gown............................ $600.00
Evening Star Cissy, 21", #46155, 2007, navy blue taffeta dress $550.00
Riviera Posh Cissy, 21" #47040, 2007, long pink dotted chiffon skirt, bra top....................... $400.00
Happy Feet Rockette 1990 Cissy, 21", #47650, 2007, gold and maroon dance costume $300.00
Shimmering Touch Cissy, 21", #48825, 2008, turquoise dress with black lacy overdress........... $400.00
Brilliant Cascade Cissy, 21", #47655, 2008, gold lace layered evening gown $650.00
85th Anniversary Cissy, 21", #48295, 2008, silk dress, black hat, brocade and fur coat...... $1,700.00
Timeless Beauty Rose Cissy, 21", #48305, 2008, pink taffeta torso gown with ruffles.......... $1,400.00
Timeless Beauty Violet Cissy, 21", #48300, 2008, purple ball gown, opera coat $1,800.00
Scarlett Visits the Mill Cissy, 21", #48165, 2008, white long dress, blue jacket, parasol $500.00

Cissy Bride — 21", #52011, porcelain portrait, 1994 only.. $350.00

Cissy Boutique Shadow Cissette — 10", #47010, 2007, black dress, feather hat,
    wig, jewelry $180.00

Cissy by Scassi — (see FAO Schwarz under Special Events/Exclusives)

Cissy Godey Bride — 21", #011, porcelain, 1993 only... $350.00

City Mouse — 8", #45825, 2007, print dress, mouse figurine... $75.00

Civil War — 18" h.p., #2010B, 1953 only, Glamour Girls Series, white taffeta with red
    roses (Margaret) .... $1,800.00 up

Clara — 8", #25330, 2000 – 2001, long blue gown with nutcracker $90.00

Clara & the Nutcracker — 14", #1564, 1992 only (Louisa/Jennifer) $75.00

Clarabell Clown — 19", 1951 – 1953 .... $375.00
    29" $575.00
    49" $1,000.00

Clara's Party Dress — 8", #14570, 1995, Nutcracker Series... $70.00

Classic Ballerina — 16", #22700, white tulle and satin (1999).. $100.00

Classic Bride — 16", #22690, white tulle and lace gown (1999) $100.00

Classic Lenox Ornament and Doll — 8", #48450, 2008, snowflake ornament, plaid dress $200.00

Claudette — 10", #1123 (in peach), 1988 – 1989, Portrette (Cissette)................................... $70.00

Claudia — 14", #34360, 2003, blue dress with lace $80.00

Cleopatra — 12", #1315, 1980 – 1985, Portraits of History Series.. $60.00
    10", #86002, 1996 Platinum Collection $75.00
    10", #40830, 2005, white dress $85.00

Cleveland, Frances — 1985 – 1987, fourth set Presidents' Ladies/First Ladies Series (Mary Ann) ... $100.00

Closet Full of Couture Shadow Cissette — 10", 2007, #47005, silver suit, nude dress,
    magenta wig $180.00

Clover Kid — 7" compo., 1935 – 1936 (Tiny Betty) $375.00

Clown — 8", #305, 1990 – 1992 only, Americana Series, has painted face (Wendy) $70.00
    Baby — 8", #464, 1955, painted face (Wendy Ann), dog.............................. $1,000.00 up
    Bobo — 8" h.p., #310, 1991 – 1992 (Wendy Ann)... $65.00
    Pierrot — 8", #561, 1956 only (Wendy Ann) .... $1,000.00 up
    14", 1991 only, #1558, white costume with red trim $90.00
    Stilts — 8", #320, 1992 – 1993, doll on stilts... $125.00

Clue Game Doll — 8", #25255, 2000, maid costume $60.00

Coca-Cola Carhop — 10", #17400, 1997 – 2000, roller skates, #17401, brunette....................... $90.00

Coca-Cola Celebrates American Aviation — 10", #17380, 1998 – 1999........................... $90.00

Coca-Cola Fantasy — 10", #31210 – white, #31213 – black, 1997 – 1998........................... $110.00

Coca-Cola 1920s — 10", #28280, 2001, long white dress with lace.................................... $125.00

Coca-Cola Nostalgia — 16", #17490, 1999, white lace dress $100.00

Coca-Cola Off to the North Pole — 8", #25245, 2001, with bear $100.00

Coca-Cola School Days — 8" #28275, 2001 – 2002, includes lunchbox............................. $100.00

Coca-Cola Sock Hop — 10", #26255, 2001, red checked skirt... $110.00

Coca-Cola Victorian Calendar Doll — 10", #17360, 1998 – 1999.................................... $125.00

Coca-Cola Winter Fun Wendy — 8", #17370, 1999, red ski outfit................................... $85.00

Coco — 21" plastic/vinyl, 1966, in various clothes (other than Portrait)............................ $2,000.00 up
    In sheath style ball gown .... $2,200.00 up

**Baby Clown, 8", SLW, #464, 1955.
Painted face. All original with dog.
$1,000.00 up.**

14", #1558, 1991 – 1992, Classic Series (Mary Ann) $80.00

10", #1140, 1989 – 1992, Portrette, dressed in all black (Cissette) $70.00

16", #31240, 1997 – 1998, travel wardrobe and dog, Cleo.....................................$300.00

16", #22400, 1998, Belle Epoque, includes houndstooth and glitter gown outfits..................$275.00

Collecting Bears, Teddy and Me — 8", #33020, 2002 – 2003, 8" doll and 5" bear
in matching blue outfits $85.00

Collecting Butterflies — 8", #28240, 2001, lavender dress with butterflies $55.00

Collecting Buttons — 8", #28245, 2001, white dress trimmed in pink $55.00

Collecting Dolls — 8", #30940, 2001 – 2002, pink lacy dress with doll and dollhouse case........$80.00

Collecting Seashells — 8", #28250, 2001, yellow dress with seashells.....................$55.00

Collecting Trains — 8", #28585, 2001 – 2002, striped overalls with Bachmann train $85.00

Collector Pin Series — 1999, 2½" polyresin miniature doll $10.00

Collectors United — (see Special Events/Exclusives)

Colleen — 10", #1121, 1988 only, Portrette, in green (Cissette) $75.00

Colonial — 7" compo., 1937 – 1938 (Tiny Betty) $375.00

9" compo., 1936 – 1939 (Little Betty)...$400.00

8" h.p., BKW, #389, #789, 1962 – 1964 (Wendy Ann) $300.00

Columbian Sailor — (see U.F.D.C. under Special Events/Exclusives)

Columbine — 8", #14575 – 1995, Nutcracker Series $60.00

Columbus, Christopher — 8" h.p., #328, 1992 only, Americana Series $125.00

Comedienne — 10", #20120, clown, 1996 Cirque du Soleil Series............................$90.00

Computer Age Wendy — 8", #17820, 1999, comes with laptop and cell phone...........$70.00

Confederate Officer — 12", 1990 – 1991, Scarlett Series (Nancy Drew) $80.00

8" h.p., 1991 – 1992, Scarlett Series (see Ashley)

Contemporary Bride — 10", 2001 ....$100.00

Cookie — 19" compo./cloth, 1938 – 1940, must be in excellent condition $650.00

Coolidge, Grace — 14", 1989 – 1990, sixth set Presidents' Ladies/First Ladies Series
(Louisa) $100.00

Coppelia — 16", #28390, 2001, pink ballerina $100.00

Coppertone Beach Set — 8", #12110, 1998 – 1999, bikini, umbrella, suntan lotion.................$100.00

Coquette Cissy — 10", #39255, pants, sweater, purse, 2004....................................$75.00

10", #39600, red suit, 2004..$75.00

10", #40670, 2005, elegant Simplicity Coquete Jacqui, print dress, blue sweater $75.00

10", #40660, 2005, Dressed to Thrill Coquette Cissy, Latin, green evening dress $85.00

10", #40665, 2005, Sight to See Coquette Cissy, African-American, yellow beaded gown.........$90.00

10", #40666, 2005, Sight to See Coquette Cissy, yellow beaded gown $90.00

10", #40710, 2005, Like No Other Coquette Cissy, strapless evening gown $85.00

10", #40650, 2005, Well Suited Coquette Cissy, white pants outfit.............................$80.00

10", #41635, 2006, Triple Take Coquette Cissy, blue evening gown $90.00

10", #40025, 2006, Signature Style Coquette Cissy Trunk Set, three outfits with trunk.........$220.00

10", #41250, 2006, Rose Shimmer, pink gown, silver accents $100.00

10", #41655, 2006, Classic with a Twist Coquette Jacqui, blue dress and coat..........................$95.00

10", #41620, 2006, Crowd Pleaser Coquette Cissy, brown feather outfit $95.00

10", #41640, 2006, Club Hopping Coquette Cecee, African-American, blue pants outfit.........$90.00

Coral and Leopard Travel Ensemble — 10", #22180, 1997.................................$110.00

Cornelia — Cloth and felt, 1930s..$700.00 up

21", #2191, 1972, Portrait, dressed in pink with full cape (Jacqueline) $400.00

#2191, 1973, pink with ¾ length jacket...$375.00

#2296, 1974, blue with black trim..$325.00

#2290, 1975, rose red with black trim and hat $350.00

#2293, 1976, pink with black trim and hat $300.00

#2212, 1978, blue with full cape..$300.00

Coroner — 8", #38395, 2004 – 2005, Wizard of Oz series, has death certificate for
Wicked Witch $80.00

Cossack — 8" h.p., #511, 1989 – 1991 (Wendy Ann) $55.00

Costume Party — #37785, 2003 – 2004, mask, dog, black hat...............................$80.00

Country Christmas — 14", #1543, 1991 – 1992 only, Classic Series (Mary Ann) $110.00
    8", #20190, 1999 – 2000, calico dress, snowman $60.00
Country Club — 8", #37980, Latin, 2004 – 2005, blue flower dress, large straw hat $85.00
Country Cousins — 10" cloth, 1940s..$575.00
    26" cloth, 1940s $650.00
    30" cloth, 1940s $750.00
    16½", 1958, mint (Mary-Bel) $350.00
Country Fair — (see Wendy Loves)
Country Mouse — 8", # 45860, 2007, overalls, Maggie, mouse figurine $75.00
Count Your Blessings Angel — 10", #36575, 2004 – 2005, pink costume.............................$110.00
Courtney and Friends — (see Madame Alexander Doll Company under Special Events/Exclusives)
Courtyard — 8", #38840, 2004, pink elaborate gown, limited to 1,000.....................................$125.00
Cousin Grace — 8" h.p., BKW, #432, 1957 only (Wendy Ann) .... $1,900.00 up
Cousin Karen — 8" h.p., BKW, #620, 1956 only (Wendy Ann) .... $1,800.00 up
Cousin Marie & Mary — 8" h.p. (Marie, #465; Mary, #462), 1963 only (Wendy Ann), each.... $1,000.00 up
Cowardly Lion — 8", #431, 1993, Storybook Series, #140431, 1994 – 1996......................$75.00
    #13220, #13211, 1997, 2003 – 2006 (Wizard of Oz), tan lion costume....................$70.00
    5", #28695, 2001 – 2002, porcelain...$70.00
    5", #36350, 2005, petitie $25.00
    9", #39795, 2005 – 2007, lion outfit $35.00
    8", #46330, 2007 – 2008, lion outfit, Medal of Courage $70.00
Cowboy — 8" h.p., BK, #732, 1967 – 1969, Americana Series (Wendy Ann).........................$350.00
    8", 1987 (see M.A.D.C. under Special Events/Exclusives)
Cowgirl — 8" h.p., BK, #724, 1967 – 1970, Americana/Storybook Series (Wendy Ann) $350.00
Congratulations — 8" h.p., #21180, 1998 (Maggie), pink dress, balloons.............................$55.00
    10", #1132, 1990 – 1991, Portrette, white/red outfit (Cissette) $75.00
Crayola, Americana — 8", #17840 – 17873, felt outfits, with Crayola crayons ....$45.00 ea.
Crayola Meagan — 14", #25470, 2000, brown dress, with Crayola crayons $65.00
Crete — 8" straight legs, #529, 1987 only $65.00
Croatia — 8" h.p., #110543, 1994 (Wendy Ann) $60.00
Crockett, Davy, Boy or Girl — 8" h.p., 1955 only (Boy – #446; Girl – #443)
    (Wendy Ann) ....$700.00 up, ea.
Croquet Match — 8", #39725, 2005, white dress, green sweater, croquet set $85.00
Cruella DeVille — 10", #38370, 2004 – 2005, with three 2" puppies $150.00
Cry Dolly — 14" – 16" vinyl, 1953, 12-piece layette..$250.00
    14", 16", 19", in swimsuit..$100.00 – 185.00
    16" – 19" all vinyl, dress or rompers ....$125.00 – 250.00
Cuba — 8", #11548, 1995 only, has round brown face $65.00
    8", #38600, 2004 – 2005, includes maracas $70.00
Cuddly — 10½" cloth, 1942 – 1944 ....$375.00
    17" cloth, 1942 – 1944..$400.00
Cupid — 8", #13860, 1998 – 1999 (Maggie), white costume, bow, arrow $65.00
Curly Locks — 8" h.p., #472, 1955 only (Wendy Ann) .... $950.00 up
    8" straight leg, #421, 1987 – 1988, Storybook Series, 1997 (Wendy Ann) $65.00
    8", #28315, 2001 – 2002, print dress with flowers...$65.00
Cute Little Baby — 14", 1994 – 1995, doll only, $85.00. With layette and basket...................$150.00
Cutie Patootie — 18", #28320, 2001, cloth, Mary Engelbreit, pink dress.............................$45.00
Cynthia — 15" h.p., 1952 only (black "Margaret")...$850.00 up
    18", 1952 only ....$900.00 up
    23", 1952 only ....$1,200.00 up
Cyrano — 8" h.p., #140505, 1994 only, Storyland Series (Pinocchio) $65.00
Czarina Alexandra — 8", #12620, 1999, blue satin and gold..$75.00
Czechoslovakia — 7" compo., 1935 – 1937 (Tiny Betty) $325.00
    8" h.p., BK, #764, 1972 (Wendy Ann) $90.00
      Straight legs, #0764, #564, 1973 – 1975, marked "Alex" $65.00
      Straight legs, #536, 1976 – 1987, marked "Alexander".................................$50.00

Daisy, 10", #1110, 1987 – 1989 (Cissette). White lace over yellow gown. $60.00.

Deborah Bride, 21", 1950 (Margaret). Very unusual gown with five-piece layered bustle. Extremely rare doll. $9,000.00 up.

8", #536, 1985 – 1987, #521, 1992 – 1993 (Wendy Ann) $55.00

Daddy's Little Princess — 8", #38920, 2004 – 2005, pink dress, tiara.....................................$85.00

Daddy's My Hero — 8", #36765, 2003 – 2004, blue pleated dress, police hat $80.00

Daddy's #1 Girl — 8", #47875, 2008, pink dotted dress...$50.00

Daffy Down Dilly — 8" straight legs, #429, 1986 only, Storybook Series
(Wendy Ann or Maggie) $60.00

Dahl, Arlene (Pink Champagne) — 18" h.p., 1950 – 1951, red wig, lavender gown
(Maggie), mint ....$7,500.00 up

Daisy — 10", #1110, 1987 – 1989, Portrette Series, white lace over yellow (Cissette) ... **$60.00**

Daisy Fairy — 8", #36890, 2003 – 2004, long pink dress, yellow petal trim $90.00

Daisy Munchkin — 8", #28770, 2001, white outfit with daisies..$75.00

Daisy Resort Cissette Ensemble — 10", #22380, 1998, silk, linen outfit, chair $140.00

Daisies and Bees — 8", #45845, 2007, black checked dress, beekeeper's box $75.00

Dance of the Flowers — 8", #25225, 2000 – 2001, blue embroidered tutu $60.00

Dancing Clara — 8", #34305, 2002, pink dress, holding nutcracker $75.00

Dancing Princess Blue — 10", #32050, 2000, blue tulle gown $90.00

Dancing Princess Gold — 10", #32055, 2000, gold tulle gown $90.00

Dancing Princess Magenta — 10", #32045, 2000, tulle and lace gown $90.00

Dancing Queen Total Moves Wendy — 8", #38265, 2004 ....$75.00

Danger's Bath — 8", #38490, 2004 – 2005, swimsuit with dog, tub, etc. $95.00

Danger's First Easter — 8", #45430, lavender dress, dog 2006 – 2007 ....$80.00

Danish — 7" compo., 1937 – 1941 (Tiny Betty)...$350.00
9" compo., 1938 – 1940 (Little Betty) $350.00

Dare, Virginia — 9" compo., 1940 – 1941 (Little Betty)..$450.00

Darlene — 18" cloth/vinyl, 1991 – 1992 ....$75.00

Darling Little Dancer — 8", #30335, 1999, pink tulle, limited to 2,500.............................$85.00

David and Diana — (see FAO Schwarz under Special Events/Exclusives)

David Copperfield — 7" compo., 1936 – 1938 (Tiny Betty)..$375.00
14" compo., 1938 only (Wendy Ann) $750.00
16" cloth, early 1930s, Dickens character ....$850.00 up

David Quack-a-Field or Twistail — cloth/felt, 1930s ....$700.00 up

David, the Little Rabbi — (see Celia's Dolls under Special Events/Exclusives)

Daydreaming in the Park — 8", #46010, 2007, bench, birds, feed....................................$80.00

Day at the Mall, A — 8", #48545, 2008, jeans, sunglasses $70.00

Day at the Races, A — 8", #47915, 2008, white vintage outfit, hat, binoculars....................$85.00

Day of Week Dolls — 7", 1935 – 1940 (Tiny Betty) ....$375.00 ea.
9" – 11" compo., 1936 – 1938 (Little Betty)..$375.00 ea.
13" compo., 1939 (Wendy Ann) $450.00

Day to Remember — 10", 2001, bride...$100.00

Dazzling Winter Skater — 8", #45425, 2006 – 2008, blue and white costume $85.00

Dear America Series — 18" re-creations from Dear America book series
Abigail Jane Stewart, 1999 – 2000, 18", blue print dress $75.00
Catherine Carey Logan, 1999 – 2000, 18", Pilgrim costume $75.00
Margaret Ann Brady, 1999 – 2000, 18", pink dress $75.00
Remember Patience Whipple, 1999 – 2000, 18", red vest, skirt $75.00
Clotee, a Slave Girl, 2000, #25665, African-American, brown outfit..............................$85.00
Emma Simpson, a Southern Belle, 2000, #25660, long beige dress $75.00
Sara Nita, a Navajo Girl, 2000, #25655, black Indian outfit $75.00
Zipporah Feldman, a Jewish Immigrant, 2000, #25650...$75.00

Dearest — 12" vinyl baby, 1962 – 1964 ....$125.00 – 175.00

Deborah Bride — 16", #25595, 2000, remake of 1949 – 1951 costume $185.00

Debra (Deborah) — 21", 1949 – 1951, Portrait, ballerina with extra make-up (Margaret).....$7,000.00 up
21", 1950, bride with five-piece layered bustle in back (Margaret) ....$9,000.00 up

Debutante — 18" h.p., 1953 only (Maggie) ....$1,250.00 up

December — 14", #1528, 1989 only, Classic Series (Mary Ann)..$75.00

Deck the Halls — 8", #35990, 2003 – 2004, red print dress with garland $70.00

Decorating the Tree — 8", #41145, 2006, green dress, ornament $70.00
DeFoe, Dr. Allen — 14" – 15" compo., 1937 – 1939...$1,600.00 up
Degas — 21" compo., 1945 – 1946, Portrait (Wendy Ann) ....$2,300.00 up
Degas Ballerina (The Star) — 10", #13910, 1998 – 1999 (Cissette), white tutu $80.00
   10", #25305, 2000 – 2001, long pink tutu with flowers $80.00
Degas Ballerina Wendy Ann Felt — 12", #42015, 2006, limited to 400 ....$275.00
Degas "Dance Lesson" — 14", #241598, 1994 ....$75.00
Degas Girl — 14", #1475 (#1575 from 1974), 1967 – 1987 (20-year production), Portrait
   Children and Fine Arts Series (Mary Ann) $60.00
Degas' Rehearsal Shadow Box — 10", 2001, #28410, white costume,
   gold shadow box $150.00
Delicious Wishes — 8", #41970, 2006, plum and plaid trimmed dress $75.00
Delightful Afternoon — 10", #30410, 2001, long pink gown $120.00
Delilah — 8" h.p., #14583, 1995 only, Bible Character Dolls Series.............................$100.00
Denmark — 10" h.p., 1962 – 1963 (Cissette) $700.00
   8" h.p., BK, #769, 1970 – 1972 (Wendy Ann)..$100.00
   8" h.p., straight legs, 0769 – 569, 1973 – 1975, marked "Alex" (Wendy) $65.00
   8" h.p., straight legs, #546, 1976 – 1989, marked "Alexander" (1985 –1987
      white face) (Wendy), #519, 1991 only (Wendy Ann).................................$55.00
Desert Storm — (see Welcome Home)
Desperate Housewives
   Bree Van de Camp, 16", #45895, 2007, white long halter dress $100.00
   Edie Britt, 16", #45885, 2007, orange halter dress $90.00
   Susan Mayer, 16", #45880, 2007, green cocktail dress...................................... $90.00
   Lynette Scavo, 16", #45900, black pants outfit... $100.00
   Gabrielle Solis, 16", #45890, 2007, blue dress, gold wrap $90.00
   Edie Britt, 16", #47665, 2007, pink long dress $90.00
   Susan Mayer, 16", #47670, 2007, pink dress with pink sash $100.00
   Bree Van de Kamp, 16", #47680, 2007, pink stripe halter dress............................. $90.00
   Lynette Scavo, 16", #47675, 2007, eyelet halter dress.................................... $95.00
   Gabrielle Solis, 16", #47685, 2007, pink dress with elaborate circle lace design $100.00
Dewdrop Fairy — 8", #28495, 2001 – 2002, blue tulle costume $75.00
Diamond Beauty — 21", 1998, black gown...$850.00
Diamond Dance — 8", #26030, 2000, long pink gown, rhinestones $100.00
Diamond Lil — 10" (see M.A.D.C. under Special Events/Exclusives)
Diana — 14", 1993 – 1994, Anne of Green Gables Series, trunk and wardrobe $165.00
   Tea dress, came with tea set, 1993 only $125.00
   Sunday Social, 8", #260417, 1994 – 1995 (Wendy Ann) $100.00
   Sunday Social, 14", #261503, 1994 ....$100.00
Dick and Jane — 8" set, #46245, with plush dog, 2007...$100.00
Dickinson, Emily — 14", #1587, 1989 only, Classic Series (Mary Ann) $90.00
Dicksie & Ducksie — cloth/felt, 1930s.. $700.00 up
Dietrich, Marlene Shanghai Express — 16", #33485, 2002, long red coat dress,
   limited to 1,500..$125.00
Dilly Dally Sally — 7" compo., 1937 – 1942 (Tiny Betty)..$350.00
   9" compo., 1938 – 1939 (Little Betty) $350.00
Ding Dong Bell — 7" compo., 1937 – 1942 (Tiny Betty) $375.00
Dinner at Eight — 10", #1127, 1989 – 1991, Portrette, black/white dress (Cissette) $60.00
Dinner with Grandma and Grandpa — 8", #46030, Maggie, 2007, lace dress......................$75.00
Dinosaur — 8" h.p., #343, 1993 – 1994, Americana Series $70.00
Dion, Celine — 10", 1999 (Cissette), long gown, heart necklace................................$100.00
Dionne Furniture — (no dolls)
   Scooter, holds five or divided high chair, holds five .... $375.00 up
   Basket case, holds five $250.00
   Table and chairs, five-piece set...$475.00
   Ferris wheel, holds five... $500.00 up

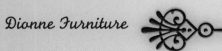

Bath/shower ....$250.00 up

Wagon, holds five...$425.00 up

Playpen, holds five ....$350.00 up

Crib, holds five ....$375.00 up

Tricycle ....$175.00 up

Merry-go-round, holds five ....$400.00 up

High chair for one..$150.00

Dionne Quints — Original mint or very slight craze. Each has own color:

    Yvonne – pink, Annette – yellow, Cecile – green, Emilie – lavender, Marie – blue

20" compo. toddlers, 1938 – 1939...$700.00 ea., $4,200.00 set

19" compo. toddlers, 1936 – 1938...$700.00 ea., $4,200.00 set

16" – 17" compo. toddlers, 1937 – 1939 ....$650.00 ea., $3,600.00 set

11" compo. toddlers, 1937 – 1938, wigs and sleep eyes ....$400.00 ea., $2,200.00 set

11" compo. toddlers, 1937 – 1938, molded hair and sleep eyes ....$400.00 ea., $2,200.00 set

11" compo. babies, 1936, wigs and sleep eyes ....$400.00 ea., $2,200.00 set

11" compo. babies, 1936, molded hair and sleep eyes ....$400.00 ea., $2,200.00 set

8" compo. toddlers, 1935 – 1939, molded hair or wigs and painted eyes .... $300.00 ea., $1,500.00 set

8" compo. babies, 1935 – 1939, molded hair or wigs and painted eyes ....$300.00 ea., $1,500.00 set

14" cloth/compo., 1938 ....$475.00 ea., $3,100.00 set

17" cloth/compo., 1938 ....$575.00 ea., $3,600.00 set

22" cloth/compo., 1936 – 1937 .... $750.00 up

24" all cloth, 1935 – 1936, must be mint ....$1,200.00 ea.

16" all cloth, 1935 – 1936, must be mint .... $900.00 up

8" h.p., 1998, 75th Anniversary Set with carousel, #12230 ....$400.00

8" Yvonne, Marie, Annette, Cecile, Emilie, 1998 ....$70.00 ea.

Nursery (cardboard) with Dr. Dafoe, nurse, 8" quints, and furniture (all composition dolls).....$7,000.00

Disney — (see Special Events/Exclusives)

Disney Princess Dress Up Trunk Set — 8", #46535, three outfits, accessories, trunk, 2007 – 2008...$150.00

Dogs — (see Poodles)

Doll Finders — (see Special Events/Exclusives)

Doll Hospital Nurse — 8" #33575, 2002, red dress and nurse's hat with 2½" doll $80.00

Dolls 'n Bearland — (see Special Events/Exclusives)

Dolls of the Month — 7" – 8" compo., 1937 – 1939, Birthday Dolls (Tiny Betty) $375.00

Dolly — 8", #436, 1988 – 1989, Storybook Series (Wendy Ann), 1997.......................................$65.00

Dolly Dears — (see Special Events/Exclusives)

Dolly Dryper — 11" vinyl, 1952 only, seven-piece layette..$300.00

Dolly Levi (Matchmaker) — 10" Portrette, 1994 only..$75.00

Dominican Republic — 8" straight leg, #544, 1986 – 1988 (1985 – 1986 white face)................$50.00

Dormouse — 8", #13090, 1998 – 2000, mouse in sugar bowl with spoon $80.00

8", #46370, 2007, painted face, beige mouse outfit $75.00

Dorothy — 14", #1532, 1990 – 1993, Wizard of Oz, all blue/white checked dress and

    solid blue pinafore (Mary Ann) $100.00

8" h.p., #464, 1991 – 1993, #140464, 1994 – 1995, blue/white checked dress, white bodice

    (Wendy Ann), Wizard of Oz..$90.00

8" h.p., emerald green dress, mid-year special (see

    Madame Alexander Doll Co. under Special Events/Exclusives)

8" h.p., #13200, 1997 – 1999, blue checked dress, basket with Toto, #13201, 2000 – 2001.......$80.00

8", #13202, 2003 – 2006, ruby slippers, Toto in basket, blue checked dress $60.00

8", #38715, 2004, limited to 1,000, blue checked silk dress $95.00

14" plastic/vinyl, #87007, 1996 ....$125.00

15" cloth, #25545, 2000 – 2001, blue checked dress, with Toto...$50.00

5" porcelain, #27065, 2000 – 2004, blue checked dress, with Toto...$70.00

10", #36775, 2003 – 2004, blue checked dress with 5" Lullaby, Flower Bonnet and

    Mayor Munchkin, Toto $165.00

21", #36355, Dorothy Cissy, flat chested torso, Toto in basket $275.00

9", #39975, 2005 – 2007, blue checked dress, red shoes $35.00

5", #36335, 2005, petite, checked dress, Toto in basket $25.00

8", #41255, 2006, Dorothy Wendy-Kin Wood with Toto $250.00

8", #42420, 2006, Off to Oz, with lunchbox and Toto $105.00

8", #46360, blue check dress, Toto, 2007 – 2008, sparkle shoes...$60.00

8", #48485, 2008, I'm Melting, checked dress with melting wicked witch $110.00

Dottie Dumbunnie — cloth/felt, 1930s...$800.00 up

Dream Dance — 10", #26180, 2000 (Cissette), blue, short party dress.................................$75.00

    10", #26175, 2000 (Cissette), black bodice, long tulle gown...$80.00

Dressed for Opera — 18" h.p., 1953 only (Margaret) ....$1,800.00 up

Dressed Like Daddy — 8", #17002, 1996, white or black...$75.00

Dressed Like Mommy — 8", #17001, 1996 – 1998, white or black....................................$75.00

Drizzly Days in Seattle — 8", #48120, 2008, raincoat, hat, umbrella $75.00

Drucilla — (see M.A.D.C. under Special Events/Exclusives)

Drum Majorette — (see Majorette)

Duchess Eliza, The — 10", #20114, 1996 Classics $85.00

Duchess, The — 8", #14613, 1996, Alice in Wonderland Series $95.00

    8", #39745, 2005, long elaborate red dress..$90.00

Dude Ranch — 8" h.p., #449, 1955 only (Wendy Ann) ....$750.00 up

Dudley Do-Right and Nell — 8", #15140, 1999, Dudley in Mounty outfit (Maggie), Nell,

    (Wendy) includes rope, train track, and backdrop $140.00

Dumplin' Baby — 20" – 23½", 1957 – 1958 ....$165.00

Dutch — 7" compo., 1935 – 1939 (Tiny Betty)..$325.00

    9" compo. boy or girl, 1936 – 1941 ....$325.00

    8" h.p., BKW, #777, 1964, boy* (Wendy) $225.00

        BK, #777, #0777, 1965 – 1972, #791, 1965 – 1972...$100.00

    8" h.p., straight leg, #777, *0777, 1972 – 1973, marked "Alex"...$75.00

    8" h.p., BKW, #391 – 791, 1961 – 1964, girl* $125.00

    8" BKW, #791, 1964 only (Maggie)..$150.00

Dutch Lullaby — 8", #499, 1993, #140499, 1994, Wynkin, Blynkin & Nod, in wooden shoe...$150.00

Earhart, Amelia — 8", #40415, 2005, comes with bear with goggles.................................$75.00

Easter — 8" h.p., #21020, 1998, hat with bunny ears, floral dress $60.00

Easter Bonnet — 14", #1562, 1992 (Louisa/Jennifer) $80.00

    8" h.p., #10383 – 10385, 1995 – 1996, three hair colors, Special Occasions Series.....................$60.00

    8" h.p., #10401, 1996, African-American $60.00

Easter Bunny — 8" (see Child at Heart Shop under Special Events/Exclusives

    8", #26675, 2001, blue dress, hat, basket with bunny $90.00

Easter Doll — 8" h.p., 1968 only, special for West Coast, in yellow dress (Wendy Ann),

    limited to 300..$1,400.00 up

    7½" SLNW, #361, 1953, organdy dress, doll carries basket with chicken.........................$925.00 up

    14" plastic/vinyl, 1968 only (Mary Ann), limited to 300..$600.00 up

Easter Egg Hunt — 8", #25020, 2000 – 2001, white dress, straw hat, basket........................$65.00

Easter Hop — 8", #37965, 2004 – 2005, pink checked dress, bunny $70.00

Easter Morning — 8", #34090, 2002, pink smocked dress, bunny purse..............................$65.00

Easter of Yesterday — 1995 (see C.U. under Special Events/Exclusives)

Easter Splendor — 8", #35445, 2003 – 2004, pink hat, white dress, basket, eggs, Bible............$80.00

Easter Sunday — 8" h.p., #340 or #340-1, 1993 only, Americana Series, black or white doll $65.00

    8", #21510 (white), #21513 (black), 1998 – 2000, yellow print dress, straw hat, basket...........$70.00

Easter Surprise — 8", #46265, 2007 – 2008, egg package, dotted dress and pinafore $85.00

Ebony and Ivory Houndstooth Suit — 10", #22190, 1997 – 1998 ....$150.00

Ecuador — 8" h.p., BK and BKW, #878, 1963 – 1966 (Wendy Ann)................................$350.00

Edith and the Duckling — 8", #31800, with duck and Mr. Bear $80.00

Edith, the Lonely Doll — 16" plastic/vinyl, 1958 – 1959 (Mary-Bel) $325.00

    22", 1958 – 1959...$375.00

    8" h.p., #850, 1958 only (Wendy Ann) ....$700.00 up

    8", #34025, 2003 – 2004, pink checked dress, 3" Mr. Bear $85.00

    8", #36930, 2004, wood doll, 3" Mr. Bear, limited to 750...$250.00

8", #37205, 2004, Holiday Trunk Set, four outfits, Mr. Bear...$200.00

12", #47760, 2007, Lissy, pink check dress, Mr. Bear $115.00

Edith with Golden Hair — 18" cloth, 1940s $675.00

Edwardian — 18" h.p., #2001A, 1953 only, pink embossed cotton long gown,

Glamour Girl Series (Margaret) ....$2,200.00 up

8" h.p., #0200, 1953 –1954 (Wendy Ann)..$1,000.00 up

80th Anniversary Cissette — 10", #34985, 2003, pink dress $125.00

80th Anniversary Cissy — 21" #34980, 2003, black crochet dress $450.00

80th Anniversary Wendy — 8", #34975, 2002, pink dress.......................................$75.00

85th Anniversary Cissette — 10", #48315, 2008, tulle evening gown, black stole.................$150.00

85th Anniversary Lissy — 12", #48320, 2008, white ballerina................................$135.00

85th Anniversary Wendy — 8", #48325, 2008, white and gold ballerina $90.00

Eisenhower, Mamie — 14", 1989 – 1990, sixth set Presidents' Ladies/First Ladies Series

(Mary Ann)...$100.00

Egypt — 8" straight leg, #543, 1986 – 1989 (round brown face)...............................$60.00

Egyptian — 7" – 8" compo., 1936 – 1940 (Tiny Betty)..$350.00

9" compo., 1936 – 1940 (Little Betty)..$375.00

Egypt with Sarcophagus — 8", #24110, 1998 – 2000, pharaoh costume $100.00

Elaine — 18" h.p., 1954 only, Me and My Shadow Series, blue organdy dress (Cissy) ..... $1,800.00 up

8" h.p., #0035E, 1954 only, matches 18" (Wendy Ann) ....$950.00 up

Elegant Emerald — 8", #32085, 2000 – 2002, long green ball gown $85.00

Elegant Simplicity Coquette Jacqui — blue sweater, pink print dress..................$80.00

Elise — 16½" h.p./vinyl arms (18", 1963 only), 1957 – 1964, jointed ankles and knees, face color

In street clothes or blouse, slacks, and sash ....$475.00 up

In ball gown, formal, or Portrait ....$800.00 up

In riding habit, 1963 (Mary-Bel head) $450.00

Ballerina, 1966 – 1991, rare yellow tutu, red hair...$900.00

With Mary-Bel head, 1962 only..$450.00

18", 1963 only, with bouffant hairstyle $475.00

17" h.p./vinyl, 1961 – 1962, one-piece arms and legs, jointed ankles and knees.....................$375.00

18" h.p./vinyl, 1963 – 1964, jointed ankles and knees, riding habit..........................$375.00

17" plastic/vinyl, 1966 only, street dress $375.00

17", 1966 – 1972, in trunk/trousseau.. $650.00 up

17", 1972 – 1973, Portrait..$175.00

17", 1966, 1976 – 1977, in formal $150.00

17", 1966 – 1987, Bride .... $125.00 up

17", 1966 – 1991, Ballerina .... $100.00 up

17", 1966 – 1989, in any discontinued costume .... $100.00 up

16", 1997, #22060, Firebird, red and gold tutu...$125.00

16", 1997, #22050, Giselle, aqua tutu, rose tiara, #22040, Swan Lake........................$125.00

Elise/Leslie — 14", #1560, 1988 only (Mary Ann)...$75.00

Eliza — 14", #1544, 1991 only, Classic Series (Louisa)..$80.00

Elizabethan Bride — 10", #25005, 2000, Cissette..$150.00

Elizabethan Pincushion — 2000 – 2001, pink #26480, gold #25645, 8", Wendy,

brocade as a pincushion...$90.00

Eliza the Flower Girl — 10", #20113, 1996 Classics...$90.00

Elle Woods — 16", #48930, 2008, Grand Finale, pink dress $135.00

Eloise — 8", #80680, 2000 – 2002, vinyl, Eloise lace, white blouse, navy pleated skirt $40.00

8", #33405, 2002, vinyl, Eloise in Paris, gray checked coat $45.00

8", #27701, 2001 – 2002, Eloise at Christmas time..$45.00

18", #80690, 2000 – 2003, cloth, Eloise face, same costume as 8" doll $45.00

36", Just Like Me, #30936, 2001, cloth with rag doll $185.00

8", Eloise Tea Party, #30810, 2001 – 2002, vinyl, white dress....................................$45.00

8", Eloise Loves to Dance, #30815, 2001, ballet..$45.00

12", Eloise Loves to Dance, #30935, 2001, cloth..$40.00

12", #27225, 2000 – 2003, poseable cloth..$30.00

8", #33410, 2002, Eloise in Moscow, gold coat, black hat..$45.00

8", #31670, Tea Party Trunk Set, trunk, tea set, clothes, 2002.................................$140.00

12", #31855, 2002 – 2003, Eloise in Paris, blue coat, travel bag, passport.................$75.00

8", #27710, 2000 – 2003, overnight kit, sleeping bag, clothes....................................$90.00

8", #47750, 2007, pink party dress, dog, turtle...$75.00

18", #46050, 2007 – 2008, cloth doll, white blouse, pleated skirt..............................$45.00

8", #46400, 2007 – 2008, Maggie, white blouse, pleated skirt, turtle, dog....................$70.00

18", #47415, 2008, cloth Eloise Christmas, green pleated skirt, red hat.......................$45.00

8", #47410, 2008, Maggie Eloise Christmas, green skirt, red hat, dog..........................$75.00

8", #48050, 2008, Maggie Eloise in Hollywood, black long dress................................$75.00

8", #48965, 2008, Eloise zip bin with ball...$60.00

Elphaba — 10", #45910, 2007, Wicked Witch of the West, Oz, green face,
    black costume and hat...$125.00

8", #46710, 2008, black costume, pointed hat, green face...$85.00

10", #48355, 2008, First Day of School, green face, blue top and pleated skirt.............$125.00

Elvis Presley Blue Suede Shoes — 8", #47690, 2008, guitar....................................$90.00

El Salvador — 8", #40635, 2005, with basket of fruit...$80.00

Emerald City and Wizard Chamber — folding playscape, #25945, 15" tall.................$325.00

Emerald City Guard — 8", #31395, 2001 – 2002, black costume with sequin hat..........$80.00

Emerald Isle — 8", #42800, 2006 – 2007, green dress, 5" Wendy, leprechaun doll........$90.00

Emerald Lass — 8", #27870, 2001, green dress..$60.00

Emily — cloth/felt, 1930s...$600.00

14", #34350, 2002 – 2003, black and white dress..$90.00

5", #27420, 2003, petite, pink dress..$20.00

Emily Elizabeth — 8", #26370, 2000 – 2002 (Maggie), with cloth 16" Clifford dog.......$85.00

5" petite Emily Elizabeth and 10" plush red Clifford dog..$45.00

Emma — 10", #25335, 2000 (Cissette) long blue gown, straw hat...............................$110.00

8", #47945, 2008, pink and white long dress, holding rose...$80.00

Emperor and Nightingale — 8", #33700, 2002, with birdcage....................................$90.00

Empire Bride — 10" (Cissette), white lace gown (1999)..$125.00

Empress Elizabeth of Austria — 10" (see My Doll House under Special Events/Exclusives)

Enchanted Doll House — (see Special Events/Exclusives)

Enchanted Evening — 21" Portrait, 1991 – 1992 only, different necklace than shown in
    catalog (Cissy)..$300.00

Endora — 10", #40125, green pant suit, 2005..$100.00

England — 8", #24040, 1997 – 1999, Beefeater guard outfit....................................$70.00

8", #28560, 2001, Queen costume..$70.00

English Guard — 8" h.p., BK, #764, 1966 – 1968, Portrait Children Series (Wendy Ann)......$350.00

8", #515, reintroduced 1989 – 1991, marked "Alexander" (Wendy Ann).........................$60.00

Entertaining the Troops — 8", #17550, 1999, red outfit, microphone.........................$70.00

Equestrian Wendy — 8", #35575, 2003 – 2005, red jacket, crop, plush horse...............$85.00

Eskimo — 8" h.p., BK, #723, 1967 – 1969, Americana Series (Wendy Ann)..................$350.00

9" compo., 1936 – 1939 (Little Betty) or 8" BKW Maggie...$350.00

Esmeralda — 9", #39960, 2005 – 2007, vinyl, long red dress...................................$35.00

10", #40350, 2005, long red dress...$100.00

Estonia — 8" straight legs, #545, 1986 – 1987 only (Wendy Ann)..............................$60.00

Estrella — 18" h.p. (Maggie), lilac gown, 1953....................................$1,200.00 up

Ethiopia — 8", #42535, 2006, white dress, coffee pot...$70.00

Eva Lovelace — 7" compo., 1935 only (Tiny Betty)...$375.00

Evangeline — 18" cloth, 1930s..$650.00 up

Evening Cissette — 10", #38745, 2004, white dress, lavender trim............................$125.00

Evening at the Opera — 8", #47916, 2008, burgandy dress.......................................$75.00

Evening of Romance — 10", #27010, 2000 (Cissette), black lace gown.........................$125.00

Evening Star — 15" porcelain, black lace over pink satin (1999 – 2000)......................$125.00

Evil Queen — 10", #42630, 2006, blue outfit, magic mirror....................................$100.00

Evil Sorceress — 8", #13610, 1997, long black velvet dress....................................$70.00

Fairy Godmother, 14", #1550, 1983 – 1990, (Mary Ann) All original. $75.00

Fashions of the Century, 18",
1954 – 1955 (Margaret). All original. Tagged dress and wrist tag.
$2,500.00 up.

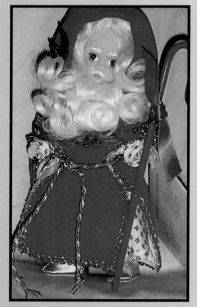

Father Christmas, 8", #100351,
1994 (Wendy). Americana Series,
red velvet coat. $75.00.

Eyre, Jane — 10", #45920, 2007, Cissette, long brown dress, green jacket $135.00
Fabulous Bloom — 8", #40850, 2005, red checked dress, curly hair $90.00
Fairie-ality Trunk Set — 8", #31825, log trunk, three outfits, accessories, 2003 – 2005..........$240.00
Fairy Godmother — 14", #1550, #1551, #1568, 1983 – 1992, Classic Series (Mary Ann, Louisa) ..$75.00
    Fairy Godmother outfit, 1983, M.A.D.C. (see Special Events/Exclusives)
    10" Portrette, #1156, 1993 only, blue/gold gown (Cissette)...$90.00
    10", #14549, 1995 only, purple gown, white wig (Cissette).......................................$80.00
    8", #13430, 1997 – 1999, dark blue hooded cloak $75.00
    8", #25920, 2000 – 2001 (Maggie), dark blue over light blue gown.........................$75.00
Fairy of Beauty — 8", #13620, 1997 – 2003, #40255, 2006 – 2007, pink tulle gown, wand
    with hearts, pointed hat $80.00
Fairy of Song — 8", #13630, 1997 – 2003, #40250, 2006 – 2007, green tulle gown, wand
    with music notes..$80.00
Fairy of Virtue — 8", #13640, 1997 – 2003, #40260, 2006 – 2007, blue tulle gown, wand
    with stars, pointed hat $80.00
Fairy Princess — 7" – 8" compo., 1940 – 1943 (Tiny Betty) $400.00
    9" compo., 1939 – 1941 (Little Betty) $400.00
    11" compo., 1939 only (Wendy Ann) $425.00
    15" – 18" compo., 1939 – 1942 (Wendy Ann) $650.00
    21" – 22" compo., 1939, 1944 – 1946 (Wendy Ann) $900.00
Fairy Queen — 14½" compo., 1940 – 1946 (Wendy Ann) $750.00
    18" compo., 1940 – 1946 (Wendy Ann) $800.00
    14½" h.p., 1948 – 1950 (Margaret) $800.00
    18" h.p., 1949 – 1950 (Margaret) $950.00
Fairy Tales — Dumas, 9" compo., 1937 – 1941 (Little Betty) $375.00
Faith — 8" h.p., #486, 1961 only, Americana Series, plaid jumper/organdy blouse (Wendy Ann) ... $1,800.00 up
    8" h.p. (see Collectors United under Special Events/Exclusives)
Fall Angel — 8", #28360, 2001 – 2002, rust gown with leaves.....................................$65.00
Falling Snowflakes with Lenox Ornament — 8", #40050, 2005 – 2006, pale pink dress......$95.00
Fancy Nancy — 8", #47955, 2008, blue ruffle dress, sunglasses $80.00
    18", #47965, 2008, purple fancy dress, sunglasses $45.00
    9", #48960, 2008, zip bin with 9" Fancy Nancy and dog $65.00
    9", #47960, 2008, Fancy Nancy and Posh Puppy $75.00
Fannie Elizabeth — (see Belk & Leggett under Special Events/Exclusives)
Fantasy — (see Doll Finders under Special Events/Exclusives)
FAO Schwarz — (see Special Events/Exclusives)
Farmer in the Dell — 8", #37990, with dog, cat, mouse, and cheese, 2004 – 2005 ....$85.00
Farmer's Daughter — (see Enchanted Doll House under Special Events/Exclusives)
Fashions of the Century — 14" – 18" h.p., 1954 – 1955 (Margaret, Maggie)....$2,500.00 up
Father Christmas — 8" h.p., #100351, Americana Series..$75.00
Father of the Bride — 10", #24623, 1996, white satin wedding gown $85.00
Father of Vatican City, The — 8", #24190, 1999, gold silk robe $75.00
Fauna — 8", #48675, 2008, Maggie, green cape, Disney $75.00
Femme Fatale — 10", #48345, 2008, couture gold gown $150.00
Festive Irish Dancer — 8", #46270, 2007 – 2008, maroon Irish costume $75.00
50's Kitsch Maggie — 8", #42035, 2006, with veggie people..$90.00
50th Anniversary Cissette — 10", #45975, gold long dress, white fur and gloves $150.00
50th Birthday Wendy — 8", #34710, 2002, blue dress..$80.00
50 Years of Friendship — 8", #37950, 2003, two dolls, pink print $135.00
    8", blue print, magnetic kiss...$140.00
Figure Eight Total Moves Wendy — 8", #39135, 2004, blue ice skating costume $80.00
Figurines — 1999, 6", polyresin replica of Alexander dolls..............................$20.00 – 30.00
Fiji — 8", #38605, 2004, with plush shark $80.00
Fillmore, Abigail — 1982 – 1984, third set Presidents' Ladies/First Ladies Series (Louisa)....$100.00
Fill My Heart — 8", #28745, 2002 – 2003, pink lace-trimmed dress, large hat $75.00
    8", #28746, 2002 – 2003, African-American $80.00

Fill My Stocking — 8", #36000, 2003, cream dress, gold checked apron,
Lenox stocking ornament **$85.00**
Findlay, Jane — 1979 – 1981, first set Presidents' Ladies/First Ladies Series (Mary Ann)......$100.00
Finland — 8" h.p., BK, #767, 1968 – 1972 (Wendy Ann) $90.00
  8" h.p., straight legs, #0767 – 567, 1973 – 1975, marked "Alex" $60.00
  8" h.p., straight legs, #567, 1976 – 1987, marked "Alexander" $55.00
  8", #42515, 2006, with shield, helmet, and sword $85.00
Finnish — 7" compo., 1935 – 1937 (Tiny Betty) $350.00
Firefighter Wendy — 8", #31270, 1998 – 1999, yellow coat, red hat, and dog $80.00
Fireplace Stocking Holder — #91005, 6¼", red fireplace $40.00
First Bloom — 8", #39245, 2005, lavender dress, straw hat $70.00
First Communion — 8" h.p., #395, 1957 only (Wendy Ann) $675.00
  8" h.p., reintroduced 1994, #100347, Americana Series $65.00
  8", #10347 – 10349, 1995, three hair colors, Special Occasions Series $65.00
  8", #17012 – 17015, 1996, black, three hair colors (Wendy Ann) #21100, 1997 – 1998 ....$65.00
  8", #21530 (white), #21534 (black), white dress, veil, Bible, 1999 – 2000 ....$65.00
  8", #30656, 2001 – 2003, Latin American, lacy white dress, veil $65.00
  8", #30655, 2001 – 2003, Caucasian, white dress, veil, gold necklace with cross $65.00
  8", #30658, 2002 – 2003, African-American (#30657, brunette) $70.00
  14", #1545, 1991 – 1992 only, Classic Series (Louisa) $80.00
First Dance — 10", #36175, 2003, long black dress, red gloves $110.00
First Dance Pair — 8", 1996 ....$125.00
First Day at School — 8", #32995, 2002 – 2003 (Maggie), sweater, plaid skirt, book $60.00
First Ladies — (see Presidents' Ladies and individual names)
First Modern Doll Club — (see Special Events/Exclusives)
1st Place at the County Fair — 8", #48080, 2008, checked dress, pickles, balloons $75.00
First Recital — 8", #17024 (white), #17037 (black), lacy dress $60.00
Fischer Quints — 7" h.p./vinyl, 1964 only, one boy and four girls (Little Genius) ....$600.00 set
Five Little Bluebirds — 8", #45835, 2007, print dress, bird cage $85.00
Five Little Peppers — 13" and 16" compo., 1936 only ....$750.00 ea.
Flapper — 10" Portrette, 1988 – 1991 (Cissette), red dress $60.00
  10", #1118, 1988, black dress (all white dress in 1991) (see M.A.D.C. under
    Special Events/Exclusives)
  8", #14105, 1995, three-tiered rose colored dress with matching headband, Nostalgia Series ..$55.00
Flies a Kite — 8", #33030, 2002 – 2003, red, white, and blue dress, patriotic outfit, with kite.....$75.00
Flora — 8", #48670, 2008, maroon cape, pink long dress...$75.00
Floral Romance Bridesmaid — 10", #42505, 2006, long pink dress $110.00
Floral Whimsey Wendy-Kin Wood — 8", #42010, 2006, wood doll, pink dress $250.00
Flora McFlimsey — (with and without "e")
  9" compo., 1938 – 1941 (Little Betty) $425.00
  22" compo., 1938 – 1944 (Princess Elizabeth) ....$800.00 up
  15" – 16" compo., 1938 – 1944 (Princess Elizabeth) ....$650.00 up
  16" – 17" compo., 1936 – 1937 (Wendy Ann)..$600.00
  14" compo., 1938 – 1944 (Princess Elizabeth) ....$600.00 up
  12" compo., 1944 only, holds 5" "Nancy Ann" doll, tagged "Margie Ann" (Wendy Ann) . $950.00 up
  15" Miss Flora McFlimsey, vinyl head (must have good color), 1953 only (Cissy) ....$750.00 up
  14", #25502, 1995, tiers of pink, white, and black, Buttons & Bows Series (Mary Ann) $85.00
  8", #46465, 2007, ruffled dress, straw hat $90.00
Flower Child — 8", #17790, 1999 (Maggie) $60.00
Flower for the Bride — 8", #36880, 2003 – 2004, pale pink short dress, with lace $80.00
Flower Girl — 16" – 18" compo., 1939, 1944 – 1947 (Princess Elizabeth) $650.00
  20" – 24" compo., 1939, 1944 – 1947 (Princess Elizabeth) ....$650.00 – 850.00
  15" – 18" h.p., 1954 only (Cissy) ....$500.00 – 950.00
  15" h.p., 1954 only (Margaret) ....$800.00 up
  8" h.p., #602, 1956 (Wendy Ann) ....$950.00 up
  8" h.p., #445, 1959 (Wendy), blue nylon pleated dress..$675.00 up

**Fill my Stocking, 8", #36000, 2003,
(Wendy). Gold check dress. Lenox
stocking ornament. $85.00.**

Garden Party, 8", #488, 1955 only (Wendy). Original box. $1,800.00 up.

8" h.p., #334, 1992 – 1993, Americana Series, white doll (Wendy Ann) $65.00
8", #334-1, 1992 only, black doll...$70.00
10", #1122, 1988 – 1990, Portrette, pink dotted Swiss dress (Cissette)...............................$80.00
8", #22620, 1999, mauve satin, rose crown, limited to 2,700 ....$75.00
Flowery Goodness — 8", #42185, 2006, with Chaos bear, watering can $90.00
Flying High with Dumbo — 8", #46580, 2007, plush Dumbo $85.00
Follow Your Dreams Angel — 8", #38580, 2004, white and gold $85.00
Forever Yours Flower Girl — 8", #46310 redhead, #46300 blonde, #46305 burnette, 2007,
    white dress...$70.00
Forget-Me-Not — 8", #28465, 2001 – 2002, yellow and pink dress with flowers, hat $70.00
8", #37890, 2004, blue dress, holding flowers...$80.00
Forrest — 8" h.p., #10750, 1998, Tyrolean outfit $60.00
40's Sweet 'N Petite — 8", #42025, 2006, with sheep..$70.00
For Your One and Only — 8", #42155, 2006 – 2007, plush bear with hearts $85.00
Four-leaf Clover Fairy — 8", #35930, 2003 – 2004, green costume.....................................$75.00
Four for the Holidays — 8", #46210, 2007 – 2008, green dress, bear, cat, dog.................$100.00
Four of Us, The — 8", #37215, 2003 – 2004, pink dress, green sweater, bear, dog, and cat......$125.00
France — 7" compo., 1936 – 1943 (Tiny Betty) $350.00
9" compo., 1937 – 1941 (Little Betty) $350.00
8" h.p., BKW, #390, #790, 1961 – 1965 (Wendy Ann) $125.00
8" h.p., BK, #790, 1965 – 1972 ....$90.00
8" h.p., straight leg, #0790, #590, 1973 – 1975, marked "Alex"..$65.00
8" straight leg, #590, #552 (1985 – 1987), #517, #582 (1976 – 1993), marked "Alexander" $60.00
8" h.p., reissued 1994 – 1995, #110538 (Wendy) $60.00
8" h.p., #11557, 1996 International, Cancan costume (#24020 – 1998).................................$60.00
French Aristocrat — 10" Portrette, #1143, 1991 – 1992 only, bright pink/white (Cissette) $175.00
French Blue Godey — 10", #33565, 2002, long blue dress, striped top, limited to 750 ....$100.00
French Court Girl — 8", #40790, 2005, powdered wig, pink vintage outfit with dress form ...$160.00
French Flower Girl — 8" h.p., #610, 1956 only (Wendy Ann) .... $800.00 up
French Kitty — 10", #40045, #40590, #39995, 2005 – 2006, Feline fashion doll......................$25.00
10", #42665, #42605, #42655, 2006, feline fashion doll...$25.00
French White Godey — 10", #33560, 2002, white dress, pink trim, limited to 750 ....$100.00
Friar Tuck — 8" h.p., #493, 1989 – 1991, Storybook Series (Maggie Mixup) $55.00
Friday's Child — 8", #27790, 2001, lavender dress $70.00
Friedrich — (see Sound of Music)
Fright Night Fun Wendy — 8", #42270, 2006, black pants, orange sweater $65.00
Frog Princess — 8", #27755, 2001 – 2002, includes frog, pink dress, puff sleeves $80.00
8", #46070, 2007 – 2008, blue and white long dress, frog, braids $90.00
Frost Fairy Boy — 8", #25140, 2000, silver costume and crown $65.00
Frost Fairy Girl — 8", #25145, 2000, silver ballerina costume $65.00
Frou-Frou — 40" all cloth, 1951 only, ballerina with yarn hair, dressed in green or lilac ..... $800.00 up
Fun Fun Chloe — 14", #30115, 2001, vinyl...$65.00
Fun with My Tricycle — 8", #48550, 2008, tricycle $80.00
Funny — 18" cloth, 1963 – 1977...$60.00
Funny Maggie — 8" (Maggie), #140506, 1994 – 1995, Storyland Series, yarn hair $55.00
Gainsborough — 20" h.p., 1957, Models Formal Gowns Series, taffeta gown,
    large picture hat (Cissy) .... $1,700.00 up
#2184, 21" h.p., vinyl arms, 1968, blue with white lace jacket (Jacqueline) $650.00
#2192, 21", 1972, yellow with full white lace overskirt (Jacqueline)...............................$675.00
#2192, 21", 1973, pale blue, scallop lace overskirt (Jacqueline) $500.00
#2211, 21", 1978, pink with full lace overdress (Jacqueline) $275.00
10" pink gown and hat, 1957 Portrette (Cissette) $750.00
10", #45201, 1995, pink with lace overlay, Madame's Portfolio Series $100.00
Garbo, Greta, Grand Hotel — 16", #33480, 2002 – 2003, wool dress, coat, limited to 1,500.$150.00
16", #31555, 2003, Greta Garbo Camille, pink gown, limited to 500 ....$175.00
Garden Fairy — 8", #28500, 2001 – 2002, pink costume with roses $75.00

Germany, 8", 1986 (Wendy). All original. $60.00.

Garden Fun — 8", #42315, 2006, green dress, trunk $100.00

Gardenia — 10", #22360, 1998 (Cissette), yellow satin long gown $100.00

Garden Party — 18" h.p., 1953 only (Margaret)... $1,700.00 up

    20" h.p., 1956 – 1957 (Cissy)... $1,600.00 up

    8" h.p., #488, 1955 only (Wendy Ann)... $1,800.00 up

Garden Party Charm — 8", #45775, 2007, purple dress..$85.00

Garden Rose — 10" (Cissette), #22530, 1999, pink tulle with roses..........................$90.00

Garfield, Lucretia — 1985 – 1987, fourth set Presidents' Ladies/First Ladies Series (Louisa)$100.00

Garland, Judy Meet Me in St. Louis — 16", #32175, 2002 – 2003, white dress,

    limited to 1,500...$150.00

Gemini — 8", #21350, 1998, African-American, two dolls, yellow outfit........................$125.00

    8", #21351, 1998, white, two dolls...$125.00

Genius Baby — 21" – 30" plastic/vinyl, 1960 – 1961, has flirty eyes.......$125.00 – 150.00

Geppetto — 8", #478, 1993, #140478, 1994, Storybook Series................................$60.00

Geppetto and Pinocchio — 8", 5", #32130, 2000, navy jacket, hat..........................$85.00

Geranium — 9" early vinyl toddler, 1953 only, red organdy dress and bonnet $150.00

German (Germany) — 8" h.p., BK, #763, 1966 – 1972 (Wendy Ann)......................$90.00

    8" h.p., straight legs, #0763 – 563, 1973 – 1975, marked "Alex".................$65.00

    10" h.p., 1962 – 1963 (Cissette)..$925.00

    8" straight legs, #563, #535, #506, 1976 – 1989, marked "Alexander".................$60.00

    8", 1990 – 1991, marked "Alexander"...$60.00

    8", #535, 1986...$60.00

    8" h.p., #110542, 1994 – 1995, outfit in 1994 Neiman-Marcus trunk set (Maggie)..................$55.00

    8", #25800, 2000 – 2001 (Maggie), blue print dress, beer stein..................$85.00

Get Well — 8" h.p., #21090, 1998 – 1999, red striped outfit, vase of flowers...............$65.00

Get Well Wishes — #10363 – 10365, 1995, three hair colors,

    nurse with bear, Special Occasions Series..$55.00

Ghost of Christmas Past — 8", #18002, 1996, Dickens, long white gown.................$60.00

Ghost of Christmas Present — 14", #18406, 1996, Dickens, sold as set only with

    8" Ignorance (boy) and 8" Want (girl)..$250.00

Gibson Girl — 10" h.p., 1962, eyeshadow (Cissette)....................................... $800.00 up

    10", 1963, plain blouse with no stripes.. $800.00 up

    16" cloth, 1930s...$850.00

    10", #1124, 1988 – 1990, Portrette, red and black (Cissette) $60.00

    10", #17750, 1999, navy blue gown...$90.00

Gidget — 14" plastic/vinyl, #1415, #1420, #1421, 1966 only (Mary Ann)..................$225.00

Gift from Grandma — 8", #38195, 2004 – 2005, pink checked dress.........................$80.00

Gift of Beauty Fairy — 8", #39045, 2004 – 2005, pink outfit................................$85.00

Gift of Song Fairy — 8", #39055, 2004 – 2005, blue gown...................................$85.00

Gift of Virtue Fairy — 8", #39050, 2004 – 2005, blue gown.................................$85.00

Gigi — **14", #1597, 1986 – 1987, Classic Series (Mary Ann), black check dress $90.00**

    14", #87011, 1996, plaid dress, straw hat (Mary Ann)..............................$100.00

    8" h.p., #13990, 1998 – 1999, pleated plaid dress, straw hat (Maggie).........$65.00

    8", #47730, 2007 – 2008, red dress, notebook, pencil $75.00

    16", #48465, 2008, long white ballgown, ltd. to 300.................................$150.00

Gilbert — 8", #260420, 1994 – 1995, Anne of Green Gables Series $85.00

Gingerbread House — Candy-trimmed house, #26595, 2001 – 2003 ....$100.00

Girl on a Swing — 8", #28640, 2001 – 2002, white dress with swing, flower rope $70.00

Girl on Flying Trapeze — 40" cloth, 1951 only, dressed in pink satin tutu (sold at FAO Schwarz) ...$950.00

Giselle — 16", #22050, 1998, aqua tutu $90.00

Glamour Girl 1953 — 10" h.p., 2000, (Cissette) pink and black gown..........................$100.00

Glamour Girls — **18" h.p., 1953 only (Margaret, Maggie) .... $1,800.00 up**

Glinda the Good Witch — 8", #473, 1992 – 1993, Storyland Series (Wendy Ann),

    #140473, 1994 – 1995..$125.00

    14" plastic/vinyl, #141573, 1994 only...$100.00

    10", #13250, 1997 – 2001 – 2007, #42405, pink tulle and taffeta dress (Cissette), silver crown ...$110.00

Gigi, 14", 1986 – 1987 (Mary Ann) Classic Series. All original. $90.00.

Glamour Girl, 18", #2010C, 1953 (Maggie). All original in pink taffeta with black velvet bodice. $1,800.00 up.

Godey, 10", #1183, 1970 (Cissette). All hard plastic and all original. $375.00.

15", #25546, 2001, cloth, pink gown $60.00
5", #33765, 2002, porcelain, pink dress............$65.00
9", #40920, 2005 – 2007, long pink dress, silver crown $45.00
10", #45905, 2007, Wicked, blue long gown $125.00
8", #45625, 2008, Wicked, blue elaborate gown $85.00
10", #42405, 2008, long pink gown, silver crown, wand............$125.00
10", #48350, 2008, Wicked, First Day of School, white top, pleated skirt, hat, purse $125.00
Glorious Angel — 10½" h.p., #54860 (see Tree Topper)
Godey — 21" compo., 1945 – 1947 (Wendy Ann), white lace over pink satin ....$2,700.00 up
14" h.p., 1950 – 1951 (Margaret) ....$1,500.00 up
21" h.p., 1951 only, lace ¾ top with long sleeves, pink satin two-tiered skirt (Margaret) ... $1,500.00 up
18" h.p., #2010A, 1953 only, Glamour Girl Series, red gown with gray fur stole (Maggie) ... $1,200.00 up
21" h.p., vinyl straight arms, 1961 only, lavender coat and hat (Cissy) $1,600.00
21", 1962, bright orange gown, white lace ruffles on bodice $1,800.00
21", #2153, 1965, dressed in all red, blonde hair (Jacqueline)............$800.00
21" plastic/vinyl, 1966 only, red with short black jacket and hat (Coco) ....$2,300.00 up
21" h.p., vinyl arms, #2172, 1967, dressed in pink and ecru (Jacqueline) $600.00
#2195, 1969, red with black trim............$600.00
#2195, 1970, pink with short burgundy jacket............$275.00
#2161, 1971, pink, black trim, short jacket............$300.00
#2298, 1977, ecru with red jacket and bonnet............$275.00
8" SLW, #491, 1955 only (Wendy Ann) ....$1,400.00 up
10" h.p., #1172, 1968, dressed in all pink with ecru lace, bows down front (Cissette) $400.00
#1172, 1969, all yellow with bows down front $450.00
#1183, 1970, all lace pink dress with natural straw hat $375.00
Godey Bride — 14" h.p., 1950, lace ¾ top over satin gown with long train (Margaret) ... $1,000.00 up
18" h.p., 1950 – 1951 (Margaret)............$1,400.00 up
21" porcelain, 1993 (Cissy)............$350.00
Godey Groom/Man — 14" h.p., 1950, has curls over ears, wearing black jacket and tan pants (Margaret) ....$975.00 up
18" h.p., 1950 – 1951 (Margaret) ....$1,300.00 up
Godey Lady — 14" h.p., 1950, green velvet dress with pink/bright orange pleated ruffles, peach/white bodice (Margaret) ....$1,000.00 up
18" h.p., 1950 – 1951 (Margaret) ....$1,500.00 up
Golden Christmas Angel — 10", #38565, 2004, white and gold costume $125.00
Golden Girl 1920 — 10", #17740, 1999, black and gold dress $90.00
Goldfish — 8" h.p., #344, Americana Series, 1993 – 1994 ....$70.00
Goldilocks — 18" cloth, 1930s $875.00
7" – 8" compo., 1938 – 1942 (Tiny Betty) $325.00
18" h.p., 1951 only (Maggie) $1,200.00
14" plastic/vinyl, #1520, 1978 – 1979, Classic Series, satin dress (Mary Ann) $75.00
14", #1520, 1980 – 1983, blue satin or cotton dress (Mary Ann) $75.00
14", #1553, 1991 only, Classic Series, long side curls tied with ribbon (Mary Ann)............$85.00
8", #497, 1990 – 1991 only, Storyland Series (1991 dress in different plaid) (Wendy Ann) $70.00
8", #140500, 1994 – 1995, Storyland Series, floral print dress, bear............$70.00
8", #25965, 2000 – 2003 (Wendy), blue dress, eyelet apron with bear $60.00
8", #39860, 2005 – 2006, lavender dress with three Chaos bears $135.00
8", #46475, 2007, print dress, plush brown bear............$80.00
Gold Rush — 10" h.p., 1963 only (Cissette) $1,400.00
Golf Boy — 8", 1998, #16402 (Maggie) green coat, checked hat, pants, golf club $65.00
Golf Girl — 8", 1998, #16412 (Wendy) ivory sweater, navy skirt, golf club $65.00
Gone Batty — 8", #45840, 2007, Maggie Bear in bat costumes $65.00
Gone Fishing — 8", #28190, 2001, green dress, hat, fishing pole $75.00
8", #46630, 2007, fish bowl, rod, fish, plush cat $80.00
Gone With the Wind (Scarlett) — 14", #1490, #1590, 1969 – 1986, all white dress/green sash, made 17 years without a change (Mary Ann) (dress must be mint)............$125.00

Godey Lady, 14", 1950 – 1951. (Margaret). Hard plastic. Tagged "Godey Lady." Unique hair style, mint lavender gown. $1,500.00 up.

Good Fairy — 14" h.p., 1948 – 1949 (Margaret) .... $725.00 up
Good Little Girl — 16" cloth, 1966 only, mate to "Bad Little Girl," wears pink dress $185.00
Goya — 8" h.p., #314, 1953 only (Wendy Ann) .... $1,100.00 up
    21" h.p./vinyl arms, #2183, 1968, multi-tiered pink dress (Jacqueline) $550.00
    21", #2235, 1982 – 1983, maroon dress with black Spanish lace (Jacqueline) $275.00
Grace — 14" vinyl, #34320, 2002 – 2003, African-American baby, pajamas $80.00
Graceful Garnet — 8", #32170, 2000 – 2002, red and gold ball gown, garnet jewelry $85.00
Graduation — 8" h.p., #399, 1957 only (Wendy Ann) .... $900.00 up
    12", 1957 only (Lissy) .... $1,000.00 up
    8", #307, 1990 – 1991, Americana Series (white doll only) (Wendy Ann) $60.00
    8", #307, #307-1, 1991 – 1992, Americana Series, white or black doll $60.00
    8", #10307 – 10309 (black), #10310 (white), 1995, blue robe, Special Occasions Series $60.00
    8", #26105 (blonde), #26106 (brunette), #26107 (African-American), 2000 – 2003,
        white robe, red dress, hat, diploma $70.00
    8", #38895, 2004 – 2005, blonde, white dress, blue robe, hat $80.00
    8", #38896, 2004 – 2005, brunette, white dress, blue robe, hat $80.00
    8", #38897, 2004 – 2005, African-American, white dress, blue robe, hat $80.00
Graduation Day — 8", #46254, 2007 – 2008, Latin, pink dress, black robe, hat, diploma $70.00
    8", #46250, 2007 – 2008, blonde, pink dress, black robe, hat, diploma $70.00
    8", #46251 burnette, #46252 redhead, 2007 – 2008 .... $70.00
    8", #46253 African American, #46255 Asian, 2007 – 2008 .... $70.00
Grandma Jane — 14" plastic/vinyl, #1420, 1970 – 1972 (Mary Ann) $225.00
Grandma's Favorite Cameo — 8", #47870, 2008, pink and gray dress, cameo $80.00
Grand Ole Opry Boy — 8", #77005, 1996 Classic $70.00
Grand Ole Opry Girl — 8", #77004, 1996 Classic $70.00
Grant, Julia — 1982 – 1984, third set Presidents' Ladies/First Ladies Series (Louisa) $100.00
Grave, Alice — 18" cloth, 1930s .... $750.00 up
Grayson, Kathryn — 20" – 21" h.p., 1949 only (Margaret) .... $6,000.00 up
Great Britain — 8" h.p., #558, 1977 – 1988 (Wendy Ann) $55.00
Great Gatsby Pair — 10", #15310, 1997, Classic characters $140.00
Greece — 8", #35970, 2003 – 2004, blue and red cultural costume, bouzaki $75.00
Greece Boy — 8" h.p., #527, 1992 – 1993 only (Wendy Ann) $50.00
Greek Boy — 8" h.p., BKW, 1965, BK, 1966 – 1968, #769 (Wendy Ann) $300.00
Greek Girl — 8" h.p., BK, #765, 1968 – 1972 (Wendy Ann) $90.00
    8" h.p., straight legs, #0765, #565, 1973 – 1975, marked "Alex" $60.00
    8" h.p., straight legs, #565, #527, 1976 – 1987 (1985 – 1987), marked "Alexander" $55.00
Green Eggs and Ham — 8", #47865, 2008, Maggie, top hat, Sam, eggs, ham $80.00
Greenaway, Kate — 7" compo., 1938 – 1943 (Tiny Betty) $425.00
    9" compo., 1936 – 1939 (Little Betty) $450.00
    16" cloth, 1936 – 1938 .... $900.00
    13", 14", 15" compo., 1938 – 1943 (Princess Elizabeth) $800.00
    18", 1938 – 1943 (Wendy Ann/Princess Elizabeth) $900.00
    24", 1938 – 1943 (Princess Elizabeth) .... $950.00 up
    14" vinyl, #1538, 1993 only, Classic Series $85.00
Gretel — 7" compo., 1935 – 1942 (Tiny Betty) $350.00
    9" compo., 1938 – 1940 (Little Betty) $350.00
    18" h.p., 1948 only (Margaret) .... $1,000.00 up
    7½" – 8" h.p., SLW, #470, 1955 (Wendy Ann) .... $550.00 up
    8" h.p., BK, #754, 1966 – 1972, Storybook Series (Wendy) $100.00
    8" h.p., straight legs, #0754, #454, 1973 – 1975, marked "Alex" $65.00
    8" h.p., straight legs, #454, 1976 – 1986, marked "Alexander" $60.00
    8" h.p., #462, 1991 – 1992 only, Storyland Series, reintroduced doll (Wendy Ann) $60.00
    8" h.p., #26600, 2001 – 2003, red stripe skirt, eyelet apron, green felt hat $65.00
Gretel Brinker — 12", 1993 only (Lissy) $125.00
    8", #14650, 1996 .... $60.00
Gretl — (see Sound of Music)

Groom — 18" – 21" compo., 1946 – 1947, mint (Margaret) .... $975.00 up

18" – 21" h.p., 1949 – 1951 (Margaret)..$975.00 – 1,500.00

14" – 16" h.p., 1949 – 1951 (Margaret)... $750.00 up

7½" h.p., SL and SLW, #577, #464, #466, 1953 – 1955 (Wendy Ann) .... $550.00 up

8" BKW, #577, 1956 ....$425.00

8" BKW, #377, 1957, BKW, #572, 1958..$400.00

8" h.p., BKW, #421, #442, 1961 – 1963 (Wendy Ann) $350.00

8", #488, #388, reintroduced 1989 – 1991 only (Wendy Ann) $60.00

8", #339, 1993, black pants, peach tie, white jacket $60.00

8", #17020, 1996, black velvet tails, black pants, pink tie $60.00

8", #17023, 1996, black velvet tails, etc., black doll $65.00

8", #21071, 1997 – 2005, velvet tailcoat, top hat, #21073 – 21074, African-American (1997 – 2007) ... $90.00

Groovy Girl 1970 — 8", #17800, 1999, BK, denim pants, hat $60.00

Guardian Angel — 10", #10602 – 1995, first in series, 100th Anniversary Special, all pink
with white wings $125.00

10", #10720, 1998, rose print brocade gown, feather wings $100.00

10", of Harmony, #10691, 1996 ....$100.00

10", of Hope, #10609, 1996 ....$100.00

10", of Love, frosted ivy, #10605, 1996 ....$100.00

10", of Love, heather blue #10607, 1996 ....$100.00

10", of Love, misty rose, #10603, 1996 ....$100.00

10", Pink Pristine, #10700, 1997 – 2000, pink tulle dress $100.00

10", #10720, 1999, pink print brocade gown, feather wings $100.00

Guatemala — 8", #24180, 1999, red and black outfit $55.00

Guinevere — 10", #1146, 1992 only, Portrette, forest green/gold...........................$100.00

8", #13570, 1999, blue dress with white brocade over dress.............................$80.00

Gymnastics Class — 8", #42120, 2006 – 2007, pink bodysuit, balance beam $65.00

Gypsy of the World — 8", #28570, 2001, purple costume, tarot cards $70.00

Hairdresser — 8", #33585, 2003 (Wizard of Oz), green dress, mini scissors, blonde with curls .$75.00

Halloween Treats — 8", #38590, 2004 – 2005, with bear and treat bag $80.00

Halloween Witch — 8" (see Collectors United/C. U. under Special Events/Exclusives)

Hamlet — 12", Romance Series (Nancy Drew)...$65.00

12", 1993 only (Lissy) $90.00

Hannah — 10", #28310, 2002 – 2004, jeans, sweater, hat.....................................$40.00

10", #28300, 2002 – 2004, skirt, striped jacket $40.00

10", #40615, 2005, Summertime Fun Playset, with dog $95.00

Hannah Pepper Trunk Set — 10", #35450, 2003 – 2004, clothes, trunk $100.00

Hans Brinker — 12", 1993 only (Lissy) $100.00

8", #14649, 1996 ....$60.00

Hansel — 7" compo., 1935 – 1942 (Tiny Betty) $350.00

9" compo., 1938 – 1940 (Little Betty) $350.00

18" h.p., 1948 only (Margaret) ....$900.00 up

8" h.p., SLW, #470, 1955 only (Wendy Ann) ....$650.00 up

8" h.p., BK, #753, 1966 – 1972, Storybook Series (Wendy Ann) $100.00

8" h.p., straight legs, #0753, #543, 1973 – 1975, marked "Alex" $65.00

8" h.p., straight legs, #543, 1976 – 1986 (1986 white face), marked "Alexander".....................$60.00

8" h.p., #461, 1991 – 1992 only, Storyland Series, reintroduced doll (Wendy Ann)................$60.00

8" h.p., #26605, 2001 – 2003, green costume $65.00

Happy — 20" cloth/vinyl, 1970 only...$200.00

Happy Birthday — 1985 (see M.A.D.C. under Special Events/Exclusives)

8" h.p., #325, #325-1, 1992 – 1993, Americana Series, black or white doll (Wendy Ann) $65.00

8" h.p., #100325, 1994, white only $65.00

8", #10325 – 10327, 1995, three hair colors, Special Occasions Series $65.00

8", #17004 – 17010, 1996, three hair colors, black or white doll (Wendy, Maggie)................$60.00

14" plastic/vinyl, #241596, 1994 only $70.00

8", #21520 (blonde),#21521 (brunette), #21523 (black), pink print dress, 1999 – 2000 ....$65.00

8", #27240 (blonde), #27241 (brunette), #27242, African-American, 2001 – 2002....................$75.00

8", #35925 (blonde), 2003 –2008, pink dress, slice of cake...$70.00

8", #35926 (brunette), 2003 – 2008, with slice of cake $70.00

8", #35927, African-American, 2003 – 2008, with slice of cake....................................$70.00

8", #35928, Asian, 2007 – 2008, pink dress, slice of cake $70.00

Happy Birthday Billie — 8" h.p., #345, #345-1, Americana Series, black or white boy, 1993 only ...$60.00

Happy Birthday Maggie — 8", #21080 – white, #21083 – black, 1997 – 1998 ....$65.00

Happy Birthday Princess — 8", #48580, 2008, blue dress, tiara $110.00

Happy Chanukah — 8", #10367, 1996 Holiday, #19630, 1997 – 1999 ....$70.00

Happy the Clown — 8", #10414, 1996 Classic Circus...$60.00

Happy Feet Rockette 1990 Cissette — 10", #47660, 2007, gold outfit........................$100.00

Harding, Florence — 1988, fifth set Presidents' Ladies/First Ladies Series (Louisa) $100.00

Harlequin — 8", #14574, 1995, Nutcracker Series..$70.00

Harley-Davidson — 8" h.p., #77002, 1996 (Wendy) Classic American, #17420, 1997............$100.00

8" h.p., #77005, 1996 (Billy), Classic American, #17410, 1997............................$100.00

10" h.p., #77102, 1996, pictured 1996 catalog ....not available for sale

10", #17440, 1997, Cissette, black leather coat, boots.......................................$125.00

10", #17430, 1997, David, jeans, black leather jacket $125.00

10", #17390, 1998, Cissette, faux leather halter and skirt and backpack $135.00

Harriet the Spy — 12", #38565, 2004 – 2005, cloth dog..$30.00

Harrison, Caroline — 1985 – 1987, fourth set Presidents' Ladies/First Ladies Series (Louisa)....$100.00

Harry Potter — 8", #38415, 2004, with broom..$85.00

Harvest Greetings — 8", #40600, 2005 – 2006, with cornucopia $75.00

Hats Off to Wendy — 8", #37800, 2003, white dress, pink trim $70.00

Haunted Delight Halloween Trunk Set — 8", #46235, 2007, cat, devil, gypsy costumes,

haunted house trunk $145.00

Hawaii — 8", #301, 1990 – 1991 only, Americana Series (Wendy Ann) $60.00

Hawaiian — 8" h.p., BK, #722, 1966 – 1969, Americana Series (Wendy Ann) $350.00

7" compo., 1936 – 1939 (Tiny Betty) $325.00

9" compo., 1937 – 1944 (Little Betty) $350.00

Hayes, Lucy — 1985 – 1987, fourth set Presidents' Ladies/First Ladies Series (Louisa) $100.00

Heather — 18" cloth/vinyl, 1990 only...$75.00

8" h.p., #10760, 1998, Tyrolean outfit with basket $75.00

Heavenly Pink Angel — 8", #26285, 2000 – 2001, pink costume, white feather wings...........$100.00

Heavenly Star Angel Tree Topper — 8", #42230, 2006, blue outfit...............................$125.00

Heidi — 7" compo., 1938 – 1939 (Tiny Betty)..$350.00

8" h.p., #460, 1991 – 1992, Storyland Series (Maggie).....................................$70.00

14" plastic/vinyl, #1480, #1580, #1581, 1969 – 1985 (16-year production),

Classic Series (Mary Ann) $70.00

14", #1581, 1986 – 1988, solid green dress, floral apron $70.00

14", #25503, 1995, Ribbons & Bows Series (not on order sheet).........................not available for sale

8" h.p., #15100, 1998 – 2000, green dress, lace apron, straw hat, goat $70.00

8", #42560, 2006, red print skirt, straw hat, goat $75.00

Heiress Elegance Shadow Cissette — 10", #46995, blue skirt and blouse, brocade coat,

black wig $180.00

Helen of Troy — 10", #48140, 2008, long white and lavender gown, pink wrap.......................$120.00

Hello Baby — 22", 1962 only..$175.00

He Loves Me, He Loves Me Not — 8", #37895, 2004 (Wendy) $70.00

8", #48900, 2008, white pinafore, print skirt, flower $60.00

Henie, Sonja — 13" – 15" compo., 1939 – 1942 ....$675.00

7" compo., 1939 – 1942 (Tiny Betty) $475.00

9" compo., 1940 – 1941 (Little Betty) $575.00

11" compo. (Wendy Ann), 14" compo. $650.00

14" in case/wardrobe ....$1,800.00 up

17" – 18" compo. $950.00

20" – 23" compo. ....$1,200.00 – 1,600.00

Happy Birthday, 8", #35926, 2003 – 2008 (Wendy). Pink dress. Came with a slice of cake on a plate. $70.00.

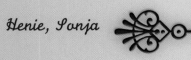

13" – 14" compo., jointed waist...$750.00

15" – 18" h.p./vinyl, 1951 only, no extra joints, must have good face color (Madeline)...........$750.00

Her Lady and Child (Thumbelina) — 21" porcelain, 8" h.p., #010, 1992 – 1994,
limited to 2,500...$400.00

Hermey the Elf & Bumble the Abominable Snow Monster — 8", #48210, 2008,
plush monster $90.00

Hermione Granger — 8", #38420, 2004, with books $75.00

10", #38640, 2004, vinyl...$30.00

Hershey's Kisses Doll — 8", #17880, 2000, pink and silver costume $60.00

Her Sunday Best — (see Wendy Loves Series)

Hey Diddle Diddle — 8", #42455, 2006, print dress, dish and spoon.....................................$75.00

Hiawatha — 8" h.p., #720, 1967 – 1969, Americana Series (Wendy Ann) $375.00

7" compo. (Tiny Betty) $350.00

18" cloth, early 1930s $800.00

Hickory Dickory Dock — 8", #11650, 1998 – 1999, clock costume $60.00

8", #42450, 2006, blue print dress, clock...$85.00

Highland Fling — 8" h.p., #484, 1955 only (Wendy Ann) $750.00

Hocus Pocus Wonder — 8", #42125, 2006, wand and rabbit..$85.00

Holiday Ballerina — 8", #28525, 2001, long white dress with gold and red trim.....................$70.00

Holiday, Billie — 10", #22070, 1997, long silver gown $90.00

Holiday Homecoming — 18", #47770, 2007, red velvet dress...$200.00

Holiday Jubilee — 8", #40360, 2005 – 2006, red dress, gift box...$85.00

Holiday on Ice — 8" h.p., #319, 1992 – 1993 only, red with white fur hat and muff,
some tagged "Christmas on Ice"...$125.00

Holiday Snowflake Skater — 8", #28520, 2001 – 2002 (Maggie), red skating outfit.................$75.00

Holland — 7" compo., 1936 – 1943 (Tiny Betty) $350.00

8", #33490, 2002, blue print pinafore, with spoon...$100.00

8", #48150, 2008, blue stripe skirt, basket of tulips...$85.00

Holly — 10", #1135, 1990 – 1991, Portrette, white/red roses Cissette $85.00

Holly Hobbie — 8", #45505, 2006 – 2008, calico dress, bonnet, flower $85.00

8", #47750, 2007 – 2008, patchwork dress, present, red bonnet $85.00

Hollywood Glamour 1930 — 10", #17760, 1999, blue taffeta dress $100.00

Hollywood Trunk Set — 8", #15340, 1997..$225.00

Homecoming — 8", 1993 (see M.A.D.C. under Special Events/Exclusives)

Homecoming Lissy — 12", #42045, 2006, navy blue dress, hat..$100.00

Home for Holidays — 14", #24606, 1995, Christmas Series $85.00

Homefront Pals — 8", pair, #34335, 2002, boy, denim, girl, star dress..................................$150.00

Honeybea — 12" vinyl, 1963 only..$175.00

Honeybun — 18" – 19", 1951 – 1952 only $225.00

23" – 26"..$300.00

Honeyette Baby — 16" compo./cloth, 1941 – 1942 ....$225.00

7" compo., 1934 – 1937, little girl dress (Tiny Betty)..$300.00

Honeymoon in New Orleans — (see Scarlett O'Hara)

Honeymoon Sweet Dreams — (see Bride or Groom)

Hooray for M.A.! — 8", #42115, 2006 – 2007, pink cheerleader, pom pons $75.00

Hoover, Lou — 14", 1989 – 1990, sixth set Presidents' Ladies/First Ladies Series (Mary Ann).....$100.00

Hope — 8" (see Collectors United under Special Events/Exclusives)

Horse Around — 8", #40760, 2005, with stick horse..$70.00

Horton Hears a Who — 8", #47860, 2008, plush elephant...$75.00

Hot Cross Buns — 8", #33055, 2002, pink dress, buns on tray $65.00

House That Wendy Built, The — 8", #42160, 2006, house, tools $100.00

How Does Your Garden Grow — 8", #34085, 2002, with watering can....................................$60.00

Howdy Doody Time, It's — 8", #15230, 1999 – 2000, marionette $100.00

How Much Is That Doggie in the Window — 8", #38780, 2004 – 2005, with store front and dog...$95.00

Huckleberry Finn — 8" h.p., #490, 1989 – 1991 only, Storybook Series (Wendy Ann).............$60.00

Huggums, Big — 25", 1963 – 1979, boy or girl..$100.00

Huggums, Little — 14", 1986 only, molded hair $50.00

 12", 1963 – 1995, molded hair, available in 7 – 10 outfits (first black version available in 1995).... $50.00

 12", 1963 – 1982, 1988, rooted hair $50.00

 1991, special outfits (see Imaginarium Shop under Special Events/Exclusives)

 1996 – 2003, variety of outfits ....$40.00 – 65.00

 12", #29700, 1998, 75th Anniversary Huggums, white dress with flowers....................$40.00 – 65.00

 12", 2006 – 2007, Christening #38900, Mint Julep #40375, Piglet #42745 ....$50.00 – 70.00

 12" assortment of outfits, vinyl, painted head..$30.00 – 80.00

Huggums, Lively — 25", 1963 only, knob makes limbs and head move $150.00

Huggums Man in the Moon Mobile — #14700, 8" boy, star costume, cloth moon, star mobiles ...$70.00

Hug Me Pets — #76001 – 76007, plush animal bodies, Huggums face $45.00

Hula Hoop Total Moves Wendy — 8", #40440, 2005 – 2006, blue outfit, hoop $75.00

Hulda — 18" h.p., 1949 only, lamb's wool wig, black doll (Margaret) ....$1,900.00 up

 14" h.p., 1948 – 1949, lamb's wool wig, black doll ....$1,300.00 up

Humpty Dumpty — 8", #13060, 1997 – 1998, plaid tailcoat, brick wall $65.00

Hungarian (Hungary) — 8" h.p., BKW, #397, #797, 1962 – 1965 (Wendy Ann) $150.00

 BK, #397, with metal crown $125.00

 BK, #797, 1965 – 1972 ....$100.00

 8" h.p., straight legs, #0797, #597, 1973 – 1976, marked "Alex" $65.00

 8" h.p., straight legs, #597, 1976 – 1986, marked "Alexander" $60.00

 8" h.p., #522, reintroduced 1992 – 1993 only (Wendy), #11547, 1995 only $60.00

Hush-You-Bye — 8", #25235, 2000 – 2001, comes with rocking horse.....................................$95.00

Hyacinth — 9" early vinyl toddler, 1953 only, blue dress and bonnet $150.00

Ibiza — 8", #510, 1989 only (Wendy Ann)...$65.00

I Can Tie My Shoes — 8", #36185, 2003, pink checked dress...$65.00

Ice Capades — 1950s (Cissy) ....$1,600.00 up

 1960s (Jacqueline)...$1,600.00 up

Ice Cream Delight Hello Kitty — 8", #46160, #46170 (Asian) with Hello Kitty in ice cream cone ...$80.00

Iceland — 10", 1962 – 1963 (Cissette) ....$750.00 up

Ice Skater — 8" h.p., BK and BKW, #555, 1955 – 1956 (Wendy Ann) ....$700.00 up

 8", #303, 1990 – 1991 only, Americana Series, purple/silver (Wendy Ann) $60.00

 8", #16371, 1997, boy, brocade vest, black pants $60.00

 8", #16361, 1997 – 1998, girl, pink knit and silver outfit $60.00

Icing on the Cake — 8", #47885, 2008, print dress, elaborate tiered cake....................................$80.00

Ignorance — 8", #18406 (see Ghost of Christmas Present) (sold as set)

I'll Love You Forever Valentine — 8", #25025, 2000, pink dress, lace front $60.00

I Love My Kitty — 8", #30420, 2001– 2002, blue checked dress, kitty $65.00

I Love My Puppy — 8", #30430, 2001, red checked dress, puppy $65.00

I Love My Rubber Duckie — 8", #41825, 2006, beach outfit, duck $70.00

I Love My Teddy — 8", #30425, 2001 – 2003, white, red dress, with teddy $65.00

I Love You — 8", #10386 – 10388, 1995, three hair colors, Special Occasions Series $55.00

I. Magnin — (see Special Events/Exclusives)

Imaginarium Shop — (see Special Events/Exclusives)

I'm a Little Teapot — 8", #28870, 2001 (Maggie), blue print teapot with tea bag $60.00

 8", #46520, 2007, pink striped dress, hat with tea bag..$100.00

I'm Gonna Like Me — 12", #35805, 2003 – 2005, cloth, Jamie Lee Curtis............................$35.00

I'm So Tall — 8", #38500, 2004, pink doll, doll and child growth charts..................................$85.00

Incredible Voyage — 8", #40455, 2005, (Maggie) with gnome and watering can $75.00

India — 8" h.p., BKW, #775, 1965 (Wendy Ann)...$125.00

 8" h.p., BK, #775, 1965 – 1972 (Wendy) $100.00

 8" h.p., straight legs, #0775, #575, 1973 – 1975, marked "Alex" $65.00

 8" h.p., straight legs, #575, #549, 1976 – 1988, marked "Alexander" (1985 – 1987).................$55.00

 8" h.p., straight legs, #11563, 1996 International, #24030, 1997 ....$55.00

 8" h.p., #39060, 2004 – 2005, Henna painted hands and plush elephant..................$90.00

Indian Boy* — 8" h.p., BK, #720, 1966 only, Americana Series (Wendy Ann) $425.00

Indian Girl* — 8" h.p., BK, #721, 1966 only, Americana Series (Wendy Ann).........................$400.00

Indonesia — 8" h.p., BK, #779, 1970 – 1972 (Wendy) $90.00
   8" h.p., straight legs, #779, #0779, #579, 1972 – 1975, marked "Alex" $65.00
   8" h.p., straight legs, #579, 1976 – 1988, marked "Alexander" $60.00
   8" BK, with Maggie Mixup face $125.00
Ingalls, Laura — 14", #1531, 1989 – 1991, Classic Series, burnt orange dress/blue pinafore (Mary Ann)...$75.00
   14", #24621, 1995, green with rose floral, Favorite Books Series (Mary Ann) $100.00
Ingalls Wilder, Laura — 8", #14110, 1998 – 1999, patchwork print outfit $80.00
Ingres — 14" plastic/vinyl, #1567, 1987 only, Fine Arts Series (Mary Ann) $80.00
Iris — 10" h.p., #1112, 1987 – 1988, pale blue (Cissette) $60.00
Irish (Ireland) — 8" h.p., BKW, #778, 1965 only (Wendy Ann) $125.00
   8" BK, #778, 1966 – 1972, long gown $100.00
   8" straight legs, #0778, #578, 1973 – 1975, marked "ALEX," long gown $65.00
   8" straight legs, #578, #551, 1976 – 1985, marked "Alexander" $60.00
   8" straight legs, #551, 1985 – 1987, short dress, 1987 – 1993 (Maggie) $55.00
   8" h.p., #100541, reissued 1994 only, green skirt with white top $55.00
   8" h.p., #17028, 1996 International, leprechaun outfit, #21000, 1997 – 1999 .....$55.00
   8", #48445, 2008, green dress, mug of stout $60.00
Irish Banshee — 8", #42510, 2006 – 2007, green satin long dress, crow $70.00
Irish Lass — 8", #11555, 1995 only $60.00
Isabelle — 14", #34345, 2002 – 2003, African-American, print dress $75.00
Isolde — 14", #1413, 1985 – 1986 only, Opera Series (Mary Ann) $75.00
Israel — 8" h.p., BK, #768, 1965 – 1972 (Wendy Ann) $100.00
   8" h.p., straight legs, #0768, 1973 – 1975, marked "Alex" $75.00
   8" h.p., straight legs, #568, 1976 – 1989, marked "Alexander" $60.00
Italy — 8" h.p., BKW, #393, 1961 – 1965 (Wendy Ann) $125.00
   8" h.p., BK, #793, 1965 – 1972 ....$90.00
   8" h.p., straight legs, #0793, #593, 1973 – 1975, marked "ALEX" $65.00
     #593, 1985, #553, #524, 1976 – 1994, marked "Alexander" $60.00
   8", #11549, 1995 only $55.00
   8", #24050, 1997 – 1998, gondolier outfit, with decorated oar $60.00
   8", #37095, 2003 – 2004, red costume, gold mask, hat with scarf $95.00
   8", #48100, 2008, maroon dress, squeeze box, plush dancing monkey $85.00
It's a Small World — 8", #46540, 2007, suitcase, extra Mickey outfit $85.00
It's Good to Be Queen — 8", #25270, 2000 – 2001 (Maggie) Mary Engelbreit $80.00
It's My Birthday — 8", #37070, 2003, brunette, blue dress with lace pinafore $80.00
It's Raining, It's Pouring — 8", #34175, 2002 – 2003, yellow raincoat, umbrella,
   boots, pink print dress $50.00
Itsy, Bitsy Spider — 8", #38785, 2004 – 2007 (Wendy), spider on dress $50.00
Itty Bitty Birdies Asian Baby — 14", #48025, 2008 ....$110.00
Ivana — 16", #25635, 2000 – 2001, Ivana Trump in black velvet gown $125.00
I've Never Seen a Purple Cow — 8", #46480, purple dress, cow $70.00
Ivory Victorian Lady — 5" porcelain, #27030, 2000, long white gown $55.00
Jabberwocky — 8", #13580, 1999 – 2000, gold costume, comes with brick tower $70.00
Jack and Beanstalk — 8", #35615, 2003 – 2005, white dress, checked top, with plush goose ...$80.00
Jack & Jill — 7" compo., 1938 – 1943 (Tiny Betty) ....$350.00 ea.
   9" compo., 1939 only (Little Betty) ....$350.00 ea.
   8" straight legs (Jack – #455, #457; Jill – #456, #458), 1987 – 1992, Storybook
     Series (Maggie) ....$60.00 ea.
   8" straight legs, sold as set, #14626, 1996 (Wendy) $100.00
Jack and Wendy — 8", pair, denim outfits, pail $100.00
Jack Be Nimble — (see Dolly Dears under Special Events/Exclusives)
Jackie — 10", #45200, 1995, Madame's Portfolio Series, pink suit $85.00
   10" h.p., #20115, 1996, wedding gown, Classic American $100.00
   21", #17450, 1997, three outfits, three pieces of luggage, jewelry, etc. $600.00
   10", #17460, 1997 – 1998, pink luncheon suit $90.00
   10", #17470, 1998, opera coat, evening dress, #17480, cocktail dress $100.00

10", #39095, suit, hat, purse (Coquette) $80.00
21", Retro Revival Jacqui, #42715, 2006, blue suit, pillbox hat.....................$400.00
Jackie and John — 10", #20117, 1996, limited edition..........................$200.00 set
Jackson, Sarah — 1979 – 1981, second set Presidents' Ladies/First Ladies Series (Louisa)....$100.00
Jacqueline — 21" h.p./vinyl arms, 1961 – 1962, street dress or suit, pillbox hat.................$950.00 up
In sheath dress and hat or slacks and top...$850.00
In gown, from cover of 1962 catalog..$950.00
Ball gown other than 1962 catalog cover..$900.00
10" h.p., 1962 only (Cissette) $750.00
1962, 1966 – 1967, exclusive in trunk with wardrobe ....$1,800.00 up
Jamaica — 8" straight legs, #542, 1986 – 1988 (round brown face)..............$60.00
Janie — 12" toddler, #1156, 1964 – 1966 only, dresses or pants and top..........$250.00
Ballerina, 1965 only $275.00
14" baby, 1972 – 1973 ....$65.00
20" baby, 1972 – 1973 ....$75.00
Japan — 8" h.p., BK, #770, 1968 – 1972 (Wendy) $100.00
8" h.p., straight legs, #0770, #570, 1973 – 1975, marked "Alex" $65.00
8" h.p., straight legs, #570, 1976 – 1986, marked "Alexander"................$60.00
8", #570, 1987 – 1991 (Maggie) $55.00
8" BK, #770, 1960s (Maggie Mixup)..$125.00
8" h.p., #526, reintroduced 1992 – 1993 only, white face (Wendy Ann)........$55.00
8", #28545, 2001 – 2002, Geisha costume, includes tea set $90.00
Japanese Bride — 10", #28590, kimono $125.00
Japanese Samurai — 8", #39820, 2005 – 2006, with sword and rack $90.00
Jasmine — 10", #1113, 1987 – 1988, Portrette, burnt orange (Cissette), 1997.....$60.00
9", #40345, 2005 – 2007, vinyl, aqua harem costume $35.00
Jeannie Walker — 13" – 14" compo., 1940s, unique jointed legs, excellent face color,
mint condition ....$675.00 up
18" compo., 1940s ....$750.00 up
Jennifer's Trunk Set — 14" doll, #1599, 1990 only...................................$165.00
Jessica — 18" cloth/vinyl, 1990 only $80.00
Jewelry Angel — 10", #28375, 2002, long pink dress $165.00
Jingle All the Way — 8", #48110, 2008, green dress, hat $65.00
Jingle Bell Skater — 8", #33460, 2002 – 2003, white skating costume, fur hat $75.00
Jingles the Juggler — 8", #10404, 1996, jester's outfit $70.00
Jo — (see Little Women)
Joanie — 36" plastic/vinyl, 1960 – 1961, allow more for flirty eyes, 36", 1960,
nurse dressed in all white with black band on cap..................................$475.00 up
36", 1961, nurse in colored uniform, all white pinafore and cap ....$425.00 up
Jo Goes to New York — 8", #14522, 1995 only, trunk set, Little Women Series ....$250.00 set
John — 8", #440, 1993 only, Peter Pan Series, wears glasses $70.00
John Powers Models — 14" h.p., 1952 only, must be mint (Maggie and Margaret).......$1,700.00 up
18", 1952 only ....$1,900.00 up
Johnson, Lady Bird — 14", 1994 only...$100.00
Jolly Old Saint Nick — 16", #19620, 1997 ....$125.00
Jones, Casey — 8" h.p., Americana Series, 1991 – 1992 only (Wendy Ann)..........$50.00
Josephine — 12", #1335, 1980 – 1986, Portraits of History (Nancy Drew) $60.00
21" Portrait, 1994 only..$300.00
10", #40130, 2005, print trimmed long dress $120.00
Joseph, the Dream Teller — 8", #14580, 1995 only, Bible Character Dolls Series.........$90.00
Joy — (see New England Collector Society under Special Events/Exclusives)
Joy Noel — (see Spiegel's under Special Events/Exclusives)
Joyous Tulip Ball Gown — 10", 2001, #28515, fancy ball gown $90.00
Judy — 21" compo., 1945 – 1947, pinch pleated flowers at hem (Wendy Ann)..........$3,200.00 up
21" h.p./vinyl arms, 1962 only (Jacqueline) ....$1,800.00 up
Judy Loves Pat the Bunny — 14", blue dress, plush bunny.......................$75.00

Jugo-Slav — 7" compo., 1935 – 1937 (Tiny Betty) $275.00
Julia — 10", #31455, 2002, tan pants, print top (Hannah) $40.00
    10", #35820, 2003 – 2005 (Hannah), Let's Celebrate, yellow dress, blue trim $40.00
Juliet — 21" compo., 1945 – 1946, Portrait (Wendy Ann) ....$2,500.00 up
    18" compo., 1937 – 1940 (Wendy Ann) ....$1,250.00 up
    8" h.p., #473, 1955 only (Wendy Ann) ....$950.00 up
    12" plastic/vinyl, 1978 – 1987, Portrait Children Series (Nancy Drew), 1991 – 1992..............$60.00
    8" (see Madame Alexander Doll Co. under Special Events/Exclusives)
    8", #40785, 2005 – 2006, pink and blue gown $80.00
Jumping Rope — 8", #38015, Caucasian, pastel dress, jumprope, 2004 – 2005 ....$75.00
    8", #38016, African-American, pastel dress, jumprope, 2004 – 2005 ....$75.00
June Bride — 21" compo., 1939, 1946 – 1947, Portrait Series, embroidered
    flowers near hem (Wendy Ann) ....$2,500.00 up
June Wedding — 8" h.p., 1956 (Wendy Ann) $750.00
Jungle Book — 8", #48695, 2008, Maggie, boy, plush bear $70.00
Just Add Love Flower Girl — 8", #42495, 2006, white dress with flowers $75.00
Just Because You're Special — 8", #35935, 2003 (Maggie), blue dress, bouquet....................$65.00
Just Darling — 8", #40430, 2005 – 2006, polka dot dress, pink purse $60.00
Just Four More — 8", #42190, 2006, with Chaos, Danger, and Mischief $125.00
Just Grape — 8", #31305, 2002, lavender checked dress, red hair $60.00
Just Heavenly — 8", #37880, car coat set, 2004 ....$85.00
Just Like Mommy — 8", #39240, 2004 – 2007, pink frilly dress, straw hat, high heel shoes $90.00
Karen — 15" – 18" h.p., 1948 – 1949 (Margaret) ....$875.00 up
Karen Ballerina — 15" compo., 1946 – 1949 (Margaret) ....$950.00 up
    18" compo., 1948 – 1949 (Margaret) ....$1,200.00 up
    18" – 21" h.p., can be dressed in pink, yellow, blue, white, or lavender ....$950.00 up
    15" porcelain (1999 – 2000), #90200, remake of 1940s Ballerina...............................$125.00
    10" h.p., 2000, #25551 (Cissette), remake of 1940s Ballerina...................................$100.00
Kathleen Toddler — 23" rigid vinyl, 1959 only $200.00
Kathy — 17" – 21" compo., 1939, 1946 (Wendy Ann) ....$650.00 – 850.00
    15" – 18" h.p., 1949 – 1951, has braids (Maggie) ....$550.00 – 750.00
Kathy Baby — 13" – 15" vinyl, 1954 – 1956, has rooted or molded hair ....$75.00 – 150.00
    11" – 13" vinyl, 1955 – 1956, has rooted or molded hair ....$85.00 – 150.00
    18" – 21", 1954 – 1956, has rooted or molded hair ....$100.00 – 175.00
    11" vinyl, 1955 – 1956, doll has molded hair and comes with trousseau..........................$200.00
    21", 1954 only $200.00
    21" and 25", 1955 – 1956..$100.00 – 175.00
Kathy Cry Dolly — 11" – 15" vinyl nurser, 1957 – 1958 ....$75.00 – 175.00
    18", 21", 25"..$125.00 – 250.00
Kathy Tears — 11", 15", 17" vinyl, 1959 – 1962, has closed mouth........................$75.00 – 175.00
    19", 23", 26", 1959 – 1962 ....$100.00 – 225.00
    12", 16", 19" vinyl, 1960 – 1961 (new face)..$75.00 – 175.00
Katie (black Smarty) — 12" plastic/vinyl, 1963 only...$325.00
    12" (black Janie), #1156, #1155, 1965 only..$325.00
    12" h.p., 1962, 100th Anniversary doll for FAO Schwarz (Lissy) $800.00
    12", Shopping in Paris, 2000, #26475, white dress, red checked jacket............................$60.00
Keane, Doris — cloth, 1930s $750.00
    9" – 11" compo., 1936 – 1937 (Little Betty)...$225.00 – 350.00
Keepsake Silk Victorian — 8", #28725, 2001 – 2002, cream silk dress............................$85.00
Kelly — 12" h.p., 1959 only (Lissy) **$500.00**
    15" – 16", 1958 – 1959 (Mary-Bel)..$300.00
    16", 1959 only, in trunk/wardrobe..$625.00
    18", 1958, 22", 1958 – 1959 ....$375.00
    8" h.p., #433, 1959, blue/white dress (Wendy Ann)...$575.00
    15", Shopping in Paris, #26470, 2000, black checked outfit...................................$75.00
Kelly and Kitty — 20", #29770, 1999, pink checked outfit with kitten............................$85.00

Kathy Baby, 11", #2901, 1956.
Mint with wrist tag and bottle.
$85.00 – 150.00.

Kelly Blue Dupionne — 20", #29380, 1998, blue silk dress $90.00
Kelly Blue Gingham — 18", #29100, 1997 – 1998, vinyl..$85.00
Kelly Good Morning — 20", #29930, 1999, white dress trimmed in blue $80.00
Kelly Happy Birthday — 18", #29230, 1997, vinyl..$85.00
Kelly Pink Butterfly — 20", #29920, 1999, pink dress and pinafore $85.00
Kelly Pink Dot Tulle — 18", #29230, 1997, vinyl...$85.00
Kelly Pink Snowflake — 18", #29110, 1997, vinyl..$85.00
Kelly's Little Sister, Katie — 12", #29940, 1999, pink plaid dress $55.00
Kelly Teacher's Pet — 15", #29760, 1999, plaid dress and hat $70.00
Kelly Teatime — 15", #29300, 1998, blue dress, straw hat...$70.00
Kelly Tree Trimming — 18", #29240, 1997, vinyl...$95.00
Kelly White Floral Party — 15" vinyl, #29390, 1998 – 1999 ....$80.00
Kennedy, Jacqueline — 14", 1989 – 1990, sixth set Presidents' Ladies/First Ladies Series
    (Mary Ann) $150.00
Kenya — 8", 1994, outfit tagged, in Neiman-Marcus trunk set....................................$70.00
    8", issued 1995 only, same outfit but sold as Nigeria..$65.00
Kick It — 8", #38890, 2004 – 2006, with soccer ball $50.00
Kikki — 9", #39965, 2005, vinyl, jeans, red bag...$30.00
King — 21" compo., 1942 – 1946 , extra make-up, red chest ribbon, gold-trimmed cape
    (Wendy Ann) ....$2,700.00 up
King of Hearts — 8", #14611, 1996, Alice in Wonderland Series $60.00
Kiss Me I'm Irish — 8", #46860, 2007 – 2008, green plaid dress, clover $70.00
Kitten — 14" – 18" cloth/vinyl, 1962 – 1963 ....$50.00 – 95.00
    24", 1961 only, has rooted hair $95.00
    20" nurser, 1968 only, has cryer box, doesn't wet...$100.00
    20", 1985 – 1986 only, dressed in pink...$90.00
    8", 1998, #29310 Powder Pink or #29423 Sunny $55.00
Kitten Kries — 20" cloth/vinyl, 1967 only $100.00
Kitten, Littlest — (see Littlest Kitten)
Kitten, Lively — (see Lively Kitten)
Kitty Baby — 21" compo., 1941 – 1942 ....$175.00
Klondike Kate — 10" h.p., 1963 only, Portrette (Cissette) ....$1,500.00 up
Knave — 8", #13040, 1997 – 1998, brocade suit, large playing card, 5 of spades.........$70.00
Knight — 8", #25915 (Wendy), 2000 – 2001, Alice in Wonderland Series...................$70.00
Kong, the 8th Wonder of the World — 10" doll, 20" gorilla $150.00
Korea — 8" h.p., BK, #772, 1968 – 1970 (Wendy)...$200.00
    BKW and BK, #772 (Maggie Mixup) $225.00
    #522, reintroduced 1988 – 1989 (Maggie Mixup) $60.00
    #47830, 8", 2008, green, red, blue outfit, drum $90.00
Kukla — 8", #11101, 1995 only, International Folk Tales (Russia) (Wendy) $60.00
Kwanzaa Celebration — 10" h.p., #10368, 1996 Holiday $80.00
Lady and Her Child — 21" porcelain, 8" h.p., 1993...$475.00 set
Lady and the Tramp — 8", #45665, 2007 – 2008, Maggie with plush Lady and the Tramp dogs...$85.00
Lady Bird — 8", #438, 1988 – 1989, Storybook Series (Maggie).................................$55.00
Ladybug — 8", #27725, 2001 – 2002, red checked dress, green jacket and hat..............$65.00
Ladybug, Ladybug — 8", #40100, 2005, red dress $65.00
Lady Godiva — 10", #40835, 2005, brown over dress..$100.00
Lady Hamilton — 20" h.p./vinyl arms, 1957 only, Models Formal Gowns Series,
    picture hat, blue gown with shoulder shawl effect (Cissy)...........................$1,300.00 up
    11" h.p., 1957, pink silk gown, picture hat with roses (Cissette) ....$750.00 up
    21", #2182, 1968, beige lace over pink gown (Jacqueline)..............................$475.00
    12" vinyl, #1338, 1984 – 1986, Portraits of History (Nancy Drew)..................$60.00
Lady in Red — 20", #2285, 1958 only, red taffeta (Cissy).................................$2,900.00 up
    10", #1134, 1990, Portrette (Cissette) $85.00
Lady in Waiting — 8" h.p., #487, 1955 only (Wendy Ann) ....$1,700.00 up
Lady Jane Grey — 10", #40840, 2005, green court gown..$120.00

Kelly, 12", 1959 (Lissy). Original tagged nylon dress with lace trim. $500.00.

Lady Lee — 8", #442, 1988 only, Storybook Series $60.00
Lady Lovelace — cloth/felt, 1930s..$650.00
Lady Valentine — 8", #140503, 1994 only (Wendy Ann) $60.00
Lady Windermere — 21" compo., 1945 – 1946, extra make-up, Portrait Series .... $2,500.00 up
Lady with the Alligator Purse — 8", #39830, 2005, red plaid dress..................$80.00
Lancelot — 8", #79529, 1995, 100th Anniversary (copy of 1995 Disney auction doll) $100.00
    8", #13550, 1999, blue and black outfit with sword $75.00
Lane, Harriet — 1982 – 1984, third set Presidents' Ladies/First Ladies Series (Mary Ann)....$100.00
Laos — 8" straight legs, #525, 1987 – 1988 ....$55.00
La Petit Arlequin — 8", #45700, 2007, white face, striped outfit $90.00
La Petite Mademoiselle — 8", #37210, 2003 –2004, toile dress, bear in wagon $90.00
Lapland — 8" h.p., #537, 1993 ....$60.00
Lassie — 8", #11102, 1995 only, International Folk Tales (Norway) $60.00
Latvia — 8" straight legs, #527, 1987 only $60.00
Laughing Allegra — cloth, 1932 ....$650.00
Laurie, Little Men — 8" h.p., BK, #781, #755, 1966 – 1972 (Wendy Ann) $150.00
    Straight legs, #0755, #416, 1973 – 1975, marked "Alex" $75.00
    Straight legs, #416, #410, 1976 – 1992..$65.00
    8", #14620, 1996, waistcoat, houndstooth trousers $60.00
    12" all h.p., 1966 only (Lissy) $600.00
    12" plastic/vinyl, 1967 – 1988 (Nancy Drew) $60.00
Laurie, Piper — 14" h.p., 1950 only (Margaret) .... $2,400.00 up
    21", h.p., 1950 only (Margaret)... $2,900.00 up
Lavender Bouquet — 8", #30895, 2001 – 2002, white, long black gown with lavender flowers ...$75.00
Lavender Sachet — 8", #33645, 2004 – 2005, lavender dress $80.00
Laverne and Shirley Set — 10", #25755, 2000, with Boo Boo Kitty $175.00
Lazy Mary — 7" compo., 1936 – 1938 (Tiny Betty) $275.00
Leaf Fairy — 8", #28505, 2001 – 2002, rust costume with leaves.....................$70.00
Legacy of Green Gables — 10", #48805, 2008, maroon and green long dress $140.00
Legally Blonde — 16", #48925, 2008, jeans, pink top and jacket, purse, dog.......$140.00
Lemonade Girl — 8", #14130, 1998 – 1999 (Maggie), doll with stand, etc $80.00
Lennox, Mary — 14" Classic Series, 1993 – 1994 ....$75.00
Leo — 8", #21370, 1998, golden lion costume $85.00
Leopard with Shopping Bag — 10", Cissette, 1997 – 1998 ....$100.00
Le Petit Boudoir — 1993 (see Collectors United under Special Events/Exclusives)
Leslie (black Polly) — 17" vinyl, 1965 – 1971, in dress $275.00
    1966 – 1971, as bride $300.00
    1965 – 1971, in formal or ball gown..$375.00
    In trunk with wardrobe .... $650.00 up
    1966 – 1971, as ballerina $400.00
Let's Ride Total Moves Wendy — 8", #40435, with scooter $75.00
Letty Bridesmaid — 7" – 8" compo., 1938 – 1940 (Tiny Betty)........................$375.00
Lewis, Shari — 14", 1958 – 1959 ....$675.00
    21", 1958 – 1959 ....$850.00
Liberace with Candelabra — 8", #22080, 1997, velvet cape $100.00
Liberty Angel — 10", #34300, 2002, white gown, feather wings with jewels...........$100.00
Libra — 8", #21390, 1998, balanced scale headpiece, purple costume $75.00
Liesl — (see Sound of Music)
Lila Bridesmaid — 7" – 8" compo., 1938 – 1940 (Tiny Betty) $325.00
Lilac Fairy — 21", 1993, Portrait Ballerina..$300.00
    10", 2008, #48365, lilac tutu (Sleeping Beauty) $115.00
Lilac Rococo Lady — 5", #27020, porcelain, 2000, embroidered gown $60.00
'Lil Christmas Candy — 8" h.p., #100348, 1994 only, Americana Series..............$65.00
'Lil Christmas Cookie — 8", #341, 1993 – 1994, Americana Series $65.00
'Lil Clara and the Nutcracker — 8", #140480, 1994, Storyland Series $65.00
Lil' Cowgirl Wendy — 8", #47845, 2008, red and white dress, hat, gun...............$65.00

Lil' Indian — 8", #47850, 2008, Maggie, feather in hair, tomahawk $60.00
Lilibet — 16" compo., 1938 (Princess Elizabeth) .... $750.00 up
'Lil Miss Genius — 7", #702 and #400702 vinyl, painted eyes, 1993 – 1995, pink lacy dress $40.00
'Lil Sir Genius — 7", #701 and #400701 vinyl, painted eyes, 1993, blue jumpsuit........................$40.00
Lilly Loves Sushi — 8", #47825, 2008, print dress, tray of sushi..$55.00
Lily — 10", #1114, 1987 – 1988, red/black (Cissette) $60.00
Lily of the Valley — 10", satin gown with lilies of the valley $100.00
Lily of the Valley Fairy — 8", #36885, 2003 – 2004, lace and tulle gown $90.00
Lincoln, Mary Todd — 1982 – 1984, third set Presidents' Ladies/First Ladies Series (Louisa)....$150.00
  8", #47920, 2008, white long dress with embroidery and ruffles.......................................$80.00
Lind, Jenny — 21" h.p./vinyl arms, #2191, 1969, dressed in all pink, no trim (Jacqueline)...$1,400.00
  21", #2181, 1970, all pink with lace trim $1,500.00
  10", #1171, 1969, Portrette, all pink, no trim (Cissette) $575.00
  10", #1184, 1970, Portrette, pink with lace trim (Cissette)...$650.00
  14" plastic/vinyl, #1491, 1970 only, Portrait Children Series (Mary Ann), pink, lace trim.....$350.00
  10", #27375, 2000, long white gown..$90.00
  10", #48135, 2008, blue long satin dress, fan...$130.00
Lind, Jenny and Listening Cat — 14", #1470, 1969 – 1971, Portrait Children Series,
  blue dot dress apron and holds plush kitten (must have kitten) (Mary Ann) $325.00
Linus — 10", #26435, 2001 – 2002, Peanuts Gang, red stripe shirt, blue blanket $30.00
  10", #35895, 2003 – 2004, Trick or Treat, blanket, sign, pumpkin.....................................$45.00
Lion Tamer — 8", #306, 1990, Americana Series (Wendy Ann) $60.00

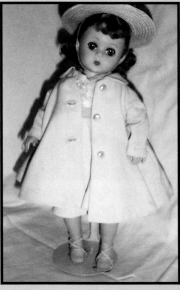

Lissy, 12", 1957. Pink circular skirt and coat. Nylon blouse and straw hat. Tagged and all original. $400.00 up.

Dating Lissy Dolls

12" Lissy and Lissy face dolls are all hard plastic with glued-on wigs. Lissy is not marked anywhere on the body. Only the clothes were tagged.

1956 – 1958: Lissy had jointed elbows and knees which allowed her to sit. Her feet were slightly arched to wear sandals with hose or white socks. The 1957 – 1958 Lissy Little Women wore black sandals.

1959 – 1967: The Lissy face dolls had the Lissy face but have non-jointed arms and legs. The feet were flat.

1959 – 1967: Lissy face Little Women were made.

1959: Kelly (Lissy face) was produced in 1959 only, in a variety of outfits.

1962: Pamela (Lissy face) had three interchangeable outfits with extra clothing in a gift set. Pamela had a Velcro strip to attach the wigs. Pamelas were made for several years as store specials. Pamela was also made with the later Nancy Drew vinyl head.

1962: Lissy face Katie and Tommy were made for FAO Schwarz's 100th Anniversary.

1963: McGuffey Ana, Southern Belle, and Scarlett O'Hara were made using the Lissy face doll.

1965: Brigitta of the large set of the Sound of Music was made using the Lissy face doll in an Alpine outfit and the rare sailor costume.

1966: Lissy face Cinderella was available in "Poor" outfit or in blue satin ball gown. A gift set featured the doll and both outfits.

1967: Only year Laurie of Little Women was made using the Lissy face.

1993: Nine Lissy face dolls were made for the regular line: Amy, Beth, Jo, Meg, Ballerina, Greta Brinker, Hans Brinker, Hamlet, and Ophelia.

1993: Special for Horchow. Pamela Plays Dress Up was a Lissy face doll with wigs, clothes, and a trunk. Lissy face Alice in Wonderland with Jabberwocky was made for Disney, and the Columbian Sailor was made for the U.F.D.C. Luncheon.

Little Colonel, 8½", 1935, composition (Betty). Closed mouth, original wrist tag, tagged dress and straw bonnet. $650.00.

Lissy — 11½" – 12" h.p., 1956 – 1958, jointed knees and elbows
  1956 – 1958, as ballerina or bride .... $475.00 up
  1956 – 1957, as bridesmaid.. $750.00 up
  1958, dressed in formal.. $800.00 up
  1956 – 1958, in street dresses... $400.00 up
  1956, in window box with wardrobe $1,600.00
  21", one-piece arm, pink tulle pleated skirt (Cissy) .... $2,200.00 up
  21", #2051, 1966, pink with tiara (Coco) $2,200.00
  12" h.p., 1957, jointed elbows and knees, in window box with wardrobe (Lissy) ....$1,500.00 up

Little Edwardian, 8", SLW, #0200, 1954. All original. $1,000.00 up.

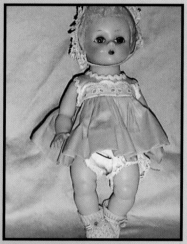

Little Genius, 8", 1961. Polished cotton dress and bonnet. $225.00 up.

Little Genius, 8", 1956 – 1962, vinyl. Pictured in lacy organdy dress and bonnet. MADC blue ribbon winner. $350.00 up.

12" h.p., one-piece arms and legs in window box/wardrobe, 1959 – 1966 (Lissy) .... $1,000.00 up

12", Spring Parade, #42050, 2006, blue coat, straw hat $100.00

12", Homecoming Lissy, #42045, 2006, blue dress and hat $100.00

12", Lissy's Sock Hop Trunk Set, #46110, 2007, five outfits, trunk accessories, plush dog, duck toy $220.00

12", Forever Darling Lissy, #45520, 2007, pink plaid dress $90.00

Lithuania — 8" h.p., #110544, 1994 only (Maggie) $55.00

Little Angel — 9" latex/vinyl, 1950 – 1957 .... $200.00

Little Audrey — Vinyl, 1954 only .... $475.00 up

Little Betty — 9" – 11" compo., 1935 – 1943, must be mint .... $250.00 – 375.00

Little Bitsey — 9" all vinyl nurser, 1967 – 1968 (Sweet Tears) $150.00

Little Boop Beep — 10", #28970, 2001 (Betty Boop), pink dress $100.00

Little Bo Peep — (see Bo Peep, Little)

Little Boy Blue — 7" compo., 1937 – 1939 (Tiny Betty) $350.00

Little Butch — 9" all vinyl nurser, 1967 – 1968 (Sweet Tears) $150.00

Little Cherub — 11" compo., 1945 – 1946 .... $275.00

7" all vinyl, 1960 only $225.00

Little Christmas Princess — 8", #10369, 1996 Holiday $70.00

Little Colonel — 8½" – 9" compo. (rare size), 1935, closed mouth (Betty) $650.00

11" – 15" compo. (rare size), closed mouth (Betty) .... $550.00 – 850.00

17" compo., closed mouth (Betty) .... $750.00 up

14", open mouth (Betty) .... $650.00 up

17" – 23", open mouth .... $700.00 – 950.00

26" – 27", open mouth .... $1,300.00 up

Little Countess — 8", #28890, 2001, white lacy dress $80.00

Little Devil — 8" h.p., Americana Series, 1992 – 1993 only $65.00

Little Dorrit — 16" cloth, early 1930s, Dickens character $700.00

Little Edwardian — 8" h.p., SL, SLW, #0200, 1953 – 1955, long dotted navy gown ... $1,000.00 up

Little Emily — 16" cloth, early 1930s, Dickens character $650.00

Little Emperor — (see U.F.D.C. under Special Events/Exclusives)

Little Gardenia Bridesmaid — 8", 2001, white dress $85.00

Little Genius — 12" – 20" compo./cloth, 1935 – 1940, 1942 – 1946 .... $250.00

24" – 25", 1936 – 1940 .... $275.00

8" h.p./vinyl, 1956 – 1962, nude (clean condition), good face color $100.00

In cotton play dress .... **$225.00 up**

In dressy, lacy outfit with bonnet and/or coat .... **$350.00 up**

In christening outfit $375.00

Sewing or Gift Set, 1950s .... $850.00 up

7" vinyl, 1993 – 1995, reintroduced doll with painted eyes $40.00

#701 and #400701, 1993 – 1995, dressed in blue jumpsuit ('Lil Sir Genius) $40.00

#702 and #400702, 1993 – 1995, dressed in pink lacy dress ('Lil Miss Genius) $40.00

1993, extra packaged outfits .... $25.00 ea.

Christening Baby, #400703, 1994 – 1995 .... $45.00

Super Genius, #400704, 1994 – 1995, dressed in Superman style outfit $40.00

Birthday Party, #400705, 1994 only $45.00

Genius Elf, #400706, 1994 – 1995, dressed in Christmas outfit $45.00

Little Genius Toddler — 8" h.p., 1954 – 1955 (Wendy Ann), caracul hair .... $275.00 up

Little Girl with a Curl — 8", #28965, 2001, pink dress $65.00

Little Godey — 8" h.p., #491, 1953 – 1955 (Wendy Ann) .... $1,400.00 up

Little Granny — 14" plastic/vinyl, #1431, 1966 only, floral gown (Mary Ann) $185.00

14", #1430, 1966 only, pinstriped gown (also variations) (Mary Ann) $225.00

Little Huggums — (see Huggums, Little)

Little Irish Dancer — 8", #32125, 2000 – 2004, navy decorated dress, bend knees $85.00

8", #48570, 2008, blue decorated dress, Maggie $85.00

Little Irish Lass — 8", #42260, 2006 – 2007, green dress, shillelagh $75.00

Little Jack Horner — 7" compo., 1937 – 1943 (Tiny Betty) $300.00

Little Jumping Joan — 8", #487, 1989 – 1990, Storybook Series (Maggie Mixup) $55.00
Little Lady Doll — 8" h.p., #1050, 1960 only, Gift Set in mint condition (Maggie Mixup).... $850.00 up
   8" doll only, must have correct hairdo and excellent face color..$325.00
   21" h.p., 1949, has braids and colonial gown, extra make-up, Portrait Series (Wendy Ann) $2,400.00
Little Lord Fauntleroy — cloth, 1930s...$750.00
   13" compo., 1936 – 1937 (Wendy Ann) .... $650.00 up
Little Love Angel — 8", #28350, 2001 – 2002, pink costume with wings...................................$90.00
   10", #28355, 2001, lavender dress, feather wings $100.00
Little Lucy Locket — 8", #40445, 2005, blue dress, black hat.......................................$65.00
Little Madeline — 8" h.p., 1953 – 1954 (Wendy Ann) .... $750.00 up
Little Maid — 8" straight legs, #423, 1987 – 1988, Storybook Series (Wendy Ann)...................$55.00
Little Men — 15" h.p., 1950 – 1952 (Margaret and Maggie) ....$850.00 up, ea.
Little Men — Set with Tommy, Nat, and Stuffy, must be in excellent condition ....$2,600.00 set
Little Mermaid — 10", #1145, 1992 – 1993, Portrette, green/blue outfit (Cissette)..................$100.00
   8", #14531, 1995, Hans Christian Andersen Series, long black hair $60.00
   8", #42550, 2006 – 2007, mermaid body, shell, and pillow..$90.00
Little Minister — 8" h.p., #411, 1957 only (Wendy Ann) .... $3,200.00 up
Little Miss — 8" h.p., #489, 1989 – 1991 only, Storybook Series (Maggie Mixup)...................$60.00
Little Miss Godey — (see M.A.D.C. under Special Events/Exclusives)
Little Miss Magnin — (see I. Magnin under Special Events/Exclusives)
Little Miss Matched — 12", #45640, 2007, mismatched clothes, cloth doll $40.00
Little Miss Sunshine — 8", #35065, 2003 – 2004 (Maggie), yellow print dress.........................$50.00
Little Nannie Etticoat — #428, 1986 – 1988, straight legs, Storybook Series........................$55.00
Little Nell — 16" cloth, early 1930s, Dickens character .... $650.00 up
   14" compo., 1938 – 1940 (Wendy Ann)..$700.00
Little Orphan Annie — 8", #13740, 1999 – 2002, red dress, comes with dog Sandy $70.00
Little Pearl Bridesmaid — 8", 2001, white dress, rose crown.......................................$75.00
Little Princess — 14", #26415, 1995 only, has trunk and wardrobe (Louisa) $200.00
Little Princess, A — 8", #14120, 1998 – 1999, pink taffeta, with doll $75.00
Little Princess, The — 8", #48595, 2008, pink dress, porcelain doll $95.00
Little Shaver — 10" cloth, 1940 – 1944 .... $475.00 up
   7" cloth, 1940 – 1944 ....$550.00
   15" – 22" cloth, 1940 – 1944... $650.00 up
   12" plastic/vinyl, 1963 – 1965, has painted eyes...$225.00
   10", #26820, 2000, cloth, gray/cream, remake of 1940s, #26825, 2000 – 2001, pink/cream.......$55.00
   6", #26830, 2000 – 2001, cloth, gray/cream, remake of 1940s......................................$55.00
Little Southern Boy/Girl — 10" latex/vinyl, 1950 – 1951 .... $195.00 ea.
Little Southern Girl — 8" h.p., #305, 1953 only (Wendy Ann) ....$950.00 up
Littlest Kitten — 8" vinyl, 1963, nude, clean, good face color...$125.00 up
   Dressed in lacy dress outfit with bonnet ....$275.00 up
   Dressed in christening outfit ....$375.00 up
   In Sewing or Gift Set...$750.00 up
   Dressed in play attire or dress.. $225.00 up
Little Thumbkins — 8", #14532, Hans Christian Andersen Series, lavender/pink/yellow tiers..$60.00
Little Victoria — 7½" – 8", #376, 1953 – 1954 only (Wendy Ann)....................................$1,200.00 up
Little Women — Meg, Jo, Amy, Beth (Marme in sets when available)
   16" cloth, 1930 – 1936..$750.00 up, ea.
   7" compo., 1935 – 1944 (Tiny Betty) ....$375.00 ea.
   9" compo., 1937 – 1940 (Little Betty) ....$350.00 ea.
   13" – 15" compo., 1937 – 1946 (Wendy Ann)..$375.00 ea.
   14" – 15" h.p., 1947 – 1956, plus Marme (Margaret and Maggie) .... $450.00 ea., $2,200.00 set
   14" – 15" h.p., widespread fingers, ca. 1949 – 1952....................................$575.00 ea.
   14" – 15" h.p., BK, plus Marme (Margaret and Maggie) .... $450.00 ea., $2,200.00 set
   14" – 15", Amy with loop curls, must have good face color (Margaret) ....$600.00 ea.
   8", Amy with loop curls, 1991, #411...$100.00
   7½" – 8" h.p., SL, SLW, all #609, 1955, plus Marme (Wendy Ann) .... $450.00 ea., $2,300.00 set

Little Genius, 8", 1956 – 1962, vinyl. Tagged original cotton dress and bonnet. $225.00 up.

Little Shaver, 12", 1963 – 1965, plastic/vinyl. Painted eyes. All original. $225.00.

Littlest Kitten, 8", 1963, vinyl. Pictured in tagged butterfly outfit. Hard to find. $225.00.

8" h.p., BKW, all #609, all #409, all #481, 1956 – 1959 (Wendy Ann)........ $350.00 ea., $1,600.00 set
8" BKW, all #381, 1960 – 1963 (Wendy Ann).. $250.00 ea., $1,200.00 set
 #781, 1966 – 1972 .... $125.00 ea., $650.00 set
 #7811 to #7815, 1973 .... $75.00 ea., $375.00 set
8" straight legs, #411 – #415, 1974 – 1986 .... $70.00 ea., $325.00 set
 #405 – #409, 1987 – 1990, #411 – #415, 1991 – 1992 .... $60.00 ea., $275.00 set
 #14523 – #14528, 1995 (Wendy Ann) .... $60.00 ea., $275.00 set
 #33375, #33380, #33385, #33386, 2002, Amy, Meg, Jo, Beth................ $65.00 ea.
 #36120, Marme, 2003, brown plaid dress.. $70.00
 #36125, Laurie, 2003, brown three-piece suit $75.00
 #33375, #33380, #33385, #33386, 2004, Amy, Meg, Jo, Beth................ $70.00 ea.
 #39070, 2004, Amy's Party Dress, long pink party dress with roses $85.00
 #28140 – #28180, 2000 .... $65.00 – $325.00 set
 #40325, #40320, #40335, #40330, 8", 2005 – 2007, Amy, Meg, Jo, Beth .... $75.00 ea.
 #48405, #48415, #48410, #48420, Meg, Beth, Jo, Amy, #46530 Marmee.......... $75.00
 #48400, 2008, 10", Beth's Trunk Set, 4 outfits, etc.................................. $270.00
10", #14630 – #14633, 1996 .... $70.00 ea., $325.00 set
10", #40315, 2005 – 2006, Jo Goes to New York, doll, extra clothes, 5-drawer trunk,
 bed with accessories.. $275.00
10", #40265, 2006 – 2007, Amy in Paris Trunk Set, three outfits, trunk.................. $325.00
10", #45935, 2007, Meg's Wedding Trunk Set, Cissette, three outfits, trunk, accessories....... $310.00
11½" – 12" h.p., jointed elbows and knees, 1957 – 1958 (Lissy) .... $475.00 ea., $2,300.00 set
11½" – 12" h.p., one-piece arms and legs, 1959 – 1968 (Lissy) .... $250.00 ea., $1,300.00 set
12" plastic/vinyl, 1969 – 1982 (Nancy Drew) .... $65.00 ea., $325.00 set
12" plastic/vinyl, 1983 – 1989, new outfits (Nancy Drew) .... $60.00 ea., $300.00 set
12", 1989 – 1990 only (see Sears-Roebuck under Special Events/Exclusives)
12", 1993 only, no Marme (Lissy) .... $90.00 ea.
16", 1997 – 2000, plastic/vinyl, Little Women Journal Series (no Marme)........... $85.00 ea.
16", 1999 – 2000, Marme, #28040, Little Women Journals $85.00
Lively Huggums — 25", knob makes limbs and head move, 1963 .... $150.00
Lively Kitten — 14", 18", 24", 1962 – 1963, knob makes limbs and head move .... $100.00 – 250.00
Lively Pussy Cat — 14", 20", 24", 1966 – 1969, knob makes limbs and head move ..... $75.00 – 225.00
Lola and Lolly Bridesmaid — 7" compo., 1938 – 1940 (Tiny Betty) .... $375.00 up, ea.
Lollie Baby — rubber/compo., 1941 – 1942 .... $100.00
Lollipop Munchkin — (see Munchkin Peasant)
Looby Loo — 15½" h.p., ca. 1951 – 1954... $675.00 up
Lord Fauntleroy — 12", 1981 – 1983, Portrait Children (Nancy Drew) $70.00
Lord Valentine — 8", #140502, 1994 only (Wendy Ann) $60.00
Louisa — (see Sound of Music)
Love — (see Collectors United/C. U. under Specials Events/Exclusives), 8", made for public in 1994
 (only differences on C.U. doll are gold locket, pearls set into cap, and gold metal braids
 on slippers, heart box) $65.00
Love Is in the Details Felt Wendy — 8", #48455, 2008, blue dress, mohair wig.............. $250.00
Love Notes for Grandma — 8", #36915, 2003 – 2004, red checked dress, notes $70.00
10", #35890, 2003, trick or treat, mask, bag with candy $90.00
Love's Bloom — 8", #49880, 2008, pink sweater, heart skirt, flowers $70.00
Love to Be Loved — 8", #40040, 2005 – 2006 (Asian) with panda $80.00
Lovey Dove (Dovey) — 19" vinyl baby, 1958 – 1959, closed mouth, molded or
 rooted hair, few are mistagged $175.00
19" h.p./latex, 1950 – 1951.. $175.00
12" all h.p. toddler, 1948 – 1951 (Precious)... $375.00 up
1951, dressed as "Ringbearer"... $675.00 up
"Answer Doll" with lever in back to move head .... $525.00 up
Lucinda — 12" plastic/vinyl, 1969 – 1970 (Janie) $225.00
14" plastic/vinyl, #1435, #1535, 1971 – 1982 (11-year production), blue gown (Mary Ann)....$65.00
14", #1535, 1983 – 1986, Classic Series, pink or peach gown (Mary Ann) $70.00

Lucinda, 14", #1535, 1983 – 1986 (Mary Ann). Harder to find pink dress. $70.00.

Luck of the Irish — 8", #327, 1992 – 1993 only, Americana Series (Maggie Mixup) $65.00
    8", #38595, 2004 – 2005, with 5" leprechaun and pot of gold $85.00
Lucy — 8", Chronicles of Narnia, #46410, fur coat, sword, 2007..$90.00
Lucy — 8" h.p., #488, 1961 only, Americana Series, strip cotton/poke bonnet (Wendy Ann)......$1,800.00 up
    10", #26420, 2001 – 2004, Peanuts Gang, blue dress, includes backdrop...................................$45.00
    10", #33715, 2002, School Days Lucy (Peanuts), plaid coat, books $45.00
Lucy and Ricky — 9" set, Vitameatavegamin episode..$175.00
Lucy Bride — 14" h.p., 1949 – 1950 (Margaret)..$1,000.00 up
    18" h.p., 1949 – 1950 (Margaret) ....$1,100.00 up
    21" h.p., 1949 – 1950 (Margaret) ....$1,200.00 up
    21", #2155, 1955 (Cissy) pale pink gown, very red hair, heavily painted face..............$10,000.00 up
    14" compo., 1937 – 1940 (Wendy Ann) $450.00
    17" compo., 1937 – 1940 (Wendy Ann) $600.00
    21" compo., 1942 – 1944, Portrait, extra make-up (Wendy Ann) $2,500.00
Lucy Gets in Pictures — 10", #31450, 2001, long pink gown, feather headpiece....................$160.00
Lucy Locket — 8" straight legs, #433, 1986 – 1988, Storybook Series...................................$60.00
    14", #25501, 1995, Ribbons & Bows Series, purple floral skirt (Louisa) $75.00
Lucy Ricardo — (see FAO Schwarz under Special Events/Exclusives)
    9", 1950s gingham dress, with bottle and spoon..$100.00
    21", #50003, 1996 Timeless Legends, black dress with black and white polka dots $350.00
    10", #14071, Shadow Polka Dot Lucy, 1998 – 1999 ....$150.00
    10", #15160, 1999 – 2000, Lucy's Italian Movie, peasant outfit, grape vat..........................$150.00
Lucy's Rhumba — 10", #25760, 2001, Be a Pal episode, white dress, ruffles $130.00
Lullaby Munchkin — (see Munchkin Peasant)
Madame (Alexander) — 21", 1984 only, one-piece skirt in pink.......................................$250.00
    21", 1985 – 1987, pink with overskirt that unsnaps $225.00
    21", 1988 – 1990, blue with full lace overskirt...$225.00
    21", #79507, 1995, 100th Anniversary, pink with lace jacket, limited edition of 500 ....$375.00
    8", 1993 only, introduced mid-year (see Madame Alexander Doll Co. under Special Events/Exclusives)
    8" in blue gown (see Doll & Teddy Bear Expo under Special Events/Exclusives)
    8", #79527, 1995, 100th Anniversary $90.00
    10", #47700, 2007, red 1920s outfit, Alice in Wonderland doll $125.00
Madame Alexander Celebrates American Design — 10" h.p. (Cissette), 2000, pink gown...$125.00
Madame Alexander Collector's Phonograph Album — 1978, Madame's voice
    reading children's stories $35.00
M.A.D.C. (Madame Alexander Doll Club) — (see Special Events/Exclusives)
Madame Butterfly — 10" (see Marshall Fields under Special Events/Exclusives)
    8" h.p., #22000, 1997 – 1998, shadow, kimono $85.00
    21", #22010, 1997, kimono over silk robe $325.00
Madame de Pompadour — 10", #25010, 1999 (Cissette), elaborate taffeta costume $175.00
    10", #45630, 2006 – 2007, Madame de Pompadour Spring, green dress $270.00
    10", #42095, 2006 – 2007, Madame de Pompadour Winter, elaborate ball gown $270.00
Madame Doll — 21" h.p./vinyl arms, 1966 only, pink brocade (Coco) ....$2,300.00 up
    14" plastic/vinyl, #1460, #1561, 1967 – 1975, Classic Series (Mary Ann) $150.00
Madame Pompadour — 21" h.p./vinyl arms, #2197, 1970, pink lace overskirt (Jacqueline)...$400.00
Madame's Best — 8", #38045, 2004, dress and pinafore $80.00
Madame X, John Singer Sargent's — 10", #25300, 2000, long black gown $100.00
Madelaine — 14" compo., 1940 – 1942 (Wendy Ann) ....$650.00 up
    8" h.p., 1954, FAO Schwarz special..$800.00 up
Madelaine du Bain — 11" compo., closed mouth, 1937 (Wendy Ann) $500.00
    14" compo., 1938 – 1939 (Wendy Ann) ....$600.00 up
    17" compo., 1939 – 1941 (Wendy Ann) $650.00
    21" compo., 1939 – 1941 (Wendy Ann) ....$950.00 up
    14" h.p., 1949 – 1951 (Maggie) ....$950.00 up
Madeline — 17" – 18" h.p./jointed elbows and knees, 1950 – 1953 ....$800.00 up
    18" h.p., 1961 only, vinyl head, extra jointed body, wears short dress, must be mint ....$750.00 up

Maggie, 17", 1972 – 1973 (Elise), plastic/vinyl. $800.00.

Maggie Mix-up Angel, 8", BKW, #618, 1961. Blue taffeta costume with silver wings. $800.00.

Ball gown 1961 only .... $800.00 up
18", #46045, 2007 – 2008, cloth doll, blue coat, yellow hat $45.00
8", #46395, 2007 – 2008, Maggie, blue coat, yellow hat, dog $70.00
Maggie Loves Gumby — 8", #48945, 2008, green dress, Gumby $75.00
12", #48625, 2008, Lissy Madeline Trunk Set $240.00
8", #47375, Madeline Christmas (Wendy), green coat $75.00
18", #47370, cloth Madeline Christmas, 2008, green coat $45.00
29", #48970, 2008, cloth, blue coat, yellow hat $70.00
Mad Hatter — 8", #14510, 1995, Alice in Wonderland Series $75.00
8", #38880, 2004 – 2005, with teapot, cup, and mouse $80.00
Madison, Dolly — 1976 – 1978, first set Presidents' Ladies/First Ladies Series (Martha), 14" $125.00
8", #48935, 2008, blue long dress, lace fan $60.00
Madonna and Child — 10", #10600, 1995, Christmas Series $100.00
10", #39750, 2005, with baby Jesus and 12" stained glass window $180.00
Maggie — 15" h.p., 1948 – 1954 (Little Women only to 1956) $550.00
17" – 18", 1949 – 1953 .... $650.00 up
20" – 21", 1948 – 1954 .... $750.00 up
22" – 23", 1949 – 1952 .... $800.00 up
17" plastic/vinyl, 1972 – 1973 only (Elise) **$150.00**
Maggie Elf — 8", #14585, 1995, Christmas Series $65.00
Maggie Loves Golf — 8", #48540, 2008, white tennis outfit, golfbag, clubs $70.00
Maggie Loves PB&J — 8", #47940, 2008, braids, strawberry print, PB&J sandwich ... $50.00
Maggie Mixup — 16½" h.p./vinyl, 1960 only (Elise body) $350.00
17" plastic/vinyl, 1961 only $400.00
8" h.p., #600, #611, #617, #627, 1960 – 1961, freckles $450.00
8" Wendy Ann face, freckles .... $650.00 up
8" h.p., #618, 1961, as angel **$800.00**
8", #610, 1960 – 1961, dressed in overalls and has watering can $800.00
8", #626, 1960 – 1961, dressed in skater outfit .... $750.00 up
8", #634, 1960 – 1961, dressed in riding habit $550.00
8", #593, 1960, dressed in roller skating outfit .... $750.00 up
8", #598, #597, #596, 1960, wearing dresses or skirts/blouses .... $475.00 up
8", #31000, 1997 – 1998, Post Office commemorative, blue gingham $50.00
Maggie's Bake Sale — 8", #48520, 2008, plaid dress, cake $75.00
Maggie's Best Memories — 8", #38905, 2004, plaid dress, scrapbook $75.00
Maggie's Trip to the Farmers Market — 8", #48095, 2008, bag with fruit $70.00
Maggie Teenager — 15" – 18" h.p., 1951 – 1953 .... $475.00 – 650.00
23", 1951 – 1953 .... $650.00 up
Maggie Visits Christmas Town — 8", #47735, 2007 – 2008, Maggie, elf costume, two tiny elves $85.00
Maggie Visits Halloween Town — 8", #48510, 2008, Lock, Shock & Barrel $75.00
Maggie Visits the World's Fair — 8", #48060, 2008, pants outfit, brochure $50.00
Maggie Walker — 15" – 18" h.p., 1949 – 1953 .... $400.00 – 650.00
20" – 21", 1949 – 1953 .... $600.00
23" – 25", 1951 – 1953 (with Cissy face) .... $650.00 up
Magnolia — 21", #2297, 1977 only, many rows of lace on pink gown $350.00
21", #2251, 1988 only, yellow gown $275.00
Maid Marian — 8" h.p., #492, 1989 – 1991 only, Storybook Series (Wendy Ann) ... $135.00
21", 1992 – 1993 only, Portrait Series (Jacqueline) $325.00
Maid of Honor — 18" compo., 1940 – 1944 (Wendy Ann) .... $700.00 up
14" plastic/vinyl, #1592, 1988 – 1989, Classic Series, blue gown (Mary Ann) $85.00
10", #28645, 2001 – 2002, long pink dress, limited to 1,000 .... $100.00
Maimey Shadow Wendy — 8", #38755, blue dress, white sweater, 2004 .... $90.00
Majorette — 14" – 17" compo., 1937 – 1938 (Wendy Ann) .... $850.00 up
Majorette, Drum — 8" h.p., #482, 1955 only (Wendy Ann) .... $950.00 up
8", #314, 1991 – 1992 only, Americana Series, no baton $55.00
Making Friends on Sesame Street — 8", #39086, #39085, 2004 – 2005 with Zoe,

Cookie Monster, and Elmo...$150.00
Making Memories Porcelain Wendy — 8", #45780, 2007, white and pink dress $160.00
Making New Friends — 8", #37225, 2003 – 2005, African-American, pink dress,
two dolls, #37226, Caucasian $75.00
Maleficent — 10", black costume, staff with crow...................................$100.00
Mali — 8", #11565, 1996 International, African-American print costume $60.00
Mama Kitten — 18", #402, 1963 only, same as "Lively Kitten" but also has cryer box $125.00
Mambo — 8" h.p., #481, 1955 only (Wendy Ann) ....$850.00 up
Mammy — 8", #402, 1989 only, Jubilee II set (black "round" face)...................$125.00
   8" h.p., #635, 1991 – 1992 only, Scarlett Series (black Wendy Ann on Cissette body) $100.00
   10" h.p., #15010, 1997 – 1999 (black Wendy Ann)...............................$90.00
   8", #38825, 2004, checked dress, white apron, hat..............................$80.00
   8", #38825, 2005, gray dress, white apron, hat................................$85.00
Manet — 21", #2225, 1982 – 1983, light brown with dark brown pinstripes (Jacqueline) $225.00
   14", #1571, 1986 – 1987, Fine Arts Series (Mary Ann) $65.00
Marcella Dolls — 13" – 24" compo., 1936 only, dressed in 1930s fashions............ $650.00 – 900.00 up
Marcella with Raggedy Ann and Andy — 12", #46390, 2007, Lissy, with plush
Ann, Andy, limited to 500 ....$120.00
March Hare — cloth/felt, mid-1930s $750.00
   8", #42430, rabbit costume, teacup, pocket watch, 2006 – 2007 ....$80.00
Margaret Ann — 15", #90100, 1999, blue dress, straw hat, porcelain $100.00
Margaret (O'Brien) — 14" h.p., nude with excellent color $375.00
   18" h.p., nude with excellent color ....$600.00 up
   14" h.p., in tagged Alexander boxed clothes $800.00
   18" ....$750.00 up
   21" compo., tagged Alexander clothes ....$1,300.00 up
Margaret Rose — (see Princess Margaret Rose)
Margot — 10" – 11" h.p., 1961 only, in formals (Cissette) .... **$500.00 up**
   Street dresses, bathing suit, 1961 only.......................................$400.00
Margot Ballerina — 15" – 18", 1951 – 1953, dressed in various colored outfits
   (Margaret and Maggie) ....$650.00 – 850.00
   15" – 18" h.p./vinyl arms, 1955 only (Cissy) ....$425.00 – 700.00
Maria — (see Sound of Music)
Marie Antoinette — 21", #2248, 1987 – 1988, multi-floral print with pink front insert
   (Jacqueline) $325.00
   21" compo., 1944 – 1946, Portrait with extra make-up and in mint condition (Wendy Ann) ...$2,300.00 up
   10", #40060, 2005, mauve court gown, fan $150.00
Marilla — 10", #261-168, 1994, Anne of Green Gables Series $80.00
Marine — 14" compo., 1943 – 1944 (Wendy Ann as boy) ....$800.00 up
Marionettes/Tony Sarg — 12" – 14" compo., 1934 – 1940 ....$450.00 up
   12" compo., Disney characters .... **$550.00 up**
Marionette Theatre — by Tony Sarg, 1938..$800.00 up
Marley's Ghost — 8", #18004, 1996, Dickens, silver chains $55.00
Marme — (see Little Women)
Marme Liza — 21" compo., 1938 and 1946, extra make-up, mint condition (Wendy Ann) ....$3,200.00 up
Mayor Wendy Celebrates Groundhog Day — 8", #48845, 2008, red jacket, hat, groundhog ... $80.00
Marshall Fields — (see Special Events/Exclusives)
Marta — (see Sound of Music)
Martin, Mary — 14" – 17" h.p., 1948 – 1952, wearing jumpsuit (Margaret) ....$700.00 – 1,000.00
   14" – 17", 1948 – 1952, dressed in sailor suit or ball gown (Nell from South Pacific) ...$750.00 – 975.00
Mary Ann — 14" plastic/vinyl, 1965, tagged "Mary Ann," in red/white dress.........$225.00
     Dressed in skirt and sweater $225.00
     Ballerina $225.00
   14" ballerina, 1973 – 1982 ....$125.00
   14", reintroduced #241599, 1994 only..$70.00
Mary-Bel, "The Doll That Gets Well" — 16" rigid vinyl, 1959 – 1965, doll only $175.00

Margot, 10", #920, 1961 (Cissette). Purple satin gown with sequin straps. Mint doll with wrist tag. $500.00 up.

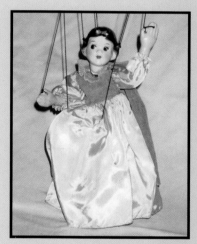

Tony Sarg, Marionette Sleeping Beauty, 12", 1934 – 1940, composition. $550.00 up.

Mary-Bel, 16", 1959 – 1965, plastic/vinyl. "The Doll That Gets Well." $300.00.

1959, 1961, 1965, doll in case **$300.00**
1960 only, doll in case with wardrobe...$350.00
1965 only, doll with very long straight hair, in case $325.00
75th Anniversary, Mary-Bel Returns, 1998, #12220 ....$100.00
Mary Cassatt Baby — 14" cloth/vinyl, 1969 – 1970..$175.00
20", 1969 – 1970 ....$250.00
14" plastic/vinyl child, #1566, 1987 only, Fine Arts Series (Mary Ann)................$75.00
Mary Ellen — 31" rigid vinyl, walker, 1954 only ....$650.00 up
31" plastic/vinyl arms, 1955 only, non-walker with jointed elbows.............$525.00 up
Mary Ellen Playmate — 16" plastic/vinyl, 1965 only, Marshall Fields exclusive (Mary Ann)... $350.00
12", 1965, in case with wigs (Lissy) ....$850.00 up
17", 1965, exclusive..$350.00
Mary Engelbreit Pink Flower Tea Set — #33850, 2002 ....$35.00
Mary Gray — 14" plastic/vinyl, #1564, 1988 only, Classic Series (Mary Ann)......$65.00
Mary Had a Little Lamb — 8", #14623, 1996 Nursery Rhyme, #11610, 1997 – 1999 ....$65.00
8", #48090, 2008, print dress, bonnet, plush lamb..$54.00
Mary, Joseph, Baby Jesus in Manger — 8", #19470, 1997 – 2000, Nativity set $225.00
Mary Lennox — 14", #1537, 1993 – 1994, Classic Doll Series $70.00
8" h.p., #13850, 1998 – 1999 (Secret Garden), plaid jumper, holds key $75.00
Mary Louise — 21" compo., 1938, 1946 – 1947, golden brown/burnt orange (Wendy Ann) .$2,700.00
18" h.p., 1954 only, Me & My Shadow Series, burnt orange and olive green (Cissy) .... $1,500.00 up
8" h.p., #0035D, 1954 only, same as 18", Me & My Shadow Series (Wendy Ann) .... $1,200.00 up
Mary, Mary — 8" h.p., BKW, BK, #751, 1965 – 1972, Storybook Series (Wendy Ann) $125.00
8" h.p., straight legs, #0751, #451, 1973 – 1975, marked "Alex" $70.00
8" h.p., straight legs, #451, 1976 – 1987, marked "Alexander" (1985 – 1987 white face) $60.00
8", #471, reintroduced 1992 only (Wendy Ann) $60.00
8", #14556, 1996, floral dress, straw hat, #11600, 1997 – 1999, water can $60.00
8", #25930, 2000 – 2001 (Maggie), pink print dress, straw hat.........................$60.00
14", #1569, 1988 – 1991, Classic Series (Mary Ann) $65.00
14", #241595, reintroduced 1994 only...$85.00
8", #41125, 2006, print dress, straw hat...$80.00
Mary Mine — 21" cloth/vinyl, 1977 – 1989 ....$125.00
14" cloth/vinyl, 1977 – 1979...$65.00
14", reintroduced 1989 ....$65.00
Mary Muslin — 19" cloth, 1951 only, pansy eyes $500.00
26", 1951 only $575.00
40", 1951 only $850.00
Mary Poppins and the Penguins — 10", umbrella and four penguins, 2006 – 2007 ....$135.00
Mary Poppins Set — 10" Mary, 5" Michael and Jane, 2004 – 2005, #38380 ....$175.00
Mary, Queen of Scots — 21", #2252, 1988 – 1989 (Jacqueline) $325.00
Mary Rose Bride — 17" h.p., 1951 only (Margaret) ....$850.00 up
Mary Sunshine, Little — 15" plastic/vinyl, 1961 (Caroline) $325.00
Marzipan Dancer — 10", #14573, 1995, Nutcracker Series (Cissette) $75.00
Matthew — 8", #26424, 1995, Anne of Green Gables Series $70.00
Mayor of Munchkinland — 8", #37125, 2004 – 2005, Wizard of Oz Series............$75.00
McElroy, Mary — 1985 – 1987, fourth set Presidents' Ladies/First Ladies Series (Mary Ann)...$100.00
McGuffey Ana — 16" cloth, 1934 – 1936 ....$675.00 up
7" compo., 1935 – 1939 (Tiny Betty) ....$375.00 up
9" compo., 1935 – 1939 (Little Betty)..$375.00 up
15" compo., 1935 – 1937 (Betty)..$700.00
13" compo., 1938 (Wendy Ann)..$675.00
11", 1937 – 1939, closed mouth $675.00
11" – 13" compo., 1937 – 1944 (Princess Elizabeth) ....$650.00 – 800.00
14" – 16" compo., 1937 – 1944 (Princess Elizabeth) ....$675.00 – 900.00
17" – 20" compo., 1937 – 1943 (Princess Elizabeth) ....$700.00 – 1,200.00
21" – 25" compo., 1937 – 1942 (Princess Elizabeth) ....$750.00 – 1,500.00

28" compo., 1937 – 1939 (Princess Elizabeth) $1,400.00
17" compo., 1948 – 1949 (Margaret) $950.00
14½" compo., 1948, wears coat, hat, and muff $950.00
18", 25", 31", 1955 – 1956, flat feet (Cissy) ....$500.00 – 975.00
18" h.p., 1949 – 1950 (Margaret) $950.00
21" h.p., 1948 – 1950 (Margaret) $1,400.00
12" h.p. (rare doll), 1963 only (Lissy) ....$2,500.00 up
8" h.p., #616, 1956 only (Wendy Ann) $750.00
8" h.p., #788, #388, 1963 – 1965 (was "American Girl" in 1962 – 1963) $300.00
8", #496, 1990 – 1991 only, Storybook Series (Wendy Ann) $65.00
8", #36710, 2005 – 2006, red plaid dress..$50.00
29" cloth/vinyl, 1952 only (Barbara Jane) $650.00
15" porcelain, #90110, 1999 – 2000..$150.00
14" plastic/vinyl, #1450, 1968 – 1969, Classic Series, plaid dress/eyelet apron (Mary Ann) $85.00
14" plastic/vinyl, #1525, 1977 – 1986, Classic Series, plaid dress (Mary Ann) $70.00
14" plastic/vinyl, #1526, 1987 – 1988, mauve stripe pinafore, Classic Series (Mary Ann)........$75.00
14", #24622, 1995, red plaid dress, Nostalgia Series (Mary Ann) $75.00

McKee, Mary — 1985 – 1987, fourth set Presidents' Ladies/First Ladies Series (Mary Ann)..$100.00
McKinley, Ida — 1988, fifth set Presidents' Ladies/First Ladies Series (Louisa) $100.00
Meagan — 14", #29990 or #30000, 1999..$70.00
Mean Stepsister — 10", #46500, 2007, Cissette, green and brown ballet outfit..........$125.00
Me and My Scassi — (see FAO Schwarz under Special Events/Exclusives)
Medici, Catherine de — 21" porcelain, 1990 – 1991..$350.00
Meg — 8", #79530, 100th Anniversary, two-tiered blue gown with white and rose trim..........$100.00
Melanie — 21" compo., 1945 – 1947 (Wendy Ann) ....$2,300.00 up
 21" h.p./vinyl arms, 1961, lace bodice and overdress over satin (Cissy) ....$1,500.00 up
 21", #2050, 1966, blue gown with wide lace down sides (Coco) ....$2,200.00 up
 #2173, 1967, blue dress with white rickrack around hem ruffle (Jacqueline) $575.00
 #2181, 1968, rust brown dress and hat..$650.00
 #2193, 1969, blue gown, white trim, many rows of lace, bonnet..........................$425.00
 #2196, 1970, white gown with red ribbon trim $500.00
 #2162, 1971, blue gown, white sequin trim $425.00
 #2195, 1974, white gown, red jacket and bonnet $425.00
 #2220, 1979 – 1980, white dotted Swiss gown with pink trim......................$300.00
 1981, pink nylon with blue ribbon $275.00
 #2254, 1989, all orange with lace shawl $275.00
 10", #1173, 1968 – 1969, pink multi-tiered skirt (Cissette) $400.00
 10", #1182, 1970, yellow multi-tiered skirt $375.00
 8" h.p., #633, 1955 – 1956, green velvet (Wendy Ann)........................ $1,300.00 up
 12", 1987 only, Portrait Children Series, aqua green gown, brown trim (Nancy Drew) $75.00
 10", #1101, 1989 only, Jubilee II, royal blue dress with black trim (Cissette) $100.00
 8", #627, 1990, Scarlett Series, lavender/lace (Wendy Ann) $85.00
 8", #628, 1992, peach gown/bonnet with lace..$75.00
 8", #25775, 2000, blue gown and hat trimmed in lace..$90.00
 10", #16555, 1996, Melanie's Sewing Circle, blue dress $85.00
 10", #42275, 2006, white dress, straw hat, red sash $130.00

Melinda — 10" h.p., 1968 – 1969, blue gown with white trim (Cissette) $400.00
 10" h.p., 1970, yellow multi-tiered lace skirt $375.00
 22", #1912, 1962 only, wears white organdy dress with red trim $350.00
 14", 16", 22" plastic/vinyl, 1962 – 1963, cotton dress $275.00
 14", 16", 22" plastic/vinyl, 1963, party dress, ballerina............................$275.00 – 475.00

Melody and Friend — 25" and 8" (see Madame Alexander Doll Co. under Special Events/Exclusives)
Merlin — 8", #13560, 1999, red velvet robe and crystal ball $75.00
Merriweather — 8", #48680, 2008, blue cape, Disney $75.00
Merry Angel — 8" (see Spiegel's under Special Events/Exclusives)
Metroplex Doll Club — (see Special Events/Exclusives)

Melanie, 21", #2220, 1979 – 1980 (Jacqueline). White dotted Swiss gown with pink ribbon. $300.00.

Mexico — 7" compo., 1936 (Tiny Betty) $325.00
 9" compo., 1938 – 1939 (Little Betty) $325.00
 8" h.p., BKW, #776, 1964 – 1965 (Wendy Ann) $125.00
 8" h.p., BK, #776, 1965 – 1972 ....$90.00
 8" straight legs, #0776, 1973 – 1975, marked "ALEX" $60.00
 8" straight legs, #576, #550, #520, 1976 – 1991, marked "Alexander" (1985 – 1987) $60.00
 8", #11551, 1995 only (Maggie) $55.00
 8", #24100, 1997 – 1998, Mariachi outfit, guitar $70.00
 8", #38915, 2004 – 2005 (Wendy), white blouse, red skirt $85.00
Miami Beach — 8", #46060, 2007, pink flamingo, tote bag $70.00
Michael — 11" plastic/vinyl, 1969 only (Janie) (Peter Pan set), with teddy bear $375.00
Mickey Mouse and Minnie Mouse — 8", 31601, 2003 – 2005, mouse ears, yellow shoes $100.00
Midnight — 21", #2256, 1990, dark blue/black (Jacqueline) $300.00
Midnight Angel — 8", #33135, 2002 – 2003, black gown and fur wings $75.00
Midnight Exotique — 10", #48340, 2008, couture pink long dress and purple long coat $130.00
Millennium Princess — 8", #25810, 2000 only, lavender gown $90.00
Miller's Daughter — 14" with 8" Rumpelstiltskin, #1569, 1992 only, limited to 3,000 sets .....$300.00 set
Milly — 17" plastic/vinyl, 1968 only (Polly) $375.00
Mimi — 30" h.p. in 1961 only, multi-jointed body, dressed in formal $950.00
 Dressed in romper suit/skirt $600.00
 Dressed in Tyrolean outfit $950.00
 Dressed in slacks, stripe top, straw hat, sweater, plaid skirt ....$650.00 – 675.00
 21" h.p./vinyl arms, #2170, 1971, vivid pink cape and trim on white gown (Jacqueline) $575.00
 14", #1411, 1983 – 1986, Opera Series (Mary Ann) $65.00
Minister, Little — 8" h.p., #411, 1957 only ....$3,200.00 up
Miracle Santa — 10", 1996, with street sign $90.00
Miracle Wendy — 8", 1996 ....$80.00
Miss America — 14" compo., 1941 – 1943, holds flag ....$850.00 up
Miss Eliza Doolittle — 10", #20112, 1996 Classic $90.00
Miss Gulch with Bicycle, Toto — 10", #13240, 1997 – 2001, Wizard of Oz Series $125.00
 10", #46355, 2007 – 2008, long green plaid dress, bicycle, and Toto $125.00
Miss Mary Mack — 8", #45205, 2006, black outfit $50.00
Miss Muffet, Little — 8" h.p., BK, #752, 1965 – 1972, Storybook Series (Wendy Ann) $100.00
 8" straight legs, #0752, #452, 1973 – 1975, marked "Alex" $75.00
 8" straight legs, #452, 1976 – 1986 (1985 – 1986 white face), marked "Alexander" (Wendy) ..$65.00
 8" straight legs, #452, 1987 – 1988 (Maggie) $60.00
 8", #493, 1993, Storybook Series, #140493, 1994 ....$60.00
 8", #13500, 1998 – 2000, comes with bowl, spoon, and pillow $75.00
 8", #38790, 2004 – 2005 (Wendy), with spider $75.00
Miss Smarty — 8", #17610, 1999 – 2001, Mary Engelbreit (Maggie), pink checked outfit $70.00
Miss U.S.A. — **8" h.p., BK, #728, 1966 – 1968, Americana Series (Wendy Ann)....$300.00**
Miss Victory — 20" compo., 1944 – 1946, magnets in hands (Princess Elizabeth) ....$750.00 up
Misterioso — 10" h.p., #20119, 1996 Cirque du Soleil Series $75.00
Mistletoe and Holly — 10", #38555, 2004, long plaid dress, fur collar and hat $125.00
Mistress Mary — 7" compo., 1937 – 1941 (Tiny Betty) $375.00
Molly — 14", #1561, 1988 only, Classic Series (Mary Ann) $70.00
Molly Cottontail — cloth/felt, 1930s $650.00
Mommy & Me — 14" and 7" compo., 1948 – 1949 (Margaret and Tiny Betty) ....$1,700.00 up, set
Mommy & Me at Home — 8", 10", h.p., #11009, 1997 – 1998, pink floral outfits $125.00
Mommy's Make-Up — 8", #46125, 2007 – 2008, pink dot dress, purse, compact $70.00
Mommy's Pet — 14" – 20", 1977 – 1986 ....$50.00 – 175.00
Mona Lisa, DaVinci's — 8", h.p., 1997, #22140, green velvet dress $75.00
Monday's Child — 8", #27770, 2001, pink dress, mirror $70.00
 10", #28860, 2001, print skirt, 10" goose $110.00
Monet — 21", #2245, 1984 – 1985, black and white checked gown with red jacket (Jacqueline)....$225.00
Mongolia — 8", #46040, 2007, pink costume, bowls $75.00

Miss USA, 8", BK, #728, 1966 – 1968 (Wendy). All original and mint. $300.00

Monique — (see Disney Annual Showcase of Dolls under Specials Events/Exclusives)

Monkeying Around — 8", #38510, 2004 – 2005, comes with knit monkey $85.00

Monroe, Elizabeth — 1976 – 1978, first set Presidents' Ladies/First Ladies Series (Mary Ann) $125.00

Moonlight Dance — 10", #28900, 2001, blue tulle and brocade dress...$110.00

Moore, Annie — 8", #39715, 2005, pleated long skirt, white blouse, straw hat, canvas bag........$85.00

Mop-Top Annie — 8", #14486, 1995, red dress with white dots..$60.00

Mop-Top Baby Girl — 12", #29030, 1998, yarn hair, patchwork dress $50.00

Mop-Top Billy — 8", #140485, 1993 – 2000, Toy Shelf Series $60.00

Mop-Top Wendy — 8", #140484, 1993 – 2000, Toy Shelf Series $60.00

Morisot — 21", #2236, 1985 – 1986 only, lime green gown with white lace (Jacqueline)...........$250.00

Morning Glory — 14", #25505, Ribbons & Bows Series, floral dress with lace (Mary Ann) $80.00

   8", #28476, 2001– 2002, lavender dress, bonnet with flowers $65.00

Morocco — 8" h.p., BK, #762, 1968 – 1970 (Wendy Ann)...$275.00

   8" h.p., #11559, 1996 International, belly dancer $60.00

   8", #33510, 2002, Maroon belly dancer, plush camel $65.00

Moss Rose — 14", #1559, 1991 only, Classic Series (Louisa) $70.00

Mother & Me — 14" – 15" and 9" compo., 1940 – 1943, mint condition

   (Wendy Ann and Little Betty) .... $1,400.00 up

Mother Goose — 8" straight legs, #427, #459, 1986 – 1992, Storybook Series (Wendy Ann) $60.00

   8", #11620, 1997 – 1999, with goose and book of rhymes...$60.00

   10", #28860, 2001 – 2003, print dress with 10" goose $110.00

   8", #45695, 2007, print dress, plush goose $80.00

Mother Gothel and Rapunzel — 8" and 14", #1539, 1993 – 1994, limited to 3,000 sets...$225.00 set

Mother Hubbard — 8", #439, #459, 1988 – 1989, Storyland Series (Wendy) $60.00

Mother's Day — 8", #10380 – 10382, 1995, three hair colors, Special Occasions Series.............$60.00

   8", #30265, 2001, pink, white dress with porcelain flower box $75.00

   8", #45220, 2006 – 2007, blue print dress, flowers $55.00

Mr. and Mrs. Frankenstein Set — 8", 1996 ....$250.00

Mr. Monopoly — 8", #25260, 2000, tails, top hat, comes with game $70.00

Mr. O'Hara — **8", #638, 1993 only, Scarlett Series (Wendy) $125.00**

   8", #468, 1992 – 1993, Storybook Series (Peter Pan set) (Wendy) $65.00

Mrs. Quack-a-Field — cloth/felt, mid-1930s $625.00

Mrs. Snoopie — cloth/felt, 1940s $625.00

Muffin — 19" cloth, 1966 only $100.00

   14", 1963 – 1977, cloth, sapphire eyes, 1965 only..$75.00

   14" black cloth, 1965 – 1966 only..$100.00

   14" cloth, 1966 – 1970, cut slanted blue eyes $70.00

   14" cloth, eyes like sideways commas $50.00

   12" all vinyl, 1989 – 1990 (Janie)...$50.00

   12", 1990 – 1992, in trunk/wardrobe...$125.00

Mulan — 8", #36260, 2003, black wig, kimono, 2¼" Mushu...$85.00

Munchkin Peasant — 8", #140444, 1993 – 1995, Wizard of Oz Series.......................................$100.00

   Daisy, 8", #28770, 2001 – 2002, daisies on costume..$90.00

   Flower Bonnet, 8", #28775, 2001 – 2002, blue, white costume, ruffled flower-trimmed hat $85.00

   Herald, 8", #140445, 1994 – 1995, Wizard of Oz Series $85.00

   Mayor, 8", #140443, 1993 – 1995, Wizard of Oz Series $125.00

   Lollipop, 8", #14513, 1995, Wizard of Oz Series, pink/white striped outfit $100.00

   Lullaby, 8", #14512, 1995, Wizard of Oz Series, white gown $90.00

   Lullaby, 8", #13300, 1999 – 2001, pink dress and hat $90.00

   Flower, 8", #27035, 2000 – 2001, Wizard of Oz Series...$65.00

   Lullaby Munchkin, 5", #27070, porcelain, 2000 – 2002, pink costume $75.00

   Lullaby League Munchkin, 8", #47390, 2007 – 2008, pink dress, pointed hat $70.00

   Mayor of Munchkinland, 8", #37125, 2003, green coat, hat, watch............................$80.00

   Sleepy Head Munchkin, 8", #46350, 2007 – 2008, white dress, hat, egg bed $85.00

   Lollipop Munchkin, 8", #45535, 2007 – 2008, green outfit with painted lollipop.......$75.00

   Munchkin Soldier, 8", #46345, 2007 – 2008, yellow and white outfit, gun $75.00

Mr. O'Hara, 8", #638, 1993 only (Wendy). Scarlett Series. $125.00.

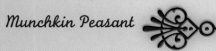
Professor Marvel, 8", #48490, 2008, with crystal ball..$75.00

My Boyfriend's Back — 10", #42820, 2006, gray skirt, black leather jacket..............................$85.00

My Doll House — (see Special Events/Exclusives)

My Favorite Ballerina — 14", #25485, 2000, lilac, ballet outfit, #25480, pink $75.00

My First Christmas Tree — 8", #36875, 2002 – 2004, Spode ornament, green dress...............$80.00

My First Christmas with Lenox Ornament — 8", #34215, 2002 ....$85.00

My First Communion — 8", #38575, 2005 – 2008, blonde, with rosary, cross necklace...........$85.00

    8", #38576, 2005 – 2008, Latin, with rosary, cross necklace.....................................$85.00

    8", #38577, 2005 – 2008, brunette, with rosary, cross necklace................................$85.00

    8", #38578, 2005 – 2008, African American, with rosary, cross necklace $85.00

My First Wendy — 8", #42600, 2007, pink dress, postcard...$50.00

My Heart Belongs to Grandma — 8", #36165, 2003 – 2004, pink dress, red heart $65.00

My Heart Belongs to You — 8", #35440, brunette, #35441, African-American, red dress, 2003...$65.00

My Little Playmates — 8", #48635, 2008, plaid dress, two resin dolls $85.00

My Little Sweetheart — (see Child At Heart Shop under Special Events/Exclusives)

My Little Valentine — 8", #47725, 2007 – 2008, red outfit, paper hearts $60.00

My New Friend Hello Kitty — 8", #42680 (#42681 Asian), with mini Hello Kitty, 2006 – 2007 ...$80.00

Mystery Dance 1951 — 14", #26035, 2000, pink lace and tulle long gown..........................$150.00

Mystery's Matriarch — 10", #48810, 2008, maroon and pink long dress, feather in hair........$120.00

Nana — 6" dog with bonnet, #441, 1993 only, Peter Pan Series.....................................$50.00

Nana/Governess — 8" h.p., #433, 1957 only (Wendy Ann) .... $2,000.00 up

Nancy Ann — 17" – 18" h.p., 1950 only (tagged Nancy Ann)...................................... $975.00 up

Nancy Dawson — 8", #441, 1988 – 1989, Storybook Series (Maggie)...............................$60.00

Nancy Drew — 12" plastic/vinyl, 1967 only, Literature Series .... $450.00 up

Nancy Jean — 8" (see Belk & Leggett under Special Events/Exclusives)

Nan McDare — cloth/felt, 1940s $650.00

Napoleon — 12", #1330, 1980 – 1986, Portraits of History (Nancy Drew)..........................$60.00

Nat (Little Men) — 15" h.p., 1952 (Maggie) .... $850.00 up

Natasha — 21", #2255, 1989 – 1990, brown and paisley brocade (Jacqueline).....................$325.00

National Velvet — 12", 1991 only, Romance Series, no riding crop (Nancy Drew)...................$75.00

    8", #10409, 1996, riding habit..$70.00

Nativity Set — 1997 – 2000, #19460, Mary, Joseph, Jesus, Angel, Créche,

    Three Wise Men, Shepherd, Drummer...$950.00

    8" #38770, 2004 – 2005, Mary, Joseph, Jesus, Créche, donkey, lambs..........................$300.00

Nature Trail — 8", #40000, 2005, print dress, wheelbarrow $70.00

Nelson, Lord — 12" vinyl, #1336, 1984 – 1986, Portraits of History (Nancy Drew)..................$60.00

Netherlands Boy — Formerly "Dutch" (Wendy)

    8" h.p., straight legs, #577, 1974 – 1975, marked "Alex" $65.00

    8" h.p., straight legs, #577, 1976 – 1989, marked "Alexander" (1985 – 1987).................$60.00

Netherlands Girl — 8" h.p., #591, #525, 1974 – 1992 (Wendy) $60.00

New Arrival — 19", #30290, 2001, stork with Baby Kisses 8" doll $50.00

New Year's Eve — 8", #42825, 2006, black dress, Chaos bear $110.00

New Zealand Moon — 8", #39805, 2005, with kiwi bird...$80.00

Nicole — 10", #1139, 1989 – 1990, Portrette, black/off white outfit (Cissette) $70.00

Nigeria — 8", #11552, 1995 only (also in 1994 Neiman-Marcus trunk set as Kenya)................$60.00

Nightingale, Florence — 14", #1598, 1986 – 1987, Classic Series.................................$80.00

Nightmare Before Christmas — 8", #42645, 2006 – 2007, black Halloween costume,

    ghost, and box...$75.00

Nikki — 9", #40865, 2005, red plaid skirt, black bag $30.00

Nina Ballerina — 7" compo., 1940 (Tiny Betty) $350.00

    9" compo., 1939 – 1941 (Little Betty)..$375.00

    14" – 17" h.p., 1949 – 1951 (Margaret).. $575.00 up

    15" h.p., 1951, came in various colors, all years (Margaret)...............................$725.00

    19" – 23", 1949 – 1951 .... $850.00 up

1920s Cissette Trunk Set — 10", #45955, 2007, green tweed suit, flapper dress,

    wooden trunk, accessories, limited to 500 ....$300.00

1950s Cissette Trunk Set — 10", #38740, 2004, hatbox, trunk, four outfits, BK Cissette.......$275.00

Nixon, Pat — (see Presidents' Ladies/First Ladies Series) 14", 1994 only................................$150.00

Noah's Ark — #33155, 2002, includes 8" Noah, wooden ark, pair zebras, camels,
giraffes, resin doves..$250.00

Normandy — 7" compo., 1935 – 1938 (Tiny Betty)................................$325.00

Northern Lights Angel — 10", #42240, 2006, white lace, organza........................$150.00

Norway — 8" h.p., BK, #584, 1968 – 1972 (Wendy Ann)................................$90.00

    8" straight legs, #584, 1973 – 1975, marked "Alex"................................$65.00

    8" straight legs, #584, 1976 – 1987, marked "Alexander" (1985 – 1987 white face).................$60.00

    8" straight legs, #11566, 1996 International Viking costume................................$65.00

    8", #35880, 2003 – 2004, red sweater, tweed skirt, troll................................$80.00

    8", #48125, 2008, vintage outfit, waist bag $90.00

Norwegian — 7" – 8" compo., 1936 – 1940 (Tiny Betty)................................$325.00

    9" compo., 1938 – 1939 (Little Betty)................................$325.00

Now I Lay Me Down to Sleep — 8", #28380, 2001– 2002, white gown, bonnet................................$70.00

Nurse — 16", 1930s, cloth and felt................................$675.00

    7" compo., 1937, 1941 – 1943 (Tiny Betty)................................$375.00

    9" compo., 1939, 1942 – 1943................................$400.00

    13" – 15" compo., 1936 – 1937 (Betty), all white outfit, Dionne nurse, mint in box..........$950.00 up

    15" compo., 1939, 1943 (Princess Elizabeth) $550.00

    14" h.p., 1948 (Maggie and Margaret) $850.00

    8" h.p., #563, 1956 only, all white dress (Wendy Ann) ....$625.00 up

    8", #429, 1961, all white dress, comes with baby................................$650.00 up

    8" BKW, BK, #329, #460, #660, #624, 1962 – 1965, wears striped dress, comes with baby... $500.00 up

    8", #308, all white uniform, Americana Series, 1991................................$60.00

    8", #17620, 1999, World War II, brown, white costume with medicine bag................................$65.00

    8", #48525, 2008, Nurse Wendy, white outfit, blue cape $50.00

Nutcracker — 16", #21700, 1998 – 1999, Clara in rose embroidered costume................................$150.00

    8", #27560, 2001 – 2002, silver pants, red jacket, black hat................................$80.00

Nutcracker Dreams — 8", #39855, 2005 – 2006, with Chaos bear................................$85.00

Nutcracker Prince — 8", #14571, 1995, Nutcracker Series, has mask................................$60.00

Oakley, Annie — 8", #42145, 2006, western outfit $85.00

O'Brien, Margaret — 14½" compo., 1946 – 1948................................$750.00 up

    17", 18", 19" compo., 1946 – 1948................................$850.00 – 1,200.00

    21" – 24" compo., 1946 – 1948................................$900.00 – 1,500.00

    14½" – 18" h.p., 1949 – 1951................................$900.00 up

    21" – 22" h.p., 1949 – 1951................................$1,400.00 up

    15" porcelain, #90100, white blouse, blue pinafore................................$125.00

O. E. O. Guard — 8", #33595, 2002 – 2004 (Wizard of Oz Series), blue fur coat, hat $85.00

Off to Class — 8", #35645, 2003, blue plaid dress, book bag and books................................$60.00

Off to the North Pole – Coca-Cola — 8", #25245, 2000, fur costume with white bear..........$90.00

Oh Christmas Tree — 8", #42055, 2007, tree dress $70.00

Old Country Rose — 8", #42130, 2006 ....$90.00

Older Stepsister — 10", #46525, Cissette, 2007, black and white dotted long gown................$120.00

Old Fashioned Christmas, An — 8", #47720, 2007, Maggie, red velvet coat candy canes......$70.00

Old Fashioned Girl — 13" compo., 1945 – 1947 (Betty)................................$550.00 up

    20" compo. (Betty)................................$700.00

    20" h.p., 1948 only (Margaret)................................$850.00 up

    14" h.p., 1948 only (Margaret)................................$650.00

Old McDonald — 8", #30785, 2001, red checked dress................................$75.00

Old Mother Hubbard — 8", #39850, 2005, with dog and cupboard $80.00

Olive Oyl — 10", #20126, 1996, Timeless Legends................................$90.00

Oliver Twist — 16" cloth, 1934, Dickens character $650.00

    7" compo., 1935 – 1936 (Tiny Betty)................................$300.00

    8", #472, 1992 only, Storyland Series (Wendy Ann)................................$55.00

Oliver Twistail — cloth/felt, 1930s................................$650.00

Olivia and the Missing Toy — 8", #36430, 2004 ....$90.00
Olivia Saves the Circus — 8", #35115, 2003 – 2005, vinyl piglet, three costumes, lion, dog, and tent $100.00
    8", At Home with Olivia Set — #35646, 2004 – 2005, bed, table..............................$100.00
    8", Olivia vinyl piglet, #35105, 2003 – 2005, red dress, purse $25.00
Olivia Trunk Set — 8", #31680, 2003, vinyl piglet, clothes, accessories, trunk.......................$75.00
O'Malley, Grace — 10", #41715, 2006 – 2007, pirate costume...$115.00
Once Upon a Time... Storyland Trunk Set — 8", #46585, 2008,
    castle trunk with bedroom, 3 outfits, etc. $190.00
One Fish, Two Fish — 8", #34095, 2002 (Maggie), smocked dress, comes with fish $65.00
One of a Kind Sisters — 8", pair, #48040, 2008, sister charms....................................$100.00
One, Two, Buckle My Shoe — 14", #24640, Nursery Rhymes (Louisa) $75.00
Only Hearts — 8", #35940, 2003, pink striped dress, tiny flower hat $70.00
On the Campaign Trail Maggie — 8", #39550, 2004...$80.00
On the Campaign Trail Wendy — 8", #39545, 2004 ....$80.00
Onyx Velvet and Lace Gala Gown and Coat — 10" h.p., #22170, 1997 – 1998 (Cissette) $125.00
Oolong Tea — 8", #46280, 2007, Asian, print dress, teacup..$85.00
Opening Night — 10", #1126, 1989 only, Portrette, gold sheath and overshirt (Cissette)...........$80.00
Ophelia — 12", 1992, Romance Collection (Nancy Drew) $75.00
    12", 1993 only (Lissy) $125.00
Ophelia and Hamlet — 8", set, #45930, 2007, vintage costumes......................................$145.00
Opulent Opal — 10", #33355, 2002, blonde, pink gown, jewel trim $125.00
Opulent Shimmer Shadow Cissette — 10", #47000, 2007, limited to 150, long silk dress,
    turquoise wig...$200.00
Orange Pekoe Tea — 8", #46285, 2007, Maggie, teacup $85.00
Orchard Princess — 21" compo., 1939, 1946 – 1947, has extra make-up (Wendy Ann) . $2,400.00 up
Orphan Annie — 14" plastic/vinyl, #1480, 1965 – 1966 only, Literature Series (Mary Ann) ...$300.00
    #1485, 1965 only, in window box with wardrobe .... $500.00 up
Our Song — 10", #36180, 2003, blue long ball gown with lace trim $110.00
Out and About with Auntie — 8", #48950, 2008, print dress and purse............................$50.00
Out for a Stroll — 10", #27815, 2001, pink long dress trimmed in lace...........................$85.00
Oz Flower Munchkin — 8", #27035, 2000 – 2001, Wizard of Oz Series $60.00
Oz Scape — #33770, 2002, Artstone backdrop $90.00
Pakistan — 8" h.p., #532, 1993 only $60.00
Palace Guard — 8", #33395, 2002, beefeater costume, limited to 1,000 ....$80.00
Pamela — 12" h.p., 1962 – 1963 only, takes wigs, excellent condition, doll only (Lissy)....... $450.00 up
    12" h.p. in case or window box, 1962 – 1963.. $1,000.00 up
    12" plastic/vinyl, 1969 – 1971, doll only (Nancy Drew) .... $200.00 up
    12" plastic/vinyl in case, 1969 .... $625.00 up
Panama — 8", #555, 1985 – 1987 ....$55.00
Pan American (Pollera) — 7" compo., 1936 – 1938 (Tiny Betty) $350.00
Pansy Fairy — 8", #38185, 2004 – 2005, gold outfit, pansy trim $90.00
Parisian Chic 1940 — 10", #17770, 1999, dress, coat, hat, purse $125.00
Park Avenue Alex the Bellhop — 8" h.p., #31180, 1997 – 1999, burgundy uniform...............$75.00
Park Avenue Cissette — 10", #35585, 2003, gray checked suit, plush puppy.......................$110.00
Park Avenue Wendy — 8" h.p., #31060, 1997 – 1999, black and white ensemble $80.00
Parlour Maid — 8" h.p., #579, 1956 only (Wendy Ann) .... $950.00 up
Party Sun Dress — 8" h.p., #344, 1957, BKW, blue or red dress with gold accents (Wendy Ann)...$675.00 up
Party Time Vintage — 8", #28910, white dress $70.00
Pat-a-Cake — 8", #12812, 1995, floral dress with white apron and chef's hat, Nursery Rhymes Series.....$60.00
Patchity Pam & Pepper — 15" cloth, 1965 – 1966...$175.00 ea.
Patriot — 8", #33506, 2002, African-American, red, white, blue dress, limited to 150 ....$85.00
    8", #33505, 2002, blonde, limited to 1,800 ....$85.00
Patterson, Martha Johnson — 1982 – 1984, third set Presidents' Ladies/First
    Ladies Series (Martha)..$100.00
Patty — 18" plastic/vinyl, 1965 only...$275.00
Patty Cake — 8", #46510, 2007, print dress, felt cake...$55.00

Patty Pigtails — 14" h.p., 1949 only (Margaret) ....$675.00 up
Paulette — 10", #1128, 1989 – 1990 only, Portrette, dressed in pink velvet (Cissette)...............$125.00
Peaches and Cream — 8", #40310, peach taffeta dress $125.00
Peach Pirouette — 8", #42350, 2006, pink ballet outfit $70.00
Peachtree Lane — 8" in blue and 14" Scarlett in green/white stripes, #16551, limited to 2,500....$250.00 set
Peacock Dreams Cissette — 10". #40205, 2005, aqua dress, peacock feather wings $130.00
Pearl (June) — 10", #1150, 1992 only, Birthstone Collection, white/silver flapper doll $75.00
Pearl of the 1920s — 10", #79700 ....$200.00
Peas Porridge Hot — 8", #48195, 2008, pot, spoon $90.00
Peasant — 7" compo., 1936 – 1937 (Tiny Betty)...$325.00
    9" compo., 1938 – 1939 (Little Betty) $325.00
Peekaboos — 8" cloth baby, vinyl face, animal peekaboo cover, 2001 – 2005 ....$12.00 – 16.00
    8", cloth, vinyl face as Pooh, Piglet, Tigger, and Eeyore, 2005 – 2007.................................$16.00 ea.
    8", #38930, 2005, set of 12 plush dolls, Sesame Street $192.00
    8", Tigger, Eeyore, Pooh, Piglet, #48720 – 48723, 2008 ....$12.00 each
Peggy Bride — 14" – 18" h.p., 1950 – 1951, very blonde hair (Margaret) ....$900.00 – 1,400.00
    21" h.p., 1950 ....$1,500.00 up
Penny — 34" cloth/vinyl, 1951 only...$500.00 up
    42", 1951 only $800.00
    7" compo., 1938 – 1940 (Tiny Betty) $300.00
Pen Pals — 8", #38505, 2004, blue checked dress, letter, photo...$60.00
Peppermint Swirl — 8", #39940, 2005 – 2006, with peppermint Chaos bear...............................$80.00
Peppermint Twist — 8", #14591, 1995, pink skirt and jacket in 1950s style, Nostalgia Series...$55.00
Perfect Bouquet — 8", #36285, 2003 – 2004, pink pleats with roses $70.00
Perfect Little Rose, A — 8", #45855, 2007, print dress...$65.00
Perfectly Polished — 8", #41995, 2006, long red dress, hat...$100.00
Perfect Pearl — 8", #33350, 2002, blonde, gold gown, pearl trim $80.00
Perfect Vintage — 8", #40810, 2005, print dress, straw hat...$85.00
Periwinkle Angel — 10", #35865, 2003, white wings, blue gown $140.00
Peron, Eva — 10", #22030, 1997, long white lace dress (Cissette)...$90.00
Persia — 7" compo., 1936 – 1938 (Tiny Betty)...$300.00
Peru — 8", #556, 1986 – 1987 ....$75.00
    8" h.p., #531, 1993 only (Wendy Ann) $60.00
    8" h.p., #35665, 2003 – 2004, colorful pink and brown costume, plush llama...........................$90.00
Peruvian Boy — 8" h.p., BK, #770, 1966 (Wendy Ann) $350.00
    8" h.p., BKW, #770, 1965...$425.00
Petal Perfection — 8", #41965, 2006, pink and white dress, bouquet $90.00
Peter and the Wolf — 8", #42580, 2006, Alpine costume, wolf, duck...$80.00
Peter Pan — 15" h.p., 1953 – 1954 (Margaret) ....$800.00 up
    8" h.p., #310, 1953 – 1954 (Wendy Ann), Quiz-Kin ....$850.00 up
    8" h.p., #465, reintroduced 1991 – 1993, #140465 in 1994, Storyland Series (Wendy Ann).....$60.00
    8" h.p., #13660, 1999 – 2001, green costume with Tinker Bell pin and sword...........................$60.00
    14" plastic/vinyl, #1410, 1969 only (Mary Ann) $225.00
    1969 only, complete set of four dolls – Peter, Michael (12" Jamie), Wendy (14" Mary Ann),
        Tinker Bell (10" Cissette) ....$1,000.00 up
Peter Pan and Wendy — 8" pair, with resin Tinker Bell, 2006 – 2007 ....$130.00
Peter Pan's Wendy — 8", #13670, 1999 – 2001, blue gown and fuzzy shoes...$65.00
Petite Playhouse — #28950, 2003, fold-up house with rooms $50.00
    5" dolls, 2002 – 2003, Kayla #27410, Emily #27420, Wendy #30360, Sarah #27415,
        Caitlin #27405 ....$20.00 ea.
Philippines — 8" straight legs, #554, 1986 – 1987 (blue gown) $70.00
    1987, #531, dressed in yellow gown...$150.00
Picking Bouquets Cissette — 10", 2006, #45235, navy dress...$110.00
Picnic Day — 18" h.p., #2001C, 1953 only, Glamour Girl Series, leaves on pink or
    blue print dress (Margaret)...$1,900.00 up
Picnic in the Park — 14", #46620, 2008, Asian baby $100.00

Picnic Time for Teddy — 8", #34080, 2002 – 2003, smocked dress with bear and basket $85.00
Picture Perfect — 8", #40420, 2005, print dress with sweater..$65.00
Pied Piper — 8", #46505, 2007, with mouse, pipe...$80.00
Pierce, Jane — 1982 – 1984, third set Presidents' Ladies/First Ladies Series (Mary Ann).......$100.00
Pierrot Clown — (see Clowns, 8" and 14")
Pig Brick — 8", #33655, 2003 – 2004, vinyl, brick house bank $50.00
Pig Stick — 8", #33657, 2003 – 2004, vinyl, stick house bank $50.00
Pig Straw — 8", #33650, 2003 – 2004, vinyl, straw house bank $50.00
Pilgrim — 7" compo., 1935 – 1938 (Tiny Betty) $350.00
    8" h.p., #100349, 1994, Americana Series, #10349, 1995..$60.00
Pink Butterfly Princess — 8", #25675, 2000 – 2001, pink wings..$70.00
Pink Carnation — 10", #25615, 2000 (Cissette), pink tiered gown...$125.00
Pink Champagne (Arlene Dahl) — 18" h.p., red hair/pink lace/rhinestone bodice gown ...$7,000.00 up
Pinkie — 12" plastic/vinyl, 1975 – 1987, Portrait Children Series (Nancy Drew).........................$60.00
    8", 1997 – 1998, #22120, chiffon gown, pink hat..$65.00
Pinking of You — 8", #37980, 2003 – 2004, hot pink dress and hat..$75.00
Pink Petals Fairy — 8", #33430 , 2002 – 2003, petal tutu, leaf wings $75.00
Pink Pirouette — 8", #33140, 2002 – 2003, pink tutu, rhinestones $75.00
    8", #33141, 2002 – 2003, African-American..$85.00
Pink Pristine Angel — 10", #10700, 1997 – 2000, pink feather wings...$125.00
Pink Sparkle — Dragonfly Fairy, 8", #36030, 2003 – 2004, pink and blue costume $80.00
Pink Sparkle Princess — 15", #22670, 1999, porcelain, pink gown $150.00
Pinky — 16" cloth, 1940s .... $475.00 up
    23" compo./cloth baby, 1937 – 1939...$300.00
    13" – 19" vinyl baby, #3561, #5461, 1954 only, one-piece vinyl body and legs.........$100.00 – 150.00
Pinocchio — 8", #477, 1992 – 1993, Storyland Series (Wendy Ann), #140477, 1994 ....$70.00
    8", 32130, 2001 – 2002, with 5" wooden Pinocchio...$90.00
    8", #38860, 2004 – 2005, with 2" Jiminy Cricket..$90.00
    8", #48705, 2008, Pinocchio, wood, 2" resin Jiminy Cricket...$250.00
Pip — All cloth, early 1930s, Dickens character $800.00
    7" compo., 1935 – 1936 (Tiny Betty) $350.00
Pippi Longstocking — 18", #16003, 1996, Rag Dolls (cloth doll)........................not available for sale
    8", #25975, 2000 – 2001 (Maggie), with monkey..$60.00
    14", #28780, 2001, cloth $35.00
Pisces — 8", #21320, 1998, blue fish costume $85.00
Pitty Pat — 16" cloth, 1950s $475.00
Pitty Pat Clown — 1950s $450.00
Place in the Sun, A — 10", #24624, lavender ball gown $100.00
Playmates — 29" cloth, 1940s .... $450.00 up
Playtime with Curious George — 8", #45440, with monkey $80.00
Pocahontas — 8" h.p., BK, #721, 1967 – 1970, Americana and Storyland Series,
    has baby (Wendy Ann) $350.00
    8" h.p., #318, 1991 – 1992, Americana Series (Wendy Ann)..$65.00
    8" h.p., #100350, 1994 – 1995, Americana and Favorite Books Series (Wendy Ann) $60.00
    10", #38390, 2004 (Cissette) with 2" raccoon, dog, and hummingbird $125.00
    14", #24613, 1995, first dark skin doll this size, Favorite Books Series (Louisa)....................$75.00
Polish (Poland) — 7" compo., 1935 – 1936 (Tiny Betty)...$325.00
    8" h.p., BKW, #780, 1964 – 1965 (Wendy Ann), BK, #780, 1965 – 1972................................$100.00
    8" BKW, #780, 1965 only (Maggie Mixup)..$125.00
    8" h.p., straight legs, #0780, #580, 1973 – 1975, marked "ALEX"......................................$65.00
    8" straight legs, #580, 1976 – 1988 (1985 – 1987 white face), marked "Alexander".................$55.00
    8", #523, reintroduced 1992 – 1993 (Maggie Mixup), 1994, #110523...............................$55.00
    8", #40730, 2005 – 2006, print dress with paper wycinanki $70.00
Polk, Sarah — 1979 – 1981, second set Presidents' Ladies/First Ladies Series (Martha) $100.00
Pollera (Pan American) — 7" compo., 1936 – 1938 (Tiny Betty)...$325.00
Polly — 17" plastic/vinyl, 1965 only, dressed in ball gown...$350.00

Dressed in street dress...$275.00
Dressed as ballerina...$250.00
Dressed as bride...$300.00
1965 only, came in trunk with wardrobe ....$750.00 up
Pollyana — 16" rigid vinyl, 1960 – 1961, marked "1958" (Mary-Bel) $400.00
16", dressed in formal...$450.00
22", 1960 – 1961...$500.00
14", #1588, 1987 – 1988, Classic Series (Mary Ann); reintroduced 1994 only, #24159............$85.00
8", #474, 1992 – 1993 only, Storyland Series (Wendy)........................$65.00
8", #25210, 2000 – 2001 (Wendy), pink dress, straw hat; #46450, 2007, pink dress, braids $70.00
Polly Flinders — 8", #443, 1988 – 1989, Storybook Series (Maggie) $60.00
Polly Pigtails — 14½" h.p., 1949 – 1951 (Maggie)...............................$500.00
17" – 17½", 1949 – 1951..$625.00
Polly Put Kettle On — 7" compo., 1937 – 1939 (Tiny Betty) $375.00
8" h.p., #11640, 1998 – 1999, teacup print dress, kettle.....................$60.00
Pom-Pom Sweetie — 10", #45715, Cissette, 2007, limited to 350, pink party dress, poodle. ...$100.00
Poodle Posh — 8", #42150, 2006, pink pants outfit, poodle $80.00
Poodles — 14" – 17", early 1950s, standing or sitting, named Ivy, Pierre, Fifi, and Inky ......$500.00 up
Popeye — 8", #10428, 1996, Timeless Legends $90.00
Popeye, Olive Oyl, and Swee' Pea — #20127, 1996 ....$175.00 set
Pop Goes the Weasel — 8", #35670, 2003, bench, monkey, and weasel...........$75.00
Poppy — 9" early vinyl, 1953 only, orange organdy dress and bonnet $125.00
Poppy Garden Ball Gown — 10", #34165, 2002, velvet, ruffled rose hem, limited to 1,000...$130.00
Portrait Elise — 17" plastic/vinyl, 1972 – 1973 ....$200.00
Portugal — 8" h.p., BK, #785, 1968 – 1972 (Wendy Ann)...............$100.00
8" straight legs, #0785, #585, 1973 – 1975, marked "Alex".................$65.00
8" straight legs, #585, #537, 1976 – 1987, marked "Alexander," 1986, white face........$60.00
8" h.p., #535, 1993, #110535, 1994..$55.00
8" h.p., #35975, 2003 – 2004, red and black costume, folk rooster $70.00
Posey Pet — 15" cloth, 1940s, plush rabbit or other animals, must be clean ....$450.00 up
Pot of Gold — 8", #39260, 2004 – 2005, green costume $75.00
Practice Makes Perfect — 8", #37885, 2004, with violin $80.00
Prairie Stroll — 8", #40005, 2005, cotton dress, basket with eggs $80.00
Precious — 12" compo./cloth baby, 1937 – 1940................................$250.00
12" all h.p. toddler, 1948 – 1951 ....$325.00
Precious Peridot — 8", #33365, 2002, green gown, lace overskirt........$90.00
Premier Dolls — (see M.A.D.C. under Special Events/Exclusives)
Present for You — 8", #42520, 2006, eyelet dress, cloisonne box $85.00
Presidents' Ladies/First Ladies —
First set, 1976 – 1978..............................$100.00 – 150.00 singles, $700.00 set
Second set, 1979 – 1981...............................$100.00 singles, $600.00 set
Third set, 1982 – 1984 ....$100.00 singles, $600.00 set
Fourth set, 1985 – 1987 ....$100.00 singles, $600.00 set
Fifth set, 1988 ....$100.00 singles, $600.00 set
Sixth set, 1989 – 1990..$100.00 singles, $600.00 set
Presley, Elvis, Blue Suede Shoes — 8", #47690, 2008, guitar $85.00
Pretty Head to Toe — 8", #37905, 2004, dress, coat, hat..................$85.00
Pretty in Pink Trunk Set — 8", #42170, 2006 – 2007, three outfits, tiny doll, accessories......$150.00
Pretty Pals — 8", #26770, pink; #26835, ivory; 2001 – 2002, smocked dresses ....$80.00 ea.
Pride and Prejudice — 10", #48435, 2008, long dress, pink coat $120.00
Prince Charles — 8" h.p., #397, 1957 only (Wendy Ann) ....$750.00 up
Prince Charles and Princess Ann Set — 8", pair, #34150, 2002 ....$150.00 set
Prince Charming — 16" – 17" compo., 1947 (Margaret) $900.00
14" – 15" h.p., 1948 – 1950 (Margaret)..$850.00
17" – 18" h.p., 1948 – 1950 (Margaret)..$950.00
21" h.p., 1949 – 1951 (Margaret) ....$1,100.00 up

Martha Randolph, 14", #1503, 1976 – 1978. President's Lady, represents daughter of Thomas Jefferson. $100.00 – 150.00.

Betty Taylor Bliss, 14", #1512, 1979 – 1981 (Mary Ann). From second set of President's Ladies. $100.00.

12", 1990 – 1991, Romance Collection (Nancy Drew) $75.00

8", #479, 1993, Storybook Series, royal blue/gold outfit...$70.00

8", #14541, 1995, Brothers Grimm Series, braid trimmed jacket with brocade vest................$70.00

Prince Phillip — 17" – 18" h.p., 1953 only, Beaux Arts Series (Margaret).........................$950.00 up

21", 1953 only ....$1,000.00 up

8", #33495, 2002, navy blue suit, red robe, limited to 500 ....$125.00

Princess — 12", 1990 – 1991 only, Romance Collection (Nancy Drew) $80.00

14", #1537, 1990 – Mary Ann, 1991 – Jennifer, Classic Series $85.00

Princess — 13" – 15" compo., 1940 – 1942 (Princess Elizabeth) ....$550.00 up

24" compo., 1940 – 1942 (Princess Elizabeth) ....$850.00 up

Princess Alexandria — 24" cloth/compo., 1937 only ....$300.00 up

Princess and the Dragon — pink and purple costume, silver dragon, 2001 – 2002.............$125.00

Princess and the Pea — 8", #27745, 2001 – 2002 (Maggie), includes mattress and pea..........$100.00

8", #46180, 2007 – 2008, pink and white dress, pillow, pea $80.00

Princess Ann — 8" h.p., #396, 1957 only (Wendy Ann)...$900.00 up

Princess Aurora — 10", #48360, 2008 (Sleeping Beauty), ballet costume........................$120.00

Princess Budir Al-Budor — 8", #483, 1993 – 1994 only, Storybook Series $60.00

Princess Diana — 10", #22500, 1998 (Cissette), white satin gown $150.00

Princess Diana Birthday — 10", white satin and gold gown $150.00

Princess Elizabeth — 7" compo., 1937 – 1939 (Tiny Betty) $425.00

8", 1937, with Dionne head (rare) $400.00

9" – 11" compo., 1937 – 1941 (Little Betty)..$350.00 – 500.00

13" compo., 1937 – 1941 (Betty) ....**$650.00 up**

14" compo., 1937 – 1941 ....$600.00 up

15" compo., open mouth ....$600.00 up

18" – 19" compo., 1937 – 1941, open mouth ....$750.00 up

24" compo., 1938 – 1939, open mouth ....$900.00 up

28" compo., 1938 – 1939, open mouth ....$1,000.00 up

Princess Flavia (also Victoria) — 21" compo., 1939, 1946 – 1947 (Wendy Ann) ....$2,000.00 up

Princess for a Day — 8", #48430, 2008, pink dress, tiara $75.00

Princess Margaret Rose — 15" – 18" compo., 1937 – 1938 (Princess Elizabeth) ....$750.00 up

21" compo., 1938 ....$975.00 up

14" – 18" h.p., 1949 – 1953 (Margaret) ....**$600.00 – 975.00**

18" h.p. #2020B, 1953 only, Beaux Arts Series, pink taffeta gown with red ribbon,
tiara (Margaret) ....$1,600.00 up

8", #35535, 2002, pink dress, red cape $125.00

Princess of Quite a Lot — 8", #25275, 2000 – 2001 (Maggie), Mary Engelbreit,
yellow dress, crown, limited to 2,800...$70.00

Princess of Storyland — 8", #25990, 2000, long pink gown $75.00

Princess Rosetta — 21" compo., 1939, 1946 – 1947 (Wendy Ann) $2,300.00

Priscilla — 18" cloth, mid-1930s $625.00

7" compo., 1935 – 1938 (Tiny Betty) $375.00

8" h.p., BK, #729, 1965 – 1970, Americana and Storybook Series (Wendy Ann) $250.00

Prissy — 8", #630, 1990 only, Scarlett Series (Wendy Ann) $100.00

8", #637, reintroduced 1992 – 1993...$75.00

8", #16650, 1995, Scarlett Series, floral gown $85.00

8", #39985, 2005 – 2007, brown checked dress, print scarf $75.00

Pristine Angel — 10", #10604, 100th Anniversary, second in series, white/gold $100.00

Psycho — 10", #14810, doll in shower, pictured in 1998 catalog, 2005 issued, #40715, 2006......$140.00

Puddin' — 14" – 21" cloth/vinyl, 1966 – 1975...$75.00 – 165.00

14" – 21", 1987 – 1993..$50.00 – 125.00

14" only, 1994 – 1995 ....$65.00

21", 1995 ....$125.00

Puerto Rico — 8", 1998 – 1999, #24120, red outfit, carries flag and frog........................$70.00

Pumpkin — 22" cloth/vinyl, 1967 – 1976, 1976 only, with rooted hair................$125.00 – 150.00

Pumpkin Full O' Treats — 8", #46230, 2007, pumpkin bucket $75.00

Princess Elizabeth, 13", 1937 – 1941, all composition, All original with original box. $650.00 up.

Princess Margaret Rose, 18", 1949 – 1953 (Margaret). Auburn hair, tagged and all original. A mint doll. $600.00 – 975.00.

Pumpkin Patch Pirouette — 8", #47775, 2008, orange tutu, green shoes, pumpkin $60.00
Pumpkin Patch Treats — 8", #26350, 2001, one doll with three Halloween costumes $150.00
Pumpkin Perfect Maggie — 8", #40425, 2006, orange skirt, black sweater $60.00
Pumpkin Pie — 8", #38180, 2003 – 2005, black jumper with pumpkin..$50.00
Punk Princess Hello Kitty Lilly — 8", #48565, 2008, green plaid dress, matching Hello Kitty bag...$75.00
Punk Princess Hello Kitty Wendy — 8", #48560, 2008, pink checked dress, matching Kitty bag $75.00
Puppet, Hand — compo. head, cloth hand mitt body, by Tony Sarg, ca. 1936
    (see also Marionettes) ....$475.00 up
Puppy Love — 8", #35825, 2003 – 2005, black checked dress, Scottie dog...................................$75.00
Purple Petals Fairy — 8", #33425, 2002, purple petal tutu, leaf wings...$80.00
Purple Sparkle Dragonfly Fairy — 8", #35580, 2003 – 2004, green wings, costume.............$80.00
Puss 'n Boots — 8", #14552, Fairy Tales Series $65.00
    8", #46490, 2007 – 2008, satin dress, Puss 'n Boots cat with sword $100.00
Pussycat — cloth/vinyl
  White dolls:
     14", 1965 – 1985 (20-year production), 1987 – 1995 ....$50.00
     14", 1966, 1968, in trunk/trousseau..$200.00 up
     18", 1989 – 1995..$80.00
     20", 1965 – 1984, 1987 – 1988 (20+ year production) $90.00
     24", 1965 – 1985 (20-year production) $125.00
     14", 1998, variety of outfits..$50.00 – 100.00
     14", 2000, #25510, pink knit layette, pink outfit...$100.00
     14" – 18", 2002 – 2007, variety of outfits ....$100.00 – 225.00
     14", #48005, #48010, 48045, 2008...$95.00 – 110.00
     18", #46705, 46675, 2008...$100.00 – 130.00
  Black dolls:
     14", 1970 – 1976, 1984 – 1995 ....$75.00
     20", 1976 – 1983..$125.00
Pussycat, Lively — 14", 20", 24", 1966 – 1969 only, knob makes head and limbs move$65.00 – 175.00
Pussycat, Pussycat — 8", #41795, 2006, blue print dress, cat...$85.00
Queen — 18" h.p., #2025, 1953 only, Beaux Arts Series, white gown, long velvet cape
    trimmed with fur (Margaret).. $1,800.00 up

18" h.p., 1953 only, Glamour Girls Series, same gown/tiara as above but no cape (Margaret)... $1,600.00 up

18" h.p., 1954 only, Me & My Shadow Series, white gown, short Orlon cape (Margaret).... $1,600.00 up
8" h.p., 1954, #0030C, #597, Me & My Shadow Series, Orlon cape attached to purple robe
    (Wendy Ann) .... $1,000.00 up
8", #499, 1955 only, scarlet velvet robe...$800.00
10" h.p., #971, #879, #842, #763, 1957 – 1958, 1960 – 1961, gold gown with blue ribbon......$450.00
    #742, #765, 1959, 1963, white gown with blue ribbon .... $375.00 up
    #1186, #1187, 1972 – 1973, white gown with red ribbon $325.00
    1959, in trunk with wardrobe, must be mint .... $1,000.00 up
14", #1536, 1990 only, Classic Series (Louisa, Jennifer)...$85.00
20" h.p./vinyl arms, 1955, Dreams Come True Series, white brocade gown (Cissy) ...... $1,600.00 up
    1957, Fashion Parade Series, white gown .... $1,000.00 up
    1958, 1961 – 1963 (1958 – Dolls to Remember Series), gold gown ....$950.00 up
18", 1963 only, white gown with red ribbon (Elise)..$750.00
    With vinyl head (Mary-Bel)..$875.00
18" vinyl, same as 1965 (21" with rooted hair, 1966 only), gold brocade gown, rare doll (Elise)...$975.00
    #2150, 21" h.p./vinyl arms, 1965, white brocade gown (Jacqueline) $750.00
    1968, gold gown..$750.00
    #33660, 8", 2002, Crowning Glory, gold robe, limited to 500..................................$175.00
    #33525, 21", 2002, Recessional, purple robe, limited to 250....................................$750.00
    #33530, 10", 2002, Processional, red robe, limited to 500.......................................$150.00
Queen Alexandrine — 21" compo., 1939 – 1941 (Wendy Ann)..$1,950.00 up
Queen Charlotte — (see M.A.D.C. under Special Events/Exclusives)

Queen Elizabeth II, 18", #2020A, 1953. Glamour Girl Series. Brocade gown with blue sash of the garter. Margaret face. $1,600.00 up.

Queen Isabella, 8", #329, 1992 only (Wendy). Green velvet over gold skirt. $125.00.

Queen Elizabeth I — 8", #12610, 1999, red velvet trimmed in gold...............$100.00
Queen Elizabeth II — 8", 1992 only (mid-year issue), commemorating reign's 40th anniversary ...$110.00
Queen Esther — 8", #14584, 1995 only, Bible Character Dolls Series $110.00
Queen Isabella — 8" h.p., #329, 1992 only, Americana Series................$125.00
Queen Mother — 10", #35715, 2002, red cape $100.00
Queen of Hearts — 8" straight legs, #424, 1987 – 1990, Storybook Series (Wendy Ann)..........$60.00
   8", #14511, 1995, Alice in Wonderland Series...............$70.00
   8", #38410, 2004 – 2005, includes flamingo, mallet, and hedgehog...............$80.00
   10" (see Disney Annual Showcase of Dolls under Special Events/Exclusives)
Queen of Storyland — 10", #26025, 2000, long white gown, limited to 2,600 ....$100.00
Queen of the Roses — 10", #22660, 1999, long yellow satin dress, limited to 1,500 ....$100.00
Quintuplets (Fischer Quints) — 7" h.p. and vinyl, 1964 (Genius), with original box .....$550.00 set
Quiz-Kins — 8" h.p., 1953, bald head, in romper only (Wendy Ann)...............$500.00 up
   1953 Peter Pan, caracul wig...............$850.00
   1953 – 1954, as groom ....$650.00 up
   1953 – 1954, as bride or 1953 Christening Baby, #318...............$700.00 up
   1953 – 1954, girl with wig ....$650.00 up
   1953, girl without wig, in romper suit...............$575.00
Rachel/Rachael — (see Belk & Leggett under Special Events/Exclusives)
Radiant Ruby — 10", #33360, red and gold gown, ruby jewelry...............$135.00
Raggedy Ann and Andy Set — 8", #47745, 2007 – 2008...............$140.00
   18", #48605, 2008, cloth pair, 48610 Andy ....$35.00 each
Raggedy Ann & Me — 8", #48615, 2008, white dress with red dots, cloth Ann...............$70.00
Raining Cats and Dogs — 8", #38850, 2004 – 2005, includes dog and cat $100.00
Randolph, Martha — 1976 – 1978, first set Presidents' Ladies/First Ladies Series (Louisa)...$100.00
Rapunzel — 10", #M31, 1989 – 1992 only, Portrette, gold velvet (Cissette)...............$90.00
   14", #1539, 1993 – 1994, Doll Classics, limited to 3,000, comes with 8" Mother Gothel ... $250.00 set
   14", #87005, 1996, purple gown (Louisa)...............$100.00
   8", #14542, 1995, Brothers Grimm Series, pink gown with gold scallops,
      pink cone hat, #13980, 1997 – 2003...............$75.00
   5", #36300, 2004, vinyl, petite, pink gown, cone hat $25.00
   14", #25460, 2000 – 2001, lavender dress, cone hat with tulle (Margaret)...............$110.00
   8", #13980, 2004, pink dress, #40300, 2005 – 2008, pink dress...............$80.00
Really Ugly Stepsister — 8" h.p., #13450, 1997 – 1998, Cinderella Series...............$85.00
Rebecca — 14" – 17", 21" compo., 1940 – 1941 (Wendy Ann) ....$600.00 – 1,000.00
   14" h.p., 1948 – 1949 (Margaret) ....$750.00 up
   14" plastic/vinyl, #1485, 1968 – 1969, Classic Series, two-tiered skirt in pink (Mary Ann)... $125.00
   #1485, #1515, #1585, 1970 – 1985, one-piece skirt, pink pindot or checked dress $60.00
   #1586, 1986 – 1987, blue dress with striped pinafore $65.00
   8", #14647, 1996...............$65.00
Rebecca of Sunnybrook Farm — 8", #48055, 2008, Maggie, pink check dress...............$80.00
Record Album — "Madame Alexander Collector's Album," 1978, children's stories told
   by Madame, cover is like Alexander box...............$35.00
Red Boy — 8" h.p., BK, #740, 1972 (Wendy)...............$100.00
   #0740, 1973 – 1975, marked "Alex"; #440, 1976 – 1988, marked "Alexander" $70.00
Red Cherries — 8", 33050, 2002, red dress, smocked with cherries...............$85.00
Red Cross Nurse — 18", #16002, Rag Doll Series...............not available for sale
Red Hat's Little Lady — 8", #45350, 2006, purple dress, red hat $80.00
Red Hat Sophisticate — 10", #40855, 2005, red hat and purse, purple dress...............$120.00
Red Riding Hood — 7" compo., 1936 – 1942 (Tiny Betty)...............$375.00
   9" compo., 1939 – 1940 (Little Betty) $395.00
   8" h.p., SLW, #608, 1955, cape sewn under arms (Wendy Ann)...............$650.00
   8" h.p., BKW, #382, 1962 – 1965, Storybook Series (Wendy Ann)...............$275.00
   8" h.p., BK, #782, 1965 – 1972...............$125.00
   8" h.p., straight legs, #0782, #482, 1973 – 1975, marked "Alex"...............$75.00
   8" h.p., straight legs, #482, 1976 – 1986 (1985 – 1987 white face), marked "Alexander"..........$60.00

8", #485, #463, 1987 – 1991 (Maggie), 1992 – 1993 (Wendy Ann), #140463, 1994, #13970, 1998 – 1999 ....$60.00

14", #24617, 1995, patchwork dress with red cape (Mary Ann).............................$85.00

14", #87004, plaid dress with red cape (Mary Ann) $75.00

8", #25970, 2000 – 2002, print dress, red cape, braided hair $70.00

14", #28620, 2001 (Margaret), print dress, red cape..$125.00

8", #33390, 2002 – 2005, red checked dress, 7½" plush wolf, basket $100.00

5", #36290, 2004, vinyl, petite, print dress, red cape $25.00

8", #42440, 2006 – 2007, print dress, red cape, basket of apples.............................$75.00

Red Queen — 8", h.p., 1997 – 1999, #13010, red and gold gown.............................$100.00

Red Queen and White King Set — 8" pair, #13030, 1997 ....$200.00

Red Sequin — 10", #19974, 1998 (Cissette), long red velvet gown.........................$125.00

Red Shoes — 8", #14533, 1995, ballerina with same head as Spain $65.00

8", #35635, 2003, white lace and tulle tutu, red shoes..$75.00

Refreshing Coca-Cola — 8", #33000, 2002, with tin box $80.00

Renaissance Bride — 10", #25000, 2000 (Cissette) $130.00

Renoir — 21" compo., 1945 – 1946, extra make-up, must be excellent condition (Wendy Ann).... $2,200.00 up

14" h.p., 1950 only (Margaret)..$875.00 up

21" h.p./vinyl arms, 1961 only (Cissy) ....$950.00 up

18" h.p./vinyl arms, vinyl head, 1963 only (Elise) ....$625.00 up

21" h.p./vinyl arms, #2154, 1965, pink gown (Jacqueline) $700.00

14", #28620, 2001 (Margaret), print dress, red cape...$125.00

21", #2062, 1966, blue gown with black trim (Coco) ....$2,200.00 up

21", #2175, 1967, navy blue gown, red hat $700.00

21", #2194, #2184, 1969 – 1970, blue gown, full lace over dress $625.00

21", #2163, 1971, all yellow gown $575.00

21", #2190, 1972, pink gown with black jacket and trim $500.00

21", #2190, 1973, yellow gold gown, black ribbon $450.00

10" h.p., #1175, 1968, all navy with red hat (Cissette)......................................$400.00

10", #1175, 1969, pale blue gown, short jacket, striped or dotted skirt..................$475.00

10", #1180, 1970, all aqua satin $400.00

Renoir Child — 12" plastic/vinyl, #1274, 1967 only, Portrait Children Series (Nancy Drew) ...$150.00

14", #1474, 1968 only (Mary Ann) $100.00

Renoir Girl — 14" plastic/vinyl, #1469, #1475, 1967 – 1968, Portrait Children Series, white dress with red ribbon trim (Mary Ann) $125.00

#1477, 1969 – 1971, pink dress, white pinafore $70.00

#1477, #1478, #1578, 1972 – 1986 (14-year production), pink multi-tiered lace gown $65.00

#1572, 1986 only, pink pleated nylon dress $65.00

Renoir Girl with Hoop — #1574, 1986 – 1987, Classic and Fine Arts Series $75.00

Renoir Girl with Watering Can — #1577, 1985 – 1987, Classic and Fine Arts Series $75.00

8" h.p., #22150, 1997, navy taffeta dress..$75.00

Renoir's on the Terrace — 8", 1999 (Wendy), blue dress with white overdress.........................$80.00

Rhett — 12", #1380, 1981 – 1985, Portrait Children Series, black jacket/gray pants (Nancy Drew) ..$75.00

8", #401, 1989 only, Jubilee II (Wendy Ann) $85.00

8", #638, #642, 1991 – 1992 only, Scarlett Series, all white/blue vest $85.00

8", #642, 1993, #160642, 1994, tan pants/vest/tie with white jacket....................$75.00

10" h.p., #15050, 1997, Gone with the Wind Series $80.00

Ribbon Celebration — 10", #36135, 2003, pink ball gown with ribbon and flowers $150.00

Riding Habit — 8", 1990 only, Americana Series (Wendy Ann) $60.00

#571, 1956 ....$500.00

#373G, 1957 ....$475.00

#541, 1958 ....$550.00

#355, 1962, #623, 1965 ....$350.00

Riley's Little Annie — 14" plastic/vinyl, #1481, 1967 only, Literature Series (Mary Ann).......$175.00

Ring Around the Rosey — 8", #12813, Nursery Rhymes Series................................$60.00

8", #13520, 1998 – 2000, pink and white lacy dress $65.00

Robin Hood, 8", #446, 1988 – 1990 (Wendy). Storybook Series. $60.00.

A Rose For You, 8", #41575, 2006 – 2007 (Wendy). Packaged in the new window box. $50.00.

8", #39885, 2005 (Maggie), red print..$70.00

Ringbearer — 14" h.p., 1951 only, must be near mint (Lovey Dove) ....$550.00 up

8", #28655, 2001 – 2002, white jacket, black pants $75.00

Ringmaster — (see Collectors United/C.U. under Special Events/Exclusives)

Riverboat Queen (Lena) — (see M.A.D.C. under Special Events/Exclusives)

Riviera Night — 16", print dress, matching hat..$135.00

Roaring 20's Bride — 10", #22630, 1999, white lace, pink roses, limited to 2,500.....$175.00

Roaring 20's Catherine — 16" porcelain, blue satin fringed costume.............$175.00

Robin Hood — 8", #446, 1988 – 1990, Storybook Series (Wendy Ann) **$60.00**

Robin Hood and Maid Marion — 8" pair, bow and arrows........................$150.00

Rock-A-Bye Baby — 8", #47900, 2008, long dress, bonnet.........................$55.00

Rock and Roll Group — #22110, 1997, four 8" dolls, mod costumes $375.00

Rocking Bear Doll — 8", #36910, 2003, lavender checked dress, bear.............$80.00

Rococo Bride — 10", pink satin and lace gown, #22460, 1999 – 2000 ....$150.00

Rococo Catherine — 16" porcelain, elaborate pink satin gown.....................$175.00

Rodeo — 8" h.p., #483, 1955 only (Wendy Ann).......................................$850.00 up

Rodeo Day in Dallas — 8", #45470, 2006 – 2007, western outfit, flags, lasso (Maggie)...........$70.00

Rodeo Rosie — 14", #87012, 1996, red checked western costume...................$85.00

Rogers, Ginger — 14" – 21" compo., 1940 – 1945 (Wendy Ann).................$2,500.00 up

Roller Blades — (see Disney Annual Showcase of Dolls under Special Events/Exclusives)

Roller Skating — 8" h.p., SL, SLW, BKW, #556, 1953 – 1956 (Wendy Ann) .....$675.00 up

Romance — 21" compo., 1945 – 1946, extra make-up, must be mint (Wendy Ann) ....$2,100.00 up

Romeo — 18" compo., 1949 (Wendy Ann)...$1,300.00 up

12" plastic/vinyl, #1370, 1978 – 1987, Portrait Children Series (Nancy Drew)....$60.00

12", reintroduced 1991 – 1992 only, Romance Collection (Nancy Drew)..............$60.00

8", 1994, mid-year introduction (see M.A.D.C. under Special Events/Exclusives)

8", #40780, 2005 – 2006, light blue costume.......................................$75.00

Ronald McDonald — 8", 2000 – 2001, red and yellow outfit........................$65.00

Ron Weasley — 8", #38425, Harry Potter Series, with Scabbers...................$85.00

10", #36635, vinyl black robe, 2004 ....$35.00

Roosevelt, Edith — 1988, fifth set Presidents' Ladies/First Ladies Series (Louisa)...........$100.00

Roosevelt, Eleanor — 14", 1989 – 1990, sixth set Presidents' Ladies/First Ladies Series (Louisa)....$100.00

8", #48940, 2008, brown dress, fur stole, black hat................................$80.00

Rosamund Bridesmaid — 15" h.p., 1951 only (Margaret, Maggie) ....$600.00 up

17" – 18" h.p., 1951 only (Margaret, Maggie)......................................$800.00 up

Rose — 9" early vinyl toddler, 1953 only, pink organdy dress and bonnet...........$125.00

Rose Blossom — 8", #38405, 2004 – 2005, red ballet costume.....................$75.00

Rose Bouquet — 10", #28880, 2001, white and red dress with red roses...........$80.00

Rosebud — 16" – 19" cloth/vinyl, 1952 – 1953 ....$150.00

13", 1953 only..$175.00

23" – 25", 1953 only...$175.00

Rosebud (Pussycat) — 14" – 20", 1986 only, white.........................$50.00 – 125.00

14", black..$75.00

Rose Fairy — 8" h.p., #622, 1956 only (Wendy Ann)..............................$1,500.00 up

8", #22640, 1999, yellow and rose costume with wings, limited to 1,500.............$75.00

Rose For You, A — 8", #41575, 2006 – 2007, white dress, red rose..........................**$50.00**

Rose Garden Ball Gown — 10", #34170, 2002, pink satin gown, limited to 1,000.........$125.00

Rosette — 10", #1115, 1987 – 1989, Portrette, pink/rose gown (Cissette) $65.00

Rosette Dreams — 8", #36275, blonde, pink satin dress, 2004 ....$70.00

8", #36276, brunette, pink satin dress, 2004 ....$70.00

8", #36277, African-American, 2004 ....$70.00

Rosey Posey — 14" cloth/vinyl, 1976 only..$75.00

21" cloth/vinyl, 1976 only...$100.00

Rosie the Riveter — 8", #17530, 1999, overalls, lunch bucket......................$75.00

Ross, Betsy — 8" h.p., Americana Series, 1967 – 1972 (Wendy Ann), bend knees, #731 ....$125.00

Straight legs, #0731, #431, 1973 – 1975, Storybook Series, marked "Alex"...............................$65.00

Straight legs, #431, 1976 – 1987 (1985 – 1987 white face)..$60.00

8", #312, reintroduced 1991 – 1992 only, Americana Series.......................................$60.00

#312, 1976 Bicentennial gown (star print) $125.00

8", #35705, 2003 – 2004, with flag..$85.00

Rosy — 14", #1562, 1988 – 1990, Classic Series, all pink dress with cream lace trim (Mary Ann)$75.00

Round Up Cowgirl — (see Disney Annual Showcase of Dolls under Special Events/Exclusives)

Row, Row, Row Your Boat — 8", #13510, 1998 – 1999, comes with boat $100.00

Roxanne — 8" h.p., #140504, 1994 only, Storyland Series...$70.00

Royal Bouquet — 8", #28895, 2001, white dress, pink sash $80.00

Royal Evening — 18" h.p., 1953 only, cream/royal blue gown (Margaret) ....$2,400.00 up

Royal Wedding — 21" compo., 1947, full circles trimmed in lace on lower skirt (Wendy Ann)... $3,200.00 up

Rozy — 12" plastic/vinyl, #1130, 1969 only (Janie) $325.00

Ruby (July) — 10", #1151, 1992 only, Birthstone Collection, all red/gold (Cissette)...............$125.00

Rudolph The Red-Nosed Reindeer — 8", #47715, 2007 – 2008, Maggie, plush deer,

paint brush, toy train $80.00

Ruffles Clown — 21", 1954 only $425.00

Rumania — 8" h.p., BK, #786, 1968 – 1972 (Wendy) $85.00

8" straight legs, #0786, #586, 1973 – 1975, marked "Alex" $65.00

8" straight legs, #586, #538, 1976 – 1987, marked "Alexander" $60.00

8", #538, 1986 – 1987..$55.00

Rumbera/Rumbero — 7" compo., 1938 – 1943 (Tiny Betty) ....$350.00 ea.

9" compo., 1939 – 1941 (Little Betty) ....$375.00 ea.

Rumpelstiltskin & Miller's Daughter — 8" and 14", #1569, 1992 only, limited to 3,000 sets ... $225.00 set

8" and 5" porcelain, #27750, 2001 ....$150.00 set

Running Away to Grandma's — 8", #34035, 2002 – 2004, with bear and suitcase,

#34036, African-American...$80.00

Russia — 8" h.p., BK, #774, 1968 – 1972 (Wendy Ann)..$100.00

8" straight legs, #0774, 1973 – 1975, marked "Alex" $65.00

8" straight legs, #574, #548, 1976 – 1988 (1985 – 1987 white face), marked "Alexander" $60.00

8", #548, 1985 – 1987, white face $60.00

8", #581, 1991 – 1992 only; #110540, 1994 only, long blue gown with gold trim $60.00

8", #24150, 1999 – 2001, comes with painted stacking doll and miniature doll....................$85.00

8", #39765, 2005 – 2006, red dress and hat..$90.00

8", #48105, 2008, maroon top, gold skirt, Fabergé egg replica..................................$90.00

Russian — 7" compo., 1935 – 1938 (Tiny Betty)...$350.00

9" compo., 1938 – 1942 (Little Betty) $350.00

Russian Ballerina — 8" h.p., #36770, 2003 – 2004, white tutu, bouquet.........................$80.00

Rusty — 20" cloth/vinyl, 1967 – 1968 only..$300.00

Sabrina — 16", #38910, 2005 (Alex), white ball gown $150.00

Sagittarius — 8", #21410, 1998 (Maggie), horse costume $90.00

Sailing the Sweet Seas — 8", #46460, 2008, pink boat $75.00

Sailor — 14" compo., 1942 – 1945 (Wendy Ann)..$750.00

17" compo., 1943 – 1944 ....$875.00

Sailorette — 10" h.p., #1119, 1988 only, Portrette Series, red, white, and blue outfit

(Cissette) $60.00

St. Patty's Day — 8", #49885, 2008, purse with coins $85.00

Sally — 9", #46260, 2007, Nightmare Before Christmas, picnic basket..........................$60.00

Sally — 10", #26430, 2001 – 2002, Peanuts Gang, red dress $35.00

10", #35900, 2003, Trick or Treat, blue dot dress, bag, candy $60.00

Sally Bride — 14" compo., 1938 – 1939 (Wendy Ann)..$475.00 up

18" – 21" compo., 1938 – 1939 ....$500.00 – 725.00

Salome — 14", #1412, 1984 – 1986, Opera Series (Mary Ann) $70.00

Salute to the Century — 8", #17630, 1999, white chiffon long gown, limited to 4,000 ....$85.00

Samantha — 14" 1989 (see FAO Schwarz under Special Events/Exclusives)

14", #1561, 1991 – 1992 only, Classic Series, gold ruffled gown (Mary Ann) $90.00

Sally, 18", composition. All original bride. $500.00 – 725.00.

10", h.p., #15300, from the Bewitched TV series $125.00

10", #40645, 2005, black dress, painted witch hat $120.00

Sami — 9", #40705, 2005, vinyl, denim skirt $30.00

Samson — 8", #14582, 1995 only, Bible Character Dolls Series $100.00

Sandy McHare — cloth/felt, 1930s $800.00

San Genero Festival — 8", #38140, 2004, red checked outfit $80.00

Santa and Mrs. Claus — 8", mid-year issue (see Madame Alexander Doll Co. under Special Events/Exclusives)

Santa Claus — 14", #24608, 1995, Christmas Series $125.00

Santa's Little Helper — 8", #19660, 1998 – 1999, elf with candy cane trim $80.00

Santa's World — 8", #38545, 2004 – 2005, Santa, reindeer, 5" elf, toys $125.00

Sapphire (September) — 10", 1992 only, Birthstone Collection $125.00

Sarah — 5", #27415, 2001 – 2003, petite, kite dress $20.00

Sardinia — 8", #509, 1989 – 1991 only (Wendy Ann) $60.00

Sargent — 14", #1576, 1984 – 1985, Fine Arts Series, dressed in lavender (Mary Ann) $70.00

Sargent's Girl — 14", #1579, 1986 only, Fine Arts Series, dressed in pink (Mary Ann) $85.00

Saturday's Child — 8", #27795, 2001, watering can $70.00

Say a Little Prayer — 8", #39755, 2005, pink dress with hymnal $80.00

Scarecrow — 8", #430, 1993, #140430, 1994 – 1996, Wizard of Oz Series, #13230, 1997 – 2005, #13231, 2006 ....$70.00

5", #28690, 2002, porcelain $65.00

9", #39790, 2005 – 2007, checked shirt $35.00

5", #36345, 2005, petite, checked shirt $25.00

8", #46335, 2007 – 2008, with dipolma, green shirt and hat $70.00

Scarlett, Miss — 14" (see Belk & Leggett under Special Events/Exclusives)

Scarlett O'Hara — (Before movie, 1937 – 1938)

7" compo., 1937 – 1942 (Tiny Betty) ....$750.00 up

9" compo., 1938 – 1941 (Little Betty) $675.00

11", 1937 – 1942 (Wendy Ann) $700.00

14" – 15" compo., 1941 – 1943 (Wendy Ann) $800.00

18" compo., 1939 – 1946 (Wendy Ann) $1,250.00

21" compo., 1945, 1947 (Wendy Ann) ....$1,500.00 up

14" – 16" h.p., 1950s (Margaret, Maggie) $1,700.00

20" h.p., 1950s (Margaret) ....$1,800.00 up

21", 1961, blue taffeta gown w/black looped braid trim, short jacket (Cissy) ....$1,700.00 up

1958, jointed arms, green velvet jacket and bonnet trimmed in light green net, rare .. $2,000.00 up

1961 – 1962, straight arms, white organdy, green ribbon inserted into tiers of lace on skirt, white picture hat, rare ....$2,000.00 up

18" h.p./vinyl arms, 1963 only, pale blue organdy with rosebuds, straw hat (Elise) ....$950.00 up

12" h.p., 1963 only, green taffeta gown and bonnet (Lissy) $1,400.00

7½" – 8", 1953 – 1954, white gown with red rosebuds, white lace hat (Wendy Ann) ....$1,400.00 up

7½" – 8" h.p., #485, 1955, two layer gown, white, yellow, and green trim (Wendy Ann) $1,500.00 up

8" h.p., BKW, 1956, pink, blue, or yellow floral gown ....$1,500.00 up

8" h.p., BKW, #431, 1957, white lace and ribbon trim (dress must be mint) ....$1,600.00 up

8" h.p., BK, #760, 1963 ....$650.00 up

8" BK, 1965, in white or cream gown (Wendy Ann) ....$750.00 up

8" BK, 1971 only, bright pink floral print $600.00

8" BK, #725, 1966 – 1972, Americana and Storybook Series, floral gown $350.00

8", #0725, #425, 1973 – 1991 (18-year production), white gown (Wendy Ann) $75.00

Straight legs, #425, #426, 1976 – 1986, marked "Alexander" $75.00

#426, 1987, white face, blue dot gown $150.00

Straight legs, #426, 1988 – 1989, floral gown $90.00

1989, #400, Jubilee II, green velvet/gold trim $125.00

Straight legs, #626, 1990 only, tiny floral print $100.00

#631, 1991 only, three-tier white gown, curly hair $90.00

#627, 1992 only, rose floral print, oversized bonnet $100.00

#641, 1993, white gown with green stripes and trim $90.00

Scarlett O'Hara, 1940 (Wendy Ann), all composition. All original. $700.00.

#643, 1993, #160643, 1994 (Honeymoon in New Orleans), trunk with wardrobe...........$275.00
#160644, 1994 only, Scarlett Bride, #160647, Scarlett Picnic.............................$100.00
#16648, 1995 – 1996, white, four-tier organdy gown with red trim......................$85.00
#16652, 1995 only, floral print picnic outfit with organdy overskirt..................$90.00
#16553, green drapery gown, 100th Anniversary...$100.00
#16653, 1996, Ashley's Farewell, maroon taffeta skirt.................................$80.00
#17025, 1996, Tomorrow Is Another Day, floral gown....................................$80.00
#86004, 1996, Ashley's Birthday, red velvet gown......................................$85.00
#15030, 1997 – 1998, Shadow, rose picnic dress..$80.00
#14970, 1998 – 1999, Poor Scarlett, floral calico, straw hat..........................$80.00
#15180, 1999 – 2000, Sweet Sixteen, white dress, red ribbons..........................$80.00
#26860, 2000, Picnic, print dress, straw hat..$80.00
#27825, 2001 – 2002, green drapery gown and hat.......................................$80.00
#28750, 2001, Honeymoon Scarlett, white dress, hat, black trim........................$85.00
#27825, 2002..$80.00
#35955, 2003, Scarlett's Sash for Ashley, red and white dress.........................$85.00
#38820, 2004, Matron of the Mansion, long red and white gown.........................$100.00
#38820, 2005 – 2007, Shadow Matron of the Mansion, red dress.........................$100.00
#46005, 2007 – 2008, In Cotton Fields, print dress....................................$80.00
#48855, 2008, Return to Tara Scarlett, green and white gown...........................$95.00
21" h.p./vinyl arms, #2153, 1963 – 1964 (became "Godey" in 1965 with blonde hair) ... $1,500.00 up
21" h.p./vinyl arms, 1965, #2152, green satin gown (Jacqueline)...................... $1,900.00 up
#2061, 1966, all white gown, red sash, and roses (also with plain wide lace hem;
  inverted "V" scalloped lace hem – allow more for this gown) (Coco) .... $2,800.00 up
#2174, 1967, green satin gown with black trim..$675.00
#2180, 1968, floral print gown with wide white hem................................. $800.00 up
#2190, 1969, red gown with white lace...$675.00
#2180, 1970, green satin, white trim on jacket......................................$475.00
#2292, #2295, #2296, 1975 – 1977, all green satin, white lace at cuffs..............$350.00
#2110, 1978, silk floral gown, green parasol, white lace............................$400.00
#2240, 1979 – 1985, green velvet...$300.00
#2255, 1986 only, floral gown, green parasol, white lace............................$325.00
#2247, 1987 – 1988, layered all over white gown.....................................$350.00
#2253, 1989, full bangs, all red gown (Birthday Party gown) $350.00
#2258, 1990 – 1993 only, Scarlett Bride, Scarlett Series $375.00
#2259, 1991 – 1992 only, green on white, three ruffles around skirt $325.00
21", #162276, 1994 (Jacqueline), tight green gown, three-layered bustle..............$300.00
#009, porcelain, 1991 only, green velvet, gold trim.................................$350.00
#50001, Scarlett Picnic (Jacqueline), floral gown $300.00
#15020, 1997, rose picnic dress, carries garden basket..............................$300.00
#15170, Black Mourning Scarlett, 1999...$325.00
#25765, 2000, Atlanta Stroll Scarlett, striped bodice...............................$375.00
#28760, 2001, Peachtree Promenade, limited to 500, blue dress, black trim...........$375.00
#33475, 2002, Matron of the Mansion Scarlett, red velvet, limited to 250............$400.00
#35950, 2003, Scarlett at the Mill, green plaid skirt, copper overdress, limited to 350....$350.00
#48165, 2008, Scarlett Visits the Mill Cissy, blue jacket, long white dress, parasol..........$500.00
10" h.p., #1174, 1968 only, lace in bonnet, green satin gown with black braid trim (Cissette) ...$450.00
#1174, 1969, green satin gown with white and gold braid $400.00
#1181, #1180, 1970 – 1973, green satin gown with gold braid trim....................$325.00
#1100, 1989 only, Jubilee II, burgundy and white....................................$125.00
#1102, 1990 – 1991 only, Scarlett Series, floral print gown.........................$125.00
#1105, 1992 only, Scarlett at Ball, all in black....................................$100.00
#161105, 1993, 1994, green velvet drapes/gold trim..................................$100.00
1994 – 1995, Scarlett in red dress with red boa.....................................$125.00
#16107, 1995 only, white sheath with dark blue jacket $125.00
#16654, 1996, mourning dress..$100.00

Scarlett, 21", #2258, 1990 – 1993 (Jacqueline). A bride gown accented with flowers. $375.00.

Scarlett, 14", #1495, 1968 only (Mary Ann). Floral gown with green velvet ribbon sash. $300.00.

#16656, 1996, Scarlett and Rhett, limited set $175.00
#15000, 1997 – 1998, Hoop-Petti outfit...$100.00
#15040, 1997, mourning outfit...$100.00
#14980, 1998 – 2000, blue satin gown, lace shawl (Cissette), Portrait Scarlett $125.00
#25770, 2000, Sewing Circle Scarlett, white top, lavender skirt....................................$100.00
#28755, 2001, Atlanta Stroll Scarlett, red/white striped dress $100.00
#33470, 2002, Scarlett dressing gown and vanity set, limited to 500............................$300.00
#36160, 2003, Sweet Sixteen Scarlett, white ruffle dress, red ribbon $125.00
#38815, 2004, Shanty Town Scarlett O'Hara, black trimmed gown $125.00
#39980, 2005, Scarlett O'Hara Visits the Mill, white dress, green jacket $125.00
#33910, 2006, Scarlett's Dinner with Rhett, black evening gown..................................$150.00
#46000, 2007, Return to Tara, green and white gown $135.00
#48160, Scarlett & Mammy, 2008, hoop petticoat, black and white outfit $200.00
12", 1981 – 1985, green gown with braid trim (Nancy Drew)......................................$125.00
14" plastic/vinyl, #1495, 1968 only, floral gown (Mary Ann)......................$300.00
#1490, #7590, 1969 – 1986 (18-year production), white gown, tagged "Gone
   with the Wind" (Mary Ann) $90.00
#1590, #1591, 1987 – 1989, blue or green floral print on beige....................................$125.00
#1590, 1990, Scarlett Series, tiny floral print gown $125.00
#1595, 1991 – 1992 only, Scarlett Series, white ruffles, green ribbon (Louisa, Jennifer) ...$125.00
#16551, 1995 (see Peachtree Lane)
#1500, 1986 only, Jubilee #1, all green velvet (Mary Ann) $150.00
#1300, 1989 only, Jubilee #2, green floral print gown (Mary Ann) $125.00
16", #46865, 2006, Scarlett Picnic, print dress, extra outfit...$225.00
#47035, 2007, Dinner with Rhett, Then and Now, black velvet gown, halter dress........$220.00

Scheherazade — 8", #42545, 2006, red, gold harem costume $65.00
School Girl — 7" compo., 1936 – 1943 (Tiny Betty) $325.00
Scorpio — 8", #21400, 1998, scorpion costume, golden spear $85.00
Scotch — 7" compo., 1936 – 1939 (Tiny Betty)...$350.00
   9" compo., 1939 – 1940 (Little Betty) $350.00
   10" h.p., 1962 – 1963 (Cissette)... $900.00 up
Scots Lass — 8" h.p., BKW, #396, 1963 only (Maggie Mixup, Wendy Ann)................$165.00
   8", #46655, 2007, Scottish Lass, hand drum $80.00
Scottish (Scotland) — 8" h.p., BKW, #796, 1964 – 1965 (Wendy Ann)......................$125.00
   8" h.p., BK, #796, 1966 – 1972 ....$100.00
   8" straight legs, #0796 – 596, 1973 – 1975, marked "ALEX" $75.00
   8" straight legs, #596, #529, 1976 – 1993 (1985 – 1987 white face), marked "Alexander" $65.00
   8" re-dressed, Scottish outfit with English guard hat, 1994.................................$60.00
   8", #28550, 2001 – 2002, Scottish costume, blue plaid, bagpipes $65.00
   8", #46655, 2008, red plaid Scottish costume, hand drum $80.00
Scouting — 8", #317, 1991 – 1992 only, Americana Series..$125.00
Scrooge — 14", #18401, 1996, Dickens (Mary Ann) $85.00
Season's Greetings Maggie — 8", #26840, 2001, green smocked dress $70.00
Season's Greetings Wendy — 8", #26845, 2001, red smocked dress $70.00
Secret Garden, My — (see FAO Schwarz under Special Events/Exclusives)
   14", #24616, 1995, trunk and wardrobe (Louisa) $225.00
   8", #48600, 2008, striped pinafore, red bird, trowel...$80.00
See No Evil, Hear No Evil, Speak No Evil — 8", #39835, 2005 – 2006, with bear, dog, cat ... $105.00
Sense and Sensibility — 10", #25340, 2000, long white gown with embroidery $100.00
September — 14", #1527, 1989 only, Classic Series (Mary Ann) $85.00
   10", #1152, 1992, Portrette, royal blue/gold flapper...$100.00
Serenade — 10", #36170, 2003, long ball gown with triangle black sequin design on skirt $125.00
Sesame Street, 1,2,3 — Trunk Set, 2004 – 2005, #39082, African-American $200.00
Sesame Street, 1,2,3 — Trunk Set, 2004 – 2005, #39080, 8", Big Bird, etc. $200.00
Setting Sail — 8", #37960, Asian, #37961, Caucasian, 2004 – 2005, dress with stars...................$80.00
Seven Dwarfs — Compo., 1937 only, must be mint ....$550.00 ea.

Scarlett Jubilee, 14", #1500 (Mary Ann). Green velvet dress and bonnet. $150.00.

Seventies Strut Shadow Cissette — 10", #38760, Caucasian, 2004, #38761, African-American, black outfit..$225.00 ea.
Seventy-Fifth Anniversary Wendy — 8", #22420, 1998, pink outfit.......................................$100.00
Shadow Madame Pompadour Fall — 10", 2007, #45635, salmon dress and jacket, 3 plush dogs ...$270.00
Shadow Madame Pompadour Spring — 10", #45630, 2006, green dress, basket of flowers.....$270.00
Shadow Madame Pompadour Summer — 10", 2007, #45615, sold long court gown, powdered wig...$300.00
Shadow Madame Pompadour Winter — 10", #42095, 2006, long gown...............................$290.00
Shadow of Madame — (see Doll & Teddy Bear Expo under Special Events/Exclusives)
Shadow Stepmother — 8", #14638, 1996 ....$110.00
Shaharazad — 10", #1144, 1992 – 1993 only, Portrette (Cissette) $80.00
    8", #33520, 2002, navy blue suit, dim sum $80.00
Shanghai — 8", #33520, 2003, navy blue silk outfit, dim sum....................................$80.00
Share Your Happiness — 8", #40825, 2005, pink coat, hat......................................$75.00
Shea Elf — (see Collectors United/C.U. under Special Events/Exclusives)
Sheer Charm — 8", #40805, 2005, Asian, plaid dress...$50.00
Sheer Delight — 8", #40815, 2005 – 2006, African American, print dress $50.00
Sheer Joy — 8", #40800, 2005 – 2006, (Wendy), print dress, straw hat............................$50.00
Sheer Warmth — 8", #40820, 2005 – 2006, Latin, print dress....................................$50.00
Shepherd and Drummer Boy Set — 8", #19490, 1997 – 2000, Nativity Set......................$200.00
Shepherdess with Lamb — 8", #20010, 1999 – 2000, red robe, headdress......................$80.00
She Sells Seashells — 8", #14629, 1996, Nursery Rhymes Series (Maggie) $70.00
    8", #42470, 2006 – 2007, sundress, umbrella, basket of shells $85.00
Shimmering Dance — 8", #30645, 2001 – 2003, ballerina, blonde................................$65.00
Shimmering 1930s Catherine — 16", porcelain, long white gown................................$125.00
Shirley's Doll House — (see Special Events/Exclusives)
Shoemaker's Elf — 8", #33665, 2002 – 2003, purple costume, 8" shoe............................$85.00
Shoemaker's Elf Boy — 8", #14637, 1996, Girl, #14636 ....$65.00
Shopping with Grandma — 8", #47880, 2008, pink straw hat, shopping bag, shoes................$80.00
Sicily — 8", #513, 1989 – 1990 (Wendy Ann) $65.00
Signature Red Hat Style Cissette — 10", #42180, 2006, purple dress $130.00
Signature Wendy — 8", #38865, 2004 – 2005, pink print dress, stationery $85.00
Signs of Spring — 8", #45340, 2006, red print dress, straw hat $100.00
Silver Star — 8", #28875, 2001, silver satin and tulle $75.00
Simone — 21" h.p./vinyl arms, 1968 only, in trunk (Jacqueline)............................$2,150.00 up
Simply Sweet Flower Girl — 8", #32985, pink dress, rose bouquet, 2002 ....$70.00
Sing a Song of Sixpence — 8", #42460, 2006, pink dress, pie with birds $70.00
Sir Lapin Hare — cloth/felt, 1930s $750.00
Sister Brenda — (see FAO Schwarz under Special Events/Exclusives)
Sisters Forever — 8", #46130, 2007 – 2008, print dress, cloth doll $70.00
Sitting Pretty — 18" foam body, 1965 only, rare $375.00
60's Go-Go Beach Party — 8", #42030, 2006, red dog......................................$50.00
Skater's Waltz — 15" – 18", 1955 – 1956 (Cissy) ....$650.00 up
Skating Doll — 16", 1947 – 1950 (untagged "Sonja Henie" after contract expired)................$700.00
Skip To My Lou — 8", #45830, 2007, print dress, jug......................................$70.00
Sky's the Limit Fairy — 8", #40770, 2005, red-trimmed fairy outfit $85.00
Sledding Wendy — 8", #36015, 2003 – 2004, pink jacket, blue pants, sled $75.00
Sleeping Beauty — 7" – 9" compo., 1941 – 1944 (Tiny Betty and Little Betty) ....$325.00 – 450.00
    15" – 16" compo., 1938 – 1940 (Princess Elizabeth) $525.00
    18" – 21" compo., 1941 – 1944 (Wendy Ann)..$650.00 – 950.00
    10", #1141, 1991 – 1992 only, Portrette, blue/white gown................................$80.00
    21", #2195, 1959 only year this head used, authorized by Disney, blue satin brocade, net cape, gold tiara ....$850.00 up
    16", #1895, same head as 21" on Elise body, authorized by Disney $650.00
    10" h.p., 1959 only, authorized by Disney, blue gown (Cissette), flat feet.........$325.00
    14" plastic/vinyl, #1495, #1595, 1971 – 1985 (14-year production), Classic Series,

Sleeping Beauty, 10", 1959 (Cissette). Taffeta gown with gold cape. Original crown. Unusual flat feet, wears vinyl shoes. $325.00.

Slumbermate, 12", 1940s, composition and cloth body. $250.00 up.

Smarty, 12", #1140, 1962, vinyl head with rooted hair. All original pink cotton dress. $275.00.

Snow White, 14", #1455, 1967 – 1977 (Mary Ann). Disney crest colors. $250.00.

gold gown (Mary Ann)	$75.00
14", #1596, 1986 – 1990, Classic Series, blue gown (Mary Ann)	$80.00
14", #87010, 1996, pink and gold ball gown (Mary Ann)	$80.00
8", #14543, 1995, Brothers Grimm Series, blue with silver crown	$65.00
8", #13600, 1997 – 2000, blue satin gown, spinning wheel	$65.00
16", #25325, 2000, gold and lilac long ballet costume	$125.00
8", #30680, 2001 – 2005, blue gown, lace and rose trim	$80.00
16", #25325, 2001, lilac ballerina costume	$125.00
10", #36570, 2004, pink satin ball gown, three 2" fairy figures	$125.00
9", #37820, 2005 – 2006 – 2007, vinyl, pink satin dress	$35.00
8", #42435, 2006 – 2008, long blue dress	$85.00
10", #48665, 2008, Disney, blue long dress, gold crown	$120.00

Sleeping Beauty's Prince — 8", #13650, 1999 – 2000 (Wendy), bend knees, purple costume....$80.00
Sleigh Riding Wendy — 8", #35650, 2003 – 2004, plaid vintage costume, sleigh, plush horse..$160.00
Slumbermate — 11" – 12" cloth/compo., 1940s .... **$250.00 up**
    21" compo./cloth, 1940s .... $475.00 up
    13" vinyl/cloth, 1951 only .... $250.00 up
Slumber Party — 8", #48175, 2008, Wendy, bear, dog, cat, sleeping bag $100.00
Slumber Party Chloe — 14", #30065, 2001, pajamas, sleeping bag $60.00
Smart Style Shadow Cissette — 10", #42778, 2005 .... $125.00
Smarty — 12" plastic/vinyl, #1160, #1136, 1962 – 1963 .... **$275.00**
    1963 only, "Smarty & Baby" $350.00
    1963 only, with boy "Artie" in case with wardrobe $950.00
Smee — 8", #442, 1993, #140442, 1994, Storybook Series (Peter Pan), wears glasses $60.00
Smiley — 20" cloth/vinyl, 1971 only (Happy) $225.00
Smokey Tail — cloth/felt, 1930s $700.00
Snap, Crackle & Pop Set — 8", #12120, 1998 – 1999, Rice Krispies Dolls set $200.00
Snips and Snails — 8", #31330, 2000 – 2002, sweater, jeans, dog $65.00
Snoopy Beagle Scout — 8" dog, #38810, 2004, with Woodstock $70.00
Snowball Fun — 8", #46200, 2007, fur coat, snowball $70.00
Snowboarding in Aspen — 8", #45475, 2006 – 2007, snowboard, pink coat $85.00
Snowflake — 10", #1167, 1993 only, Portrette, ballerina dressed in white/gold outfit (Cissette) .$75.00
Snowflake Symposium — (see M.A.D.C. under Special Events/Exclusives)
Snow Queen — 10", #1130, 1991 – 1992 only, Portrette, silver/white gown (Cisette) $100.00
    8", #14548, Hans Christian Andersen Series, white with gold trim $70.00
    8", #32150, 2000 – 2002, white gown, fur-trimmed robe $80.00
Snow White — 13" compo., 1937 – 1939, painted eyes (Princess Elizabeth) $450.00
    12" compo., 1939 – 1940 (Princess Elizabeth) $450.00
    13" compo., 1939 – 1940, sleep eyes (Princess Elizabeth) $475.00
    16" compo., 1939 – 1942 (Princess Elizabeth) $550.00
    18" compo., 1939 – 1940 (Princess Elizabeth) $750.00
    14" – 15" h.p., 1952 only (Margaret) $750.00
    18" – 23", 1952 only .... $800.00 – 1,200.00
    21" h.p., rare (Margaret) .... $1,200.00 up
    14", #1455, 1967 – 1977, Disney crest colors (Mary Ann) $250.00
    8" h.p., 1972 – 1977, Disney crest colors (Wendy) $300.00
    8", #495, 1990 – 1992 only, Storyland Series (Wendy) $80.00
    8", #14545, 1995, Brothers Grimm Series, crest colors but with red bodice, #13800, 1997 – 2005....$80.00
    12", 1990 (see Disney Annual Showcase of Dolls under Special Events/Exclusives)
    14" plastic/vinyl, #1455, #1555, 1970 – 1985 (15-year production), Classic Series,
        white gown (Mary Ann) $100.00
      #1556, #1557, 1986 – 1992, ecru & gold gown, red cape (Mary Ann, Louisa) $90.00
    14", #14300, 1995, crest colors but red bodice (Louisa) $100.00
    14", #87013, 1996, Snow White's Trunk Set (Mary Ann) $100.00
    10", Disney crest colors (see Disney Annual Showcase of Dolls under Special Events/Exclusives)
    14", #28615, 2001, white gown, red cape $125.00

10", #35520, 2002 – 2004 (Cissette), Disney colors, gift set with seven 5" vinyl dwarfs $250.00

9", #37815, 2004 – 2006 – 2007, vinyl, Disney colors $35.00

8", #42445, 2006 – 2008, yellow skirt, red striped top $65.00

16", #48650, 2008, blue top, yellow skirt, cape $150.00

Snow White's Prince — 8", #14639, 1996 ....$65.00

Snow White Wedding — 8", #30460, 2001 – 2002, white gown, red cape, flower coat............$85.00

So Big — 22" cloth/vinyl, 1968 – 1975, painted eyes...$225.00

18", #30310, 2001, cloth, Mary Engelbreit $45.00

Soccer Boy — 8", #16350, sports outfit with soccer ball, 1997 – 1998, Girl, #16341 ....$60.00 each

Sock Hop 1950 — 8", #17780, 1999, poodle skirt $75.00

Soda Shop Coca-Cola — 8", #38695, 2004 – 2005, with glass and chair................................$80.00

Soldier — 14" compo., 1943 – 1944 (Wendy Ann) $375.00

17" compo., 1942 – 1945 (Wendy Ann) $850.00

Some Bunny Loves Me — 8", #48530, 2008, plush bunny $80.00

So Lite Baby or Toddler — 20" cloth, 1930 – 1940s ....$375.00 up

Sophie — 10", #28301, 2002 – 2003, green checked dress, sweater $40.00

10", #35815, 2003, Fun Loving, blue sweater...$40.00

Sorcerer's Apprentice — 8", #42640, 2006, red cape, broom $80.00

Sound of Music —

Large set, 1965 – 1970

14", #1404, Louisa (Mary Ann), #1405 Liesl $250.00

12", #1107 Friedrich (Janie or Smarty)...**$250.00**

14", #1403 Brigitta (Mary Ann) $225.00

12" Marta, 12" Gretl (Smarty or Janie) **$225.00**

17", #1706 Maria (Elise or Polly) $275.00

Full set of seven dolls..$1,200.00

Sound of Music, Marta, 12", 1965 – 1970 (Janie). Large set. $225.00.

Small set, 1971 – 1973

12" Maria (Nancy Drew) $300.00

8", #801 Gretl (Wendy Ann) $175.00

8", #802 Marta, #807 Friedrich (Wendy Ann) $225.00

10" Brigitta (Cissette) $185.00

10" Liesl (Cissette) $225.00

10" Louisa (Cissette) $250.00

Set of seven dolls...$1,200.00

Dressed in sailor suits and tagged, dates unknown

17" Maria (Elise or Polly) $500.00

14" Louisa (Mary Ann) $500.00

10" Friedrich (Smarty), 10" Marta $375.00

14" Brigitta (Mary Ann), 14" Liesl $375.00

10" Gretl (Smarty) $350.00

Set of seven dolls...$2,700.00 up

12", 1965, Brigitta in sailor suit (Lissy) ....$800.00 up

12", 1965, Brigitta in Alpine outfit (Lissy) $650.00

All in same outfits: red skirt, white attached blouse, black vest that ties in front with gold cord,

very rare ....$500.00 – 800.00 ea.

Reintroduced 1992 – 1993

8", #390, #391, 1992 – 1993 only, Gretl and Kurt (boy in sailor suit)..............................$125.00

8", #390, #392, 1992 – 1994, Brigitta $100.00

8", #394, 1993 only, Friedrich dressed in green/white playsuit $100.00

8", #393, 1993 only, Marta in sailor dress **$175.00**

10", 1992 – 1993 only, Maria (Cissette), 10", 1993 only, Liesl $125.00

12", 1992 only, Maria Bride (Nancy Drew) $125.00

10", Maria at Abbey, dressed in nun's outfit (Cissette), 1993 only $125.00

Reintroduced 1998

8", #14060, Gretl Von Trapp (Wendy), green/gray sailor suit...$85.00

8", #14050, Marta Von Trapp (Maggie), sailor suit $85.00

Sound of Music, Gretl, 12", 1965 – 1970 (Janie). Large set. $225.00.

Sound of Music, Friedrich, 12", #1107, 1965 – 1970 (Janie). Large set. $250.00.

9", #14040, Brigitta Von Trapp (Wendy), sailor outfit..................................$100.00
10", #14030, Captain Von Trapp (Cissette), gray Tyrolean suit......................$125.00
10", #13890, Maria at the Abbey (Cissette), navy dress, guitar $125.00
10", #13870, Mother Superior (Cissette), black and white nun habit $125.00
10", #13880, Maria Travel Ensemble (Cissette), pleated skirt, bolero................$125.00
9", #14020, Friedrich Von Trapp (Maggie), blue and gray sailor suit $85.00
10", #14160, Louisa Von Trapp (Wendy), blue/gray pleated sailor suit $100.00
10", #14090, Kurt Von Trapp (Wendy), sailor uniform..................................$100.00
10", #14170, Liesl Von Trapp (Cissette), blue and gray sailor outfit.................$100.00

South American — 7" compo., 1938 – 1943 (Tiny Betty)........................$325.00
   9" compo., 1939 – 1941 (Little Betty) $325.00
Southern Belle — 10", #25985, 2000, long white gown with lace, limited to 2,000....................$150.00
Southern Belle or Girl — 8" h.p., SLNW, 1953, white dress,
    straw hat with pink silk roses .... **$900.00 up**
   8" h.p., #370, 1954 (Wendy Ann)..$1,000.00 up
   8" h.p., #437, #410, 1956, pink or blue/white striped gown (Wendy Ann)......$1,100.00 up
   8" h.p., #385, 1963 only (Wendy Ann) $650.00
   12" h.p., 1963 only (Lissy)..$1,600.00 up
   21" h.p./vinyl arms, #2155, 1965, blue gown with wide pleated hem (Jacqueline) $1,600.00
   21", #2170, 1967, white gown with green ribbon trim $450.00
   10" h.p., #1170, 1968, white gown with green ribbon through three rows of lace (Cissette)....$400.00
   1969, white gown with four rows of lace, pink sash (Cissette) $450.00
   #1185, 1970, white gown with red ribbon sash (Cissette) $300.00
   #1185 (#1184 in 1973), 1971 – 1973, white gown with green ribbon sash $275.00
   10", #48390, 2008, white long dress, white hat with black tulle..................$130.00
Southern Flower Girl — 8", #25980, 2000, long pink gown, basket, limited to 2,800 ....$90.00
Southern Girl — 11" – 14" compo., 1940 – 1943 (Wendy Ann) ....$375.00 – 750.00 up
   17" – 21" compo., 1940 – 1943 (Wendy Ann)...................$700.00 – 950.00
Southern Miss — 8", #45275, 2006, pink organdy, straw hat $100.00
Southern Rose Charmer — 10", #48385, 2008, pink long dress, straw hat $130.00
Southern Symposium — (see M.A.D.C. under Special Events/Exclusives)
Spanish — 7" – 8" compo., 1935 – 1939 (Tiny Betty), 9" compo., 1936 – 1940 (Litte Betty)......$325.00
Spanish Boy — 8" h.p., BK and BKW, #779, 1964 – 1968 (Wendy Ann).................$275.00
Spanish Girl — 8" h.p., BKW, #795, #395, 1962 – 1965, three-tiered skirt (Wendy Ann) $125.00
   8" h.p., BK, #795, 1966 – 1972, three-tiered skirt $90.00
   8" straight legs, #0795, #595, 1973 – 1975, three-tiered skirt, marked "ALEX" $60.00
   8" straight legs, #595, 1976 – 1982, three-tiered skirt, marked "Alexander" $60.00
   8" straight legs, #595, 1983 – 1985, two-tiered skirt $50.00
   8" straight legs, #541, 1986 – 1990, white with red polka dots (1986 – 1987 white face).........$55.00
   8" straight legs, #541, 1990 – 1992, all red tiered skirt.........................$50.00
   8" h.p., #110545, 1994 – 1995, red, two-tiered polka dot gown................$50.00
   8" h.p., #24160, 1999 – 2000, red rose and black gown $65.00
   8", #35605, 2003 – 2004, red satin outfit, plush ball...........................$75.00
   8", #47835, 2008, red tiered gown, castanets $75.00
Spanish Matador — 8", #530, 1992 – 1993 only (Wendy) $60.00
Sparkle Fairy — 8", #38615, 2004 – 2005, pink dress with wings................$85.00
Sparkling Sapphire — 10", #32080, 2000 – 2002, long red and blue gown $150.00
Special Girl — 23" – 24" cloth/comp., 1942 – 1946...............................$500.00
Speedy Service — 8", #42105, 2006, red striped outfit, tray with food.............$80.00
Spring — 14", 1993, Changing Seasons, doll and four outfits $100.00
   5", #25850, 2000, porcelain, pink dress, straw hat $60.00
Spring Angel — 10", #28370, 2001 – 2002, long gown, feather wings...............$100.00
Spring Bouquet — 8", #30890, 2001 – 2003, white ballet outfit, green top, blonde $60.00
Spring Chick-A-Dee — 8", #42265, 2006 – 2007, yellow dress, baby chick...........$80.00
Spring Garden Flower Girl — 8", #34390, 2002 – 2003, flower-trimmed dress $80.00
Spring Parade Lissy — 12", #42050, 2006, coat, straw hat $100.00

Sound of Music, Marta, 8", #393, 1993 (Wendy). $175.00.

Spring Promenade — 10", #27810, 2001, long white dress, straw hat $125.00
Spring Splendor — 8", #42830, 2006, pink dress, Chaos bear $80.00
Stardust Greetings Angel — 10", #39930, 2005, red angel costume $100.00
Starlight Angel — 10", #10790, 1999 – 2000 (Cissette), star-accented gown $125.00
Starlight, Starbright — 8", #43020, 2006 – 2007, pink dress with stars...........................$50.00
Starr, Belle — 10", #48205, 2008, black long coat, hat, gun.......................................$130.00
Stars and Stripes — 10", #33740, 2002, red striped overskirt $125.00
Stars and Stripes Forever — 8", #40625, 2005, with flag garland...............................$60.00
Stepmother — 8", 1997, #13820, velvet cape, satin dress $75.00
Stick Piggy — 12", 1997, #10030, sailor outfit $80.00
Stilts — 8", #320, 1992 – 1993 only, clown on stilts...$80.00
Story Princess — 15" – 18" h.p., 1954 – 1956 (Margaret, Cissy, Binnie) ....$600.00 – 950.00
   8" h.p., #892, 1956 only (Wendy Ann) ....$1,300.00 up
Straw Piggy — 12", 1997, #10020, plaid pants, straw hat $80.00
Strawberry Shortcake — 8", #47360, 2008, Maggie, strawberry hat, plush cat.....................$80.00
   18", #47430, 2008, cloth, strawberry hat $45.00
Strolling Through London — 8", #45450, 2006 – 2007, Maggie, plush dog $80.00
Stuffy (Boy) — h.p., 1952 – 1953 (Margaret) ....$850.00 up
Suellen — 14" – 17" compo., 1937 – 1938 (Wendy Ann)......................................$975.00 up
   12", 1990 only, yellow multi-tiered skirt, Scarlett Series (Nancy Drew)....................$80.00
   8" pink bodice, floral skirt, apron, #160645, 1994 – 1995.................................$75.00
Suellen O'Hara — 8", #15200, 1999 ....$90.00
Suffragette 1910 — 10", #17730, 1999...$100.00
Sugar and Spice — 8", #13530, 1998 – 1999, pink and white lace dress $80.00
   8", #32145, 2000 – 2002, three rows of ribbon on skirt, lollipop $60.00
Sugar Darlin' — 14" – 18" cloth/vinyl, 1964 only.......................................$65.00 – 125.00
   24", 1964 only $150.00
   Lively, 14", 18", 24", 1964 only, knob makes head and limbs move.................$125.00 – 250.00
Sugar Plum Fairy — 10", #1147, 1992 – 1993 only, Portrette, lavender ballerina $80.00
   8" (Wendy), 1999 – 2000, #12640, pink satin and tulle $75.00
   16", #80780, 2000, long ballet costume from The Nutcracker................................$125.00
Sugar Tears — 12" vinyl baby, 1964 only (Honeybea) $100.00
Sulky Sue — 8", #445, 1988 – 1990, marked "Alexander" (Wendy Ann).........................$60.00
Summer — 14", 1993, Changing Seasons, doll and four outfits $75.00
   5", #25855, 2000, porcelain, blue dress, straw hat..$60.00
Summer Angel — 8", #27640, 2001 – 2002, multicolored tulle, blonde...........................$80.00
Summer Cherry Picking — 8", #48555, 2008, white dress, basket of cherries $50.00
Summer Day Dreaming — 8", #42835, 2006, with Chaos bear $90.00
Summer Garden Vintage — 8", #28915, 2002 – 2003, with basket of flowers, blue striped pinafore ..$75.00
Summer of Cissette — 10", #45230, 2006, navy dot dress, red hat...............................$125.00
Summer Sailing — 8", #40640, 2005, white dress...$70.00
Summer Smiles Fairy — 8", #40765, 2005, pink and green costume...............................$80.00
Summers Past — 8", #40595, 2005, print dress $80.00
Summer Sweetie Pie — 8", #40450, Maggie, 2005, red checked dress............................$75.00
Sunbeam — 11", 16", 19", 1951 only, newborn infant, clean and in fair condition........$100.00 – 225.00
   16", 20", 24" cloth/vinyl, 1950, Divine-a-Lite Series (reg. #573, #313), scowling expression ... $125.00 up
Sunbonnet Sue — 9" compo., 1937 – 1940 (Little Betty) $300.00
Sunday Best — 8", #38845, 2004 – 2005, dress with flowers, hat................................$85.00
Sunday's Child — 8", #27800, 2001, angel costume $100.00
Sunflower Clown — 40" all cloth, 1951 only, flower eyes ....$850.00 up
Sun-Maid Raisin Girl — 8", #26190, 2000, red costume..$65.00
Sunny — (see Collectors United/C.U. under Special Events/Exclusives)
Sunrise, Sunset — 8", #45200, 2006 – 2007, pink and blue dress $50.00
Susie Q — cloth, 1940 – 1942 ....$750.00
   8", #14590, 1995, Toy Shelf Series, yarn braids and pink polka dot dress with green jacket....$65.00
Suzy — 12" plastic/vinyl, #1150, 1970 only (Janie) $325.00

Southern Girl, 8", SLNW, 1953 (Wendy). Organdy and lace dress. Hat and dress trimmed with silk roses. $900.00.

Swan Lake — 16", #22040, 1998, Odette in white tutu $150.00
    10", #35870, 2003, white tutu, feathers...$125.00
    10", #42075, 2006, Odette, white ballet outfit, #42080, Odile, black ballet outfit.....$90.00
Swan Princess — 10", #14106, 1995 only, Fairy Tales Series $85.00
    8", #33690, 2002, white dress, crown, limited to 1,000 ....$100.00
    8", #40310, 2005 – 2006, long white dress, pink trim $85.00
Sweden (Swedish) — 8" h.p., BKW, #392, #792, 1961 – 1965 (Wendy Ann) $125.00
    8" h.p., BK, #792, 1966 – 1972 ....$90.00
    8" straight legs, #0792, #592, 1973 – 1975, marked "Alex" $70.00
    8" straight legs, #592, #539, #521, 1976 – 1989, marked "Alexander" $60.00
    8", 1986, #580, reintroduced 1991 only..$60.00
    BKW with Maggie $150.00
    8", #35980, 2003 – 2004, print dress, red hat, wooden horse $75.00
Swedish — 7" compo., 1936 – 1940 (Tiny Betty) $325.00
    9" compo., 1937 – 1941 (Little Betty)..$350.00
Sweet Baby — 18½" – 20" cloth/latex, 1948 only ....$75.00 – 150.00
    14", 1983 – 1984 (Sweet Tears)..$65.00
    14", reissued 1987, 1987 – 1993 (1991 has no bottle) (Sweet Tears) $75.00
    14", 1990 – 1992 only (1991 has bottle), in carry case..................................$125.00
    14", reintroduced 1993 only, pink striped jumper or dress................................$65.00
Sweet Harmony Angel — 8", #40290, 2005, lavender costume........................$85.00
Sweetheart of the Corn — 8", #46100, 2007 – 2008, checked dress, Tony Tiger,
    Toucan Sam, cereal spoon, "vintage Kellog's" $85.00
Sweetie Baby — 22", 1962 only $125.00
Sweetie Walker — 23", 1962 only ....$275.00 up
Sweet Innocence — 8", #41985, 2006, white dress, hat, tan bear......................$90.00
Sweet Irish Dancer — 8", #36495, red hair, green decorated dress, 2003 – 2004 ....$65.00
Sweet Kisses for Grandma — 8", #36155, 2003 – 2004, white dress, red trim.......$65.00
Sweet Sentiments — 8", #41990, 2006, with Chaos bear...............................$100.00
Sweet Sixteen — 14", #1554, 1991 – 1992 only, Classic Series (Louisa) $90.00
    10", #21060, 1997, pink silk dress, lace stole $85.00
    8", #35985, 2004 – 2005, black velvet top, tulle skirt $80.00
Sweet Steps — 18" #41345, 2007, Toddler Baby, pink and white outfit................$200.00
Sweet Sunflower — 8", #46470, 2007, Asian, blue print dress...........................$70.00
Sweet Tears — 9" vinyl, 1965 – 1974 ....$85.00
    9" with layette in box, 1965 – 1973 ....$175.00
    14", 1967 – 1974, in trunk/trousseau; 1965 – 1974, in window box.................$175.00
    14", 1979, with layette $150.00
    14", 1965 – 1982; 16", 1965 – 1971...$65.00
Sweet Violet — 18" h.p., 1951 – 1954 (Cissy) ....$900.00 up
Swiss — 7" compo., 1936 (Tiny Betty)...$325.00
    9" compo., 1935 – 1938 (Little Betty) $325.00
    10" h.p., 1962 – 1963 (Cissette)...$825.00
Switzerland — 8" h.p., BKW, #394, #794, 1961 – 1965...................................$125.00
    8" h.p., BK, #794, 1966 – 1972 ....$90.00
    8" h.p., straight legs, #0794, #594, 1973 – 1975, marked "Alex" $70.00
    8" h.p., straight legs, #594, #540, #518, 1976 – 1989, marked "Alexander".......$60.00
    8", #546, 1986, #518, 1988 – 1990, costume change...............................$60.00
    8" BKW, Maggie smile face $150.00
    8", #25795, 2000, pink and white costume with watch $65.00
Symposium — (see M.A.D.C. under Special Events/Exclusives)
Taft, Helen — 1988, fifth set Presidents' Ladies/First Ladies Series (Louisa) $100.00
Take Home Coca-Cola — 8", #40310, 2005, white dress, coat and hat, six-pack Coca-Cola.....$90.00
Take to the Skies — 10", #47015, Cissette, 2007, silver stewardess outfit, hat, boots...............$100.00
Tara — #14990, 1998, two-sided home of Scarlett...$100.00
Taurus — 8", #21340, 1998 – brown and white bull costume $85.00

Swedish Boy, 9" (Little Betty), all composition with side-painted eyes. Tagged: Madame Alexander N.Y. U.S.A. $350.00.

Teacher's Pet — 8", #46115, 2007, red plaid coat, hat, bag, apple $70.00
Team Canada — 8", #24130, 1998 – 1999, hockey skater...$75.00
Team Mates — 8", #38885, 2004 – 2005, with dog, baseball, and bat...$85.00
Tea Rose Cissette — 10", #22370 – 1998, floral silk cocktail dress $100.00
Tea Time with Muffy — 8", #39990, 2005, with Muffy bear, teapot, and cup $125.00
Tea Time with Old Country Roses — 8", #46175, 2007, tea bag holder...$80.00
Teeny Twinkle — 1946 only, cloth with flirty eyes...$525.00
Teeter-Totter Fun — 8", #46730, 2007, toy, Chaos the Bear $80.00
Tennis — 8" h.p., BKW, #415, #632 (Wendy Ann)...$450.00
Tennis Boy — 8", #16331, 1997, Girl, #16320 ....$60.00
Tess — 10", #28405, 2001, green, pink vintage gown $125.00
Texas — 8", #313, 1991 only, Americana...$65.00
Texas Shriner — (see Shriner's First Ladies' Luncheon under Special Events/Exclusives)
Thailand — 8" h.p., BK, #767, 1966 – 1972 (Wendy) $90.00
    8" straight legs, #0767, #567, 1973 – 1975, marked "Alex"...$75.00
    8" straight legs, #567, 1976 – 1989, marked "Alexander" $65.00
    8" straight legs, #39770, 2005, Asian, pointed hat $75.00
Thanksgiving — 8", #35680, 2003, sweater, pumpkin print skirt, turkey...$65.00
Thank You — 8", #21110, 1997 – 1998, comes with a thank-you card...$60.00
That Girl — 10", #26345, 2000 (Cissette), navy blue suit...$90.00
"There's No Place Like Home" Doll House — trunk set, #13260, 1997 – 1999...$150.00
There Was a Little Girl — 14", #24611, 1995, Nursery Rhymes Series (Mary Ann)...$70.00
Thinking of You — 8", #21500, 1998 – 1999, print dress, straw hat...$65.00
This Little Light of Mine — 8", #39760, 2005, long beige dress, candle...$90.00
Thomas, Marlo — 17" plastic/vinyl, 1967 only (Polly) ....$650.00 up
Three Blind Mice — 8", #39945, 2005 – 2006, with three mice $85.00
Three Little Kittens — 8", #26970, 2000 – 2001, blue plaid dress, three kittens $90.00
    8", #45445, Maggie, three plush kittens, 2006 – 2007 ....$90.00
Three Little Pigs and Wolf — compo., 1938 – 1939, must be mint...$675.00 up, ea.
Three Little Pigs Set — 12", #10000, 1997, bricks, straw, and sticks Pigs...$250.00
    8", #33656, 2003, three pigs, each with house bank $150.00
Three Wise Men Set — 8", #19480, 1997 – 1999, Nativity Set...$400.00
Thumbelina & Her Lady — 8" and 21" porcelain, 1992 –1993, limited to 2,500 sets $400.00
Thursday's Child — 8", #27785, 2001, comes with suitcase $80.00
Tibet — 8" h.p., #534, 1993 only...$60.00
8", #39815, 2005 – 2006, Asian, with yak $85.00
Tickled Pink — 8", #45675, 2007 – 2008, pink checked dress...$50.00
Tierney, Gene — 14" – 17" compo., 1945, must be mint (Wendy Ann) ....$3,300.00 up
Tiger Lily — 8", #469, 1992 – 1993 only, Storybook Series (Peter Pan) (Wendy Ann) $85.00
Time Out for Coca-Cola Sock Hop — 10", #26225, 2000...$100.00
Timmy Toddler — 23" plastic/vinyl, 1960 – 1961...$150.00
    30", 1960 only...$250.00
Tinker Bell — 11" h.p., #1110, 1969 only, Peter Pan Series (Cissette)...$400.00
    Magic wand and wings, #13960 in 1998 – 2000...$75.00
    14", #87009, 1996 (Mary Ann)...$90.00
    8", #30675, 2001, pink/blue costume, lace wings, limited to 2,500 pieces...$75.00
    8", #34100, 2002 – 2005, white costume, silver wand...$80.00
    5", #30455, 2002, porcelain, pink and blue costume...$65.00
    10", #31750, 2003, green costume, shoes, gold wand...$125.00
    5", #38325, 2004, vinyl, petite, with wand...$25.00
    8", #42245, 2006 – 2008, lavender dress, wand, wings...$85.00
    10", #48700, 2008, green tulip dress, white wings...$70.00
Tinkles — 8", #10400, 1995, Christmas Series $60.00
Tin Man — 8", #13211, 1998 – 2006, Wizard of Oz Series, silver face and costume...$70.00
    5", #28685, 2001 – 2003, porcelain...$75.00
    5", #36340, 2005, silver costume...$25.00

Tibet, 8", #39815, 2005 – 2006
(Asian). With plush yak. $85.00.

9", #39780, 2005 – 2007, silver costume......$35.00

8", #46340, 2007 – 2008, silver costume, heart clock, silver hat......$70.00

Tin Woodsman — 8", #432 in 1993, #140432 in 1994 – 1995......$85.00

Tiny Betty — 7" compo., 1935 – 1942......$325.00 up

Tiny Betty Christmas — 7", #49025, 2008, red skirt, white top, blue jacket......$30.00

Tiny Betty Easter — 7", #48585, 2008, pink dress with rickrack on skirt......$30.00

Tiny Betty 1st Communion — 7" #49020, 2008, white dress, veil......$30.00

Tiny Betty Halloween — 7", #49015, 2008, orange dress, black trim......$30.00

Tiny Betty Happy Birthday — 7", #48330, 2008, reintroduced, plastic......$30.00

Tiny Betty St. Patrick's Day — 7", #48440, 2008, green dress with shamrock......$30.00

Tiny Tim — 7" compo., 1934 – 1937 (Tiny Betty)......$325.00 up

14" compo., 1938 – 1940 (Wendy Ann)......$625.00

16" cloth, early 1930s......$700.00 up

8", #18001, 1996, Dickens (Wendy Ann)......$65.00

Tiny Treasure — 8", #41975, 2006, beige dress, green bow......$90.00

Tippi Ballerina — (see Collectors United/C.U. under Special Events/Exclusives)

Tippy Toe — 16" cloth, 1940s......$600.00

Tisket, A Tasket, A — 8", #48640, 2008, print dress, straw hat, basket......$75.00

Toast to Madame Alexander — 8", #36145, 2003, long pink dress with fur at neck and hem, champagne bottle......$85.00

Today I Feel Excited and Sad — 8", #33685, 2002, cloth......$35.00

Today I Feel Silly — 14", #80710, 2000 – 2004, dressed cloth doll with four interchangeable faces...$50.00

Today I Feel Silly and Angry — 8", #33680, cloth, includes cat......$35.00

To Grandma's House — 8", #42365, 2006 – 2007, red coat, hat......$80.00

Token of My Love, A — 8", #48145, 2008, pink dress, Madame pin......$70.00

To Market, To Market — 8", #38775, 2004 – 2006, with pig, red pinafore......$50.00

Tommy — 12" h.p., 1962 only (Lissy)......$700.00

Tommy Bangs — h.p., 1952 only, Little Men Series (Maggie, Margaret)......$875.00

Tommy Snooks — 8", #447, 1988 – 1991, Storybook Series......$55.00

Tommy Tittlemouse — 8", #444, 1988 – 1991, Storybook Series (Maggie)......$55.00

Tom Sawyer — 8" h.p., #491, 1989 – 1990, Storybook Series (Maggie Mixup)......$60.00

Tony Sarg Marionettes — (see Marionettes)

Tooth Fairy — 10" Portrette, 1994 only......$75.00

8", #10389 – 10391, 1995 only, Special Occasions Series, three hair colors......$65.00

8", #21550, 1999 – 2000, pink sparkling outfit, satin pillow......$65.00

8", #30660, 2001 – 2002, lavender costume, silver bag, crown, white wings......$70.00

8", #42735, 2006, pink costume, pouch, certificate......$80.00

To Oz Bear Set — #33634, 2002, four 3" bears......$100.00 set

To Oz Cowardly Lion — 8", #33632, 2002, with 3" bear......$95.00

To Oz Dorothy — 8", #33630, 2002, with 3" plush bear......$100.00

To Oz Scarecrow — 8", #33633, 2002, with 3" plush bear......$90.00

To Oz Tin Man — 8", #33631, 2002, with 3" plush bear......$90.00

Top O' the Morning — 8", #39810, 2005, with green bear......$80.00

Topsy-Turvy — Compo. with Tiny Betty heads, 1935 only......$325.00 up

With Dionne Quint head, 1936 only......$350.00

Cinderella — #14587, 1995 only, two-headed, one side gown; other side dress with apron ...$100.00

Red Riding Hood — 8", #14555 (three-way) Red Riding Hood, Grandma, Wolf......$100.00

Wicked Stepmother — 8", #14640, 1996, evil witch, stepmother......$90.00

Toulouse-Lautrec — 21", #2250, 1986 – 1987 only, black/pink outfit......$250.00

Toy Box Wendy — 8", #36270, 2003 – 2004, print dress, toybox with toys and books......$90.00

Toy Soldier — 8", #481, 1993, #140481, 1994, #13210 – 1998, white face, red dots on cheeks....$70.00

Toy Soldier Rockette — 16", #47895, 2008, red jacket, white pants......$130.00

Train Journey — 8" h.p., #486, 1955, white wool jacket, hat, red plaid dress......$550.00

Trapeze Artist — 10", #1133, 1990 – 1991, Portrette (Cissette)......$75.00

Treasured Memories — 8", #46135, 2007, blue dress, pin......$85.00

Treena Ballerina — 15" – 21" h.p., 1952 only, must be near mint (Margaret)......$650.00 – 875.00

Tree Topper — 8" (half doll only), #850, 1992 only, red/gold dress.................................$100.00

    8" (half doll only), #852, 1992 – 1994, Angel Lace with multi-tiered ivory lace skirt (Wendy)....$100.00

    8" (half doll only), #853, 1993 – 1994, red velvet/gold and green (Wendy) $110.00

    10" (half doll only), #854, 1993 – 1994; #54854, 1995, pink Victorian (Cissette) $125.00

    8" (half doll only), #540855, 1994; #540855 – 1995, all antique white (Wendy)......................$90.00

    8", #84857, 1995 – 1996, Yuletide Angel dressed in red and gold (Wendy), #19600, 1997.....$100.00

    8", #84859, 1995 – 1996, Christmas Angel dressed in white and gold (Wendy) $100.00

    10", #54860, Glorious Angel dressed in red and white, gold crown, #19590, 1997 – 1998 (Cissette)..$100.00

    10", #19610, 1997 – 1998, Heavenly Angel, gold and ivory costume (Wendy)......................$100.00

    10", Glistening Angel, 1998 – 1999, #19700 (Wendy), silver brocade $90.00

    10", Winter Lights, #20000, 1999 – 2000 (Wendy), AC illuminated..................................$100.00

    10", Holiday Trimmings, 2000 – 2001, #2704 (Wendy), red plaid gown $100.00

    10", Golden Dream, 2000, #27055, gold and white gown $90.00

    10", Caroler, 2000, #27045, red jacket, fur muff..$90.00

    10", Star, 2000, #26100, gold star, tassels...$75.00

    8", Shining Bright fiber optic angel, #28265, 2001 – 2002, white, gold (Wendy), fur wings.....$90.00

    10", Starburst Angel, #28535, 2001, red/gold gown (Wendy).......................................$100.00

    10", Peace on Earth, #33445, 2002 – 2003, red gown, feather wings $110.00

    8", Lighting the Christmas Tree, #35920, 2003, gold wings, white dress $100.00

Trellis Rose Flower Girl — 8", #28650, 2001 – 2002, long white dress...........................$80.00

Trick and Treat — (see Child at Heart Shop under Special Events/Exclusives)

Trip to the Candy Shoppe — 8", #46080, 2007, Maggie, candy cabinet with candy $95.00

Trip to the Moon — 8", #40385, 2005, Wendy, dog wearing space helmet $90.00

Triumphant Topaz — 10", #32165, 2000 – 2002, black and gold ball gown........................$125.00

Truman, Bess — 14", 1989 – 1990, sixth set Presidents' Ladies/First Ladies Series (Mary Ann)...$100.00

Tuesday's Child — 8", #27775, 2001, white dress, blue ribbon $80.00

Tunisia — 8", #514, 1989 only, marked "Alexander" (Wendy).....................................$65.00

Turkey — 8" h.p., BK, #787, 1968 – 1972 (Wendy)...$90.00

    8" straight legs, #0787, #587, 1973 – 1975, marked "Alex".......................................$65.00

    8" straight legs, #587, 1976 – 1986, marked "Alexander" $60.00

    8", #42525, 2006, red dress and hat, felt twirl $90.00

'Twas the Night Before Christmas — 8", #27305, 2001, long white gown............................$80.00

Tweedledee & Tweedledum — 14" cloth, 1930 – 1931 ....$750.00 ea.

    8" h.p., #13080, 1998 – 1999, checked pants, red jackets, propeller caps................................$150.00

Twelve Days of Christmas — 8", #35555, 2002 – 2005, with tree and ornaments,

    plaid dress, red pinafore $100.00

    5", #31745, 2003 – 2004, set of 12 dolls, display box $225.00

20's Bride — #14103, 1995, Nostalgia Series...$125.00

20's Traveler — 10", #1139, 1991 – 1992 only, Portrette, M.A. signature logo on box (Cissette) ...$150.00

25th Anniversary — (see Enchanted Doll House under Special Events/Exclusives)

Twilight Angel — 8", #10780 (Wendy), 1999 – 2000, white organza gown................................$90.00

Twinkle Toes — 8", #36905, 2003 – 2005, ballerina, bear with tutu $80.00

Twinkle, Twinkle Little Star — 8", #11630, 1997..$65.00

    8", #48835, 2008, navy dress, star on stick $70.00

Twirling Confetti — 8", 2003, #35075, pink tutu, flower trimmed $50.00

Twirling Rose — 8", #33145, 2002 – 2003, long blue ballet costume................................$65.00

Tyler, Julia — 1979 – 1981, second set Presidents' Ladies/First Ladies Series (Martha)..........$100.00

Tyrolean Boy and Girl* — 8" h.p., BKW (girl – #398, #798; boy – #399, #799), 1962 – 1965

    (Wendy Ann) ....$150.00 ea.

    8" h.p., BK (girl – #798; boy – #799), 1966 – 1972 ....$100.00 ea.

    8" straight legs (girl – #0798; boy – #0799), 1973, marked "ALEX" ....$75.00 ea.

    8" BKW (Maggie Mixup)..$150.00 ea

Ugly Betty — 18", #47450, 2008, cloth doll, check skirt, red cape...............................$45.00

    8", #47385, 2008 (Maggie), red cape, brown check skirt $70.00

Ugly Stepsister — 10" h.p., #13340, 1997 – 1998, Cinderella Series $80.00

    10", #45985, 2007, Cissette, pink ruffled ballet outfit...$120.00

Ukraine — 8", #34325, 2002 – 2003, cultural costume, with decorated egg, flower hat...............$70.00

Ultimate Angel — 21", #10770, 1999, blue silk and lace gown...$525.00

Uncle Henry — 8", #39915, 2005 – 2007, Wizard of Oz Series, #39915, 2006.......................$60.00

Uncle Sam — 8", #10353, 1995 only (Wendy) $65.00

    8" h.p., #24170, 1999 – 2000, astronaut costume, United States of America.............................$75.00

Unconditional Love — 8", #46105, 2007 – 2008, pink check dress, doll, bear, and carriage $95.00

Union Officer — 12", #634, 1990 – 1991, Scarlett Series (Nancy Drew)...................................$80.00

    Soldier, 8", #634, 1991 only, Scarlett Series...$125.00

United States — 8" h.p., #559, straight legs, 1974 – 1975, marked "Alex" $70.00

    8", #559, Alex mold, misspelled "Untied States" $90.00

    8" straight legs, #559, 1976 – 1987, marked "Alexander" $65.00

    8", #559, #516, 1988 – 1992 (Maggie) $60.00

    8", #11562, 1996, Statue of Liberty costume, #24000, 1997 – 1998 ....$65.00

United States Air Force — 8", #12000, 1998 (Wendy), uniform and flag.................................$85.00

United States Armed Forces Set — four dolls, five flags, flag stand....................................$350.00

United States Army — 8", #12010, 1998 (Wendy)...$85.00

United States Marines — 8", #12030, 1998 (Wendy)...$85.00

United States Navy — 8", #12020, 1998 (Wendy)..$85.00

U.S.A. — 8" h.p., #536, 1993 – 1994 (#110536) (also see Neiman-Marcus, Caroline's Adventures,

    under Special Events/Exclusives)...$75.00

    Las Vegas, 8", #28565, 2001, silver costume..$65.00

    Sacajawea, 8", #28575, 2001 – 2002, includes papoose...$85.00

Valentine Kisses — 8", #27050, 2000 – 2001, red and silver outfit...$65.00

Van Buren, Angelica — 1979 – 1981, second set Presidents' Ladies/First Ladies Series (Louisa) $100.00

Velvet Party Dress — 8" h.p., #389, 1957 only, very rare (Wendy Ann)........................... $2,000.00 up

Victoria — 21" compo., 1939, 1941, 1945 – 1946 (also see Flavia) (Wendy Ann) .... $2,000.00 up

    20" h.p., 1954 only, Me & My Shadow Series (Cissy) .... $2,000.00 up

    14" h.p., 1950 – 1951 (Margaret) $900.00

    18" h.p., 1954 only, Me & My Shadow Series, slate blue gown (Maggie)....................... $2,000.00 up

    8" h.p., #2030C, 1954 only, matches 18" doll (Wendy Ann) ....$1,300.00 up

    14" baby, 1975 – 1988, 1990 – 1997, 18" baby, 1966 only...$75.00

    18", reintroduced 1991 – 1993, 1997...$50.00 – 125.00

    20" baby, 1967 – 1989 ....$65.00

    20" 1986 only, dress, jacket, bonnet $75.00

    18" vinyl, 1998, velour romper, #29420 white, #29423 African-American $100.00

    14", "Mozart Music" Concertina, #26915, 2000, plays Mozart music $75.00

    18", "Mozart Music" Symphony, #26900, 2000, plays Mozart music $115.00

    14" – 18", 2002 – 2007, variety of outfits...$75.00 – 130.00

    14", #48015, #48020, 2008, painted head..$80.00 – 90.00

Victorian — 18" h.p., 1953 only, pink taffeta/black velvet gown, Glamour Girl Series (Margaret) ..$1,500.00 up

Victorian Bride — 10", #1148, 1992 only, Portrette..$100.00

    10", blue satin and lace gown...$100.00

Victorian Catherine — 16", #90010, porcelain, elaborate gown...$175.00

Victorian Christmas — 8", #19970, red velvet and lace..$90.00

Victorian Coca-Cola — 8", #36020, 2003 – 2004, red vintage dress and hat, Coke glass..........$80.00

Victorian Countess — 10", #28885, 2001, long white dress with lace $125.00

Victorian Girl 1954 — 10" h.p., 2000 (Cissette), remake of 1954 Victoria...............................$100.00

Victorians — 8" Adorable silk, #26875, 2000, flower adorned dress.......................................$100.00

    8" Charming silk, #25035, 2000 – 2001, white silk dress...$100.00

    8" Innocent silk, #25045, 2000 – 2001, white lace trimmed silk dress.............................$100.00

    8" Sophisticated silk, #26780, 2000 – 2001, lilac silk costume.......................................$90.00

    8" Sweet silk, #25040, 2000 – 2001, pink silk dress $85.00

    8" Marigold, #27805, 2001, short yellow dress, hat with lace...$75.00

    8" Sailorette, #33555, 2002 – 2003, pleated vintage costume $75.00

Victorian Little One — 8", #46090. 2007, pink and green dress $75.00

Victorian Skater — 10", #1155, 1993 – 1994, Portrette, red/gold/black outfit (Cissette)..........$150.00

Victorian Valentine — 8", #30615, 2000 – 2003, pink pleated dress, hat
trimmed with lace, valentine..$70.00
Vietnam — 8" h.p., #788, 1968 – 1969 (Wendy Ann)...$200.00
    8", #788, 1968 – 1969 (Maggie Mixup)..$225.00
    8", #505, reintroduced in 1990 – 1991 (Maggie)...$60.00
    8", #45210, 2006 – 2007, Asian face, green pants, pink top........................$60.00
Vintage Violet Silk Victorian — 8", #30405, 2001 – 2002, pink dress....................$90.00
Violet — (see Sweet Violet)
Violet — (Nutcracker Ballerina) 10" Portrette, 1994 only..................................$65.00
Violetta — 10", #1116, 1987 – 1988, all deep blue (Cissette) $60.00
Virgo — 8", #21380, pink pleated outfit, gold helmet $80.00
Visions of Sugarplums — 8", #37805, 2003 – 2004, red and green dress, sunglasses, lollipop ..$80.00
W.A.A.C. (Army) — 14" compo., 1943 – 1944 (Wendy Ann).............................$750.00 up
W.A.A.F. (Air Force) — 14" compo., 1943 – 1944 (Wendy Ann) ....$750.00 up
Waiting for Santa Boy — 8", #37090, 2003 – 2004, red p.j.'s, plush bear, cookies, milk...........$80.00
Waiting for Santa Girl — 8", #37085, 2003 – 2004, red p.j.'s, plush bear, cookies, milk $80.00
Wales — 8", #46325, 2007, checked outfit, plush Corgi dog................................$80.00
    8", #46325, 2008, checked dress, plush Welsh corgi $80.00
Walk in the Park — 8", #42195, 2006, with three dogs......................................$100.00
Waltz — 16", 1999, pink gown trimmed in marabou...$125.00
    8" h.p., #476, 1955 only (Wendy Ann) .... $700.00 up
Want — (see Ghost of Christmas Present) (sold as set)
Want to Come Over and Play — 8", #48185, 2008, blue dress, marionette, doll house $100.00
Washington, Martha — 1976 – 1978, first set Presidents' Ladies/First Ladies Series (Martha)...$150.00
Watchful Guardian Angel — 10", #10740, 1998 – 1999, blue/white outfit................$150.00
Watchful Guardian Angel Set — three dolls, bridge, gift card $300.00
W.A.V.E. (Navy) — 14" compo., 1943 – 1944 (Wendy Ann) ....$750.00 up
Wedding Rings Ring Bearer — 8", #36280, 2003, blonde, green and white costume..............$70.00
Wedding Wishes — 16", #28455, 2001, white gown with lace around hem, bouquet with red roses ...$150.00
Weeping Princess — 8", #11104, 1995 only, International Folk Tales (Maggie) $65.00
Welcome Home — Desert Storm, 8", 1991 only, mid-year introduction, boy or girl
    soldier, black or white..$50.00
    8", #38145, 2004, blue striped dress with "Welcome Home" banner $65.00
Wendy — 8", 1989, first doll offered to club members only (see M.A.D.C. under Special Events/Exclusives)
    5", #30350, 2001 – 2003, petite, pink checked dress $20.00
Wendy and Her Radio Flyer — 8", #42360, with bear, blanket, wagon, 2006 – 2007............$90.00
Wendy and Muffy — 8", #33635, 2004, bag with tiny bear $125.00
Wendy and the Yellow Brick Road — 8", #38720, 2004 – 2005 (Wendy)...............$80.00
Wendy Angel — 8" h.p., #404, 1954 (Wendy Ann) .... $850.00 up
Wendy Ann — 11" – 15" compo., 1935 – 1948 ....$350.00 – 575.00
    9" compo., 1936 – 1940, painted eyes...$375.00
    14", 1938 – 1939, in riding habit, molded hair or wig $450.00
    14", any year, swivel waist, molded hair or wig...$475.00
    17" – 21" compo., 1938 – 1944...$600.00 – 1,100.00
    14½" – 17" h.p., 1948 – 1949 ....$600.00 – 850.00
    16" – 22" h.p., 1948 – 1950 ....$575.00 – 975.00
    23" – 25" h.p., 1949 ....$850.00 up
    8", #79516, 1995, 100th anniversary, wearing dress, coat, and bonnet, limited production $90.00
Wendy Ann Felt — 12", #37945, 2004, molded felt doll, linen dress, special for the Toy Shoppe....$250.00
Wendy Ballerina — 8" (Wendy), 1999, pink trim on white lace tutu $65.00
(Wendy) Being Just Like Mommy — 8", #801, 1993, has baby carriage, #120801, 1994....$110.00
(Wendy) Being Prom Queen — #120808, 1994...$65.00
Wendy Bride — 14" – 22" compo., 1944 – 1945 (Wendy Ann) ....$325.00 – 675.00
    15" – 18" h.p., 1951 (Margaret)...$525.00 – 875.00
    20" h.p., 1956 (Cissy).. $950.00 up
    8" h.p., SLW, #475, 1955 (Wendy Ann)...$650.00

Wendy Builds a Snowman — 8", #39925, 2005 – 2007, with snowman.....................................$75.00
Wendy Cheerleader — 8", #16500, 1998, pleated skirt, red sweater $65.00
Wendy Elf — 8", #12818, 1995, Christmas Series...$65.00
Wendy (from Peter Pan) — 15" h.p., 1953 only (Margaret) ....$550.00 up
    14" plastic/vinyl, #1415, 1969 only (Mary Ann) $275.00
    8", #466 in 1991 – 1993; #140466 in 1994; Storyland Series, pom-pons on slippers (Peter Pan)...$65.00
Wendy Go Bragh! — 8", #35435, 2002 – 2003, white dress, green shamrocks...........................$65.00
Wendy Goes Camping — 8", #42100, 2006, tent, raccoon, fire, bedroll.....................................$80.00
(Wendy) Goes to the Circus — 8", #12819, 1996 (Wendy Ann) $60.00
Wendy Goes to the North Pole — 8", #46195, 2007 – 2008, red and white holiday outfit,
    North Pole sign $90.00
Wendy Has the Sniffles — 8", #47890, 2008, pink PJs, blue robe, Kleenex...............................$55.00
(Wendy) Her Sundress — #120804, 1994 ....$50.00
Wendy-Kin Baby — 8", one-piece vinyl body with hard plastic Little Genius head, 1954 .... $375.00 up
Wendy-Kin Wood Silk Rose — 8", #40795, 2005, green dress $250.00
(Wendy) Learning to Sew — 8", #120809, 1994, in wicker case $100.00
Wendy Learns Her ABC's — (see ABC Unlimited Productions under Special Events/Exclusives)
Wendy Learns to Drive — 8", #46085, 2007 – 2008, sunglasses, convertible car, pink outfit...$90.00
Wendy Learns to Swim — 8", #45685, 2007, yellow water wings $50.00
Wendy Loves Bambi — 8", #48710, 2008, plush Bambi, Thumper $85.00
Wendy Loves Being Loved — 8", 1992 – 1993 only, doll and wardrobe....................................$100.00
Wendy Loves Cheer Care Bear — 8", #47905, 2008, Care Bear...$80.00
Wendy Loves Clifford the Big Red Dog — 8", #38730, 2004 – 2005, 3" dog...........................$80.00
Wendy Loves Curious George — 8", #42575, 2006, yellow dress, monkey $85.00
Wendy Loves Donald and Daisy — 8", 2004 – 2005, cloth Donald and Daisy $95.00
Wendy Loves Funshine Care Bear — 8", #47355, 2008, yellow Care Bear................................$80.00
Wendy Loves Goofy and Pluto — 8", #39565, 2004 – 2005 ....$95.00
(Wendy Loves) Her First Day at School — 8", #120806, 1994 – 1995......................................$60.00
(Wendy Loves) Her Sunday Best — 8", #120807, 1994 – 1995...$70.00
Wendy Loves Kermit — 8", #42615, 2006 – 2007, green dress, Kermit $80.00
Wendy Loves Mickey and Minnie — 8", #39555, 2004 – 2007, red dress..................................$95.00
Wendy Loves Mr. Rogers' Neighborhood — 8", red jacket, trolley $85.00
Wendy Loves Miss Piggy — 8", #48685, 2008, purple check dress, plush Miss Piggy $80.00
Wendy Loves Munchkinland — 8", #40160, 2005, includes mini Dorothy doll.......................$85.00
Wendy Loves Snoopy — 8", #48975, 2008, blue dot dress, plush Snoopy $85.00
Wendy Loves Sunday School — 8", pink dress, white sweater $80.00
Wendy Loves Tennis — 8", #42110, 2006, pink and white tennis outfit $70.00
(Wendy Loves) the Country Fair — 8", #802, 1993, has cow, #120802, 1994 ....$75.00
Wendy Loves the Grand Ole Opry — 8", #48955, 2008, western attire, Opry mic stand......$85.00
Wendy Loves the Grinch — 8", #46415, 2007 – 2008, red dress, plush dog................................$80.00
Wendy Loves the Lion King — 8", #40340, 2005, Lion King dress, plush lion..........................$85.00
Wendy Loves the Red Hat Society — 8", #40860, 2005, red hat, fur, and dress $70.00
Wendy Makes It Special — 8", #31050, 1998, pink satin dress...$75.00
Wendy Plays Doctor — 8", #48840, 2008, stethoscope, doctor bag, dog $85.00
Wendy Plays Hopscotch — 8", #40170, pink print dress $60.00
Wendy Salutes the Heartland — 8", #39955, 2005 – 2006, with quilt and stand $95.00
Wendy Salutes the Olympics — 8", #86005, 1996, Olympic Medal...$110.00
Wendy's Anniversary Trunk Set — 8", #36130, 2003, trunk, clothes, shoes, accessories......$200.00
Wendy's Doll House Trunk Set — 8", #12820, 1996...$250.00
Wendy's Fabulous Fifties Trunk Set — 8", #37925, 2003 – 2004, hatbox trunk,
    three sets of clothes $275.00
Wendy's Favorite Crossword Puzzle — 8", #48070, 2008, puzzle, dress newspaper.............$70.00
Wendy's Favorite Fairy Tales — 8", #35655, 2003 – 2004, pink dress with pinafore,
    rabbit, cape, book, etc...$90.00
Wendy's First Puppet Show — 8", #48075, 2008, pig, tiger, alligator puppets $55.00
Wendy's First Scrapbook — 8", #46020, 2007, with scrapbook kit $85.00

Wendy's Feathered Friends — 8', #46025, 2007, with birdhouse $75.00
Wendy's Gift for You — 8", #40465, 2005, pink-trimmed dress, gift box $85.00
Wendy's Little Sister — 8", #47840, 2008, print eyelet dress, baby $75.00
Wendy Shops FAO — (see FAO Schwarz under Special Events/Exclusives)
Wendy's Puppet Show — 8", #33780, 2002 –2003, four puppets and theaters $165.00
Wendy's Special Cheer — 8", #16500, 1998 – 1999, cheerleading outfit $65.00
Wendy's Surprise Party — 8", #40605, 2005 – 2006, pink cake and Danger the Dog $100.00
Wendy's Tiny Footprints — 8", #48770, 2008, blue outfit $50.00
(Wendy) Summer Box Set — #805, 1993; #120805, 1994 ....$100.00
Wendy's Wicked Ways — 8", #42410, 2006 – 2007 , spider costume with monkey $95.00
Wendy's Witchy Web — 8", #48575, 2008, pink dress, hat $80.00
Wendy Tap Dancer — 8" h.p., #13930, 1998, white jacket, gold tap pants $75.00
Wendy the Gardener — 8", #31400, 1998 – 1999, sunflower outfit, watering can, sunflowers ..$65.00
Wendy Visits Grandma — 8", #42200, 2006 – 2007, green print dress, suitcase $80.00
Wendy Visits the Museum — 8", #40400, 2005, striped dress $80.00
Wendy Visits the Statue of Liberty — 8", #40395, 2005 – 2006, red pants, camera $50.00
    8", #39845, 2005 – 2006, with ostrich, leopard, snake, penguin, and monkey $85.00
(Wendy) Winter Box Set — #120810, 1994, boxed doll and wardrobe $100.00
Wendy Woodkin — 8", #37910, 2004, jointed wooden doll with tiny wooden doll $250.00
Wendy Works Construction — 8", #31420, 1998 – 1999, includes tools and toolbox $80.00
Western Riding — 8", #39735, 2005 – 2006, riding outfit, horse $85.00
Wharton, Edith — 10", #42060, 2006, black vintage outfit $115.00
Wheels on the Bus, The — 8", #34135, 2002 – 2003, yellow checked dress, bus on skirt $50.00
Where Oh Where Has My Little Dog Gone — 8", #35675, 2003 – 2004, blanket, dog $70.00
Where the Wild Things Are — 8", #48505, 2008, with large cloth Carol $95.00
Where's My Blankie Total Moves Wendy — 8", #40460, 2005 – 2006 ....$50.00
White Christmas — 10", #10105, 1995 only, Christmas Series $80.00
White Christmas Pair — 10", #15380, Betty and Bob from the movie White Christmas $175.00
White Hat Doll — 8", #25315, 2000, Maud Humphrey design $70.00
White Iris — 10", #22540, 1999 – 2000 (Cissette), white lace and roses $100.00
White King — 8" h.p., #13020, 1997 – 1998, white suit, cape $100.00
White Rabbit — 14" – 17" cloth/felt, 1940s ....$500.00 – 750.00
    8", #14509, 1995, Alice in Wonderland Series, 8", #14616, 1996 ....$90.00
    8", #48130, 2008, rabbit costume, trumpet $80.00
White Witch, The — 10'', #46405, 2007, Cissette, Chronicles of Naria, white gown, fur $110.00
Who Took the Cookies — 8", #48850, 2008, black stripe dress, black hat, mask, cookie jar, bag $75.00
Wicked Stepmother — 21", #50002, 1996, limited edition $325.00
Wicked Witch of the East — 10", #42415, 2006 – 2007, black and orange costume with broom $130.00
    10", #42415, 2008, red and black outfit, red hat, broomstick $130.00
Wicked Witch of the West — 10", #13270, #42400, 1997 – 2008 (Cissette),
        black witch costume, broom $125.00
    21", #27760, 2000, long black costume with Dorothy globe, #42400, 2006 ....$425.00
Wilson, Edith — 1988, fifth set Presidents' Ladies/First Ladies Series (Mary Ann) $100.00
Wilson, Ellen — 1988, fifth set Presidents' Ladies/First Ladies Series (Louisa) $100.00
Window Shopping — 8", #37920, 2004, with store front, mannequin $90.00
Winged Monkey — 8" h.p. (Maggie), #140501, 1994 only $100.00
    8" h.p. #25950, 2000 – 2002 (Wendy), blue jacket, hat, blue feather wings $75.00
    8", #47400, 2008, blue monkey outfit with wings $70.00
Winnie the Pooh — 8", #38365, 2004 – 2008, with plush Pooh, Tigger, Piglet, and Eeyore $100.00
Winnie Walker — 15" h.p., 1953 only (Cissy) ....$350.00 up
    18" – 25", #1836 ....$350.00 – 650.00
    1953 – 1954, in trunk/trousseau ....$850.00 up
Winter — 14", 1993, Changing Seasons, doll and four outfits $75.00
    5" porcelain, #25865, 2000, fur-trimmed white coat and hat $50.00
Winter Angel — 10", #28365, 2001 –2004, blue costume, white fur wings $90.00
Winter Fun Skater — 8", #10357, 1995, Christmas Series $65.00

Yugoslavia, 8", #589, 1984 (Wendy). $60.00.

Winter Magic — 8", #42040, 2006, blue outfit, Chaos bear $85.00
Winter Wonderland — 10", #19990, 1999 – 2000, white satin, fur, jewels $125.00
Wishes Come True — 8", #33315, 2002, ballerina outfit $75.00
Wishing Fairy — 8", #36035, 2003 – 2004, pink costume, crystal snowflake $75.00
Wisteria Flower Girl — 8", #30370, 2001 – 2002 (Maggie), lavender gown $80.00
Witch — 8", #322, 1992 – 1993, Americana Series $75.00
Witches' Brew Wendy — 8", #40620, 2005 – 2006, with black cat, green hat $75.00
Witching Hour Wendy — 8", #49925, 2008, orange tulle skirt, spider $85.00
Withers, Jane — 12" – 13½" compo., 1937, closed mouth ....$1,000.00 up
    15" – 17", 1937 – 1939 ....$850.00 – 1,300.00
    17" cloth body, 1939 ....$1,500.00
    18" – 19", 1937 – 1939 ....$1,500.00
    19" – 20", closed mouth ....$1,400.00 up
    20" – 21", 1937 ....$1,700.00 up
With Love — 8", #17003, 1996, pink gown, comes with a heart............................$65.00
    8", #17001, 1996, same as above except African-American $70.00
Wizard of Oz — 8", #13281, plaid pants, green tailcoat, 1998 – 2000 ....$100.00
    8", #13280, 1998 – 2000, Wizard, with state fair balloon...........................$150.00
    5", #38200, 2003 – 2004, set of four – Daisy, Lollipop, Coroner, and Town's Lady.....$100.00
    #38400, Wizard of Oz house trunk for 8" dolls $125.00
    5", 2004 – 2005, Petite Set, Tin Man, Cowardly Lion, Scarecrow, Dorothy.........$25.00 ea.
    8", Wizard of Oz Dress Up Trunk Set, #46365, 2007 – 2008, four outfits, picnic basket trunk,
        accessories $230.00
    8", Off to Oz, #42420, 2007, Dorothy, Toto, lunch box $105.00
Women, 1860s — 10" h.p., 1990 (see Spiegel's, Beth, under Special Events/Exclusives)
Wooden Wendy — 8", #33820, 2003 – 2004, fully jointed wooden doll in pink dress............$250.00
Workin' Out with Wendy 1980 — 8", #17810, 1999, BK, striped bodysuit............$65.00
Wreath of Holiday Wishes — 8", #46035, 2007 – 2008, red holiday dress, wreath, tree box ..$90.00
Wuthering Heights — 8", #45925, 2007, blue plaid dress $85.00
Wynkin — (see Dutch Lullaby)
Yankee Doodle — 8", #35945, 2003 – 2004, blonde, vintage patriotic costume $90.00
Yellow Butterfly Princess — 8", #25680, 2000 – 2001 (Maggie)............................$70.00
Yellow Daffodil — 10", #25620, 2000, long white and yellow gown $70.00
Yellow Hat Doll — 8", #25320, 2000, Maud Humphrey design $70.00
Yes, Virginia, There Is a Santa Claus — 8", #20200, 1999 – 2001, green dress with
    lace collar and trim...$80.00
Yolanda — 12", 1965 only (Brenda Starr) ....$375.00 up
You Can't Catch the Gingerbred Man — 8", #48285, 2008, Maggie, shorts,
    striped top, skates, gingerbread man $80.00
Younger Stepsister — 10", #46495, 2007, Cissette, black long gown $100.00
Yugoslavia — 8" h.p., BK, #789, 1968 – 1972 (Wendy)....................................$90.00
    8" straight legs, #0789, #589, 1973 – 1975, marked "Alex" **$60.00**
    8" straight legs, #589, 1976 – 1986, marked "Alexander" $55.00
Yukon — 8", #38610, 2004 – 2005, with sled and three dogs................................$110.00
Yuletide Angel — (see Tree Topper)
Zoe — 10", #35821, 2003 – 2005 (Hannah), African-American, yellow dress, blue trim $40.00
Zorina Ballerina — 17" compo., 1937 – 1938, extra make-up, must be mint condition
    (Wendy Ann) ....$1,900.00 up

Special Events/Exclusives

Shops and organizations are listed alphabetically.

Wendy Learns Her ABC's, 8", 1993 (Wendy). Came with a wooden block stand. $90.00.

ABC Unlimited Productions
 Wendy Learns Her ABC's — 8", 1993, wears blue jumper and beret, ABC blocks on skirt, wooden block stand, limited to 3,200 ....$90.00

Alpha Kappa Alpha
 Ivy Rose – 16", #47435, 2007 (Paris), sheath evening gown and wrap $150.00

Amanda Callahan's Susan's Dolls
 Amanda Sue — 8", #38120, 2004 (Maggie) limited to 250.......................$100.00

Ashton-Drake Galleries
 Apple of Grandma's Eye, The — 8", 2004, denim and red checked outfit, basket of cherries ..$80.00
 Grandma's Little Honey — 8", 2004, yellow flower dress, straw hat $90.00
 Grandma's Little Sweetheart — 8", 2004, red print holiday outfit, gingerbread cookie............$80.00
 Some Bunny Loves Me, Grandma — 8", 2004, print dress and hat, with bunny $90.00
 Jacqueline Kennedy Bride — porcelain, 2004, taffeta wedding gown with rosettes of lace ...$150.00
 My First Christmas with Berta Hummel — 8", #39151, 2004, with ornament $100.00

Avon Products
 Party Dress Wendy — 8", #39150, 2004, pink dress $75.00

Bay Area Alexander Doll Club
 Now I Am Ten — 8", #33855, 2002, white dress, pink trim......................$100.00
 Sweet 16 Lissy – 12", 2008, black lace over taffeta $150.00

Belk & Leggett Department Stores
 Miss Scarlett — 14", 1988 ....$125.00
 Rachel/Rachael — 8", 1989, lavender gown.................................$65.00
 Nancy Jean — 8", 1990, yellow/brown outfit $60.00
 Fannie Elizabeth — 8", 1991, floral dress with pinafore, limited to 3,000.................................$80.00
 Annabelle at Christmas — 8", 1992, plaid dress, holds Christmas cards, limited to 3,000 ......$125.00
 Caroline — 8", 1993, limited to 3,600 ....$90.00
 Holly — 8", 1994, green eyes, freckles, red top with white skirt $85.00
 Elizabeth Belk Angel — 8", #79648, 1996, red velvet.................................$175.00

Bloomingdale's Department Store
 10", 1997, coral and leopard Cissette with Bloomie's big brown bag.................................$125.00
 Golden Holiday Tree Topper — 1999, limited to 1,000 pieces, gilded gold and silver embroidery on satin $125.00
 Millennium Angel Tree Topper — 10", #27955, 2000, gold lamé dress with jewels.................$150.00
 8", Angelic Tree Topper, #32035, 2001, burgundy velvet, limited to 300.................................$125.00
 Snowflake Skater Sarah, #32030 ....$80.00

Boscov's
 Bubbles — 8", #33815, 2003 (Wendy), pink outfit, limited to 500 ....$95.00
 Frosted Dreams — 8", #35455, 2003, white outfit with fur.................................$100.00

Celebrations Fantastic
 Let's Hop — 8", #33810, 2003, poodle skirt $90.00
 Dressed Like Mommy — 8", #39620, 2004, sunsuit, tulle petticoat $100.00
 Lavender Fairy — 8", #33875, 2006, purple petal tutu.................................$100.00

Celia's Dolls
 David, the Little Rabbi — 8", 1991 – 1992, 3,600 made, three hair colors.................................$65.00

Central Massachusetts Doll Collectors
 Winter Wonderland Cissy — 21", #36406, 2006, blue silk coat $350.00
 Winter Wonderland Coquette — 10", #36405, 2006, blue silk coat, skates.................................$125.00

Cherished Friends Doll Shoppe
 Independent Traveler Coquette Jacqui — 10", #39490, 2004, zebra coat, fuchsia scarf.........$100.00

Child at Heart Shop
 Easter Bunny — 8", 1991, limited to 3,000 (1,500 blondes, 750 brunettes, 750 redheads) $175.00

My Little Sweetheart — 8", 1992, limited to 4,500 (1,000 blondes, 1,000 brunettes with blue eyes, 1,000 brunettes with green eyes, 1,000 redheads with green eyes, 500 blacks) $60.00

Trick and Treat — 8", 1993, sold in sets only (400 sets with red-haired/green-eyed "Trick" and black-haired/ black-eyed "Treat"; 1,200 sets with red-haired/green-eyed "Trick" and brunette/ brown-eyed "Treat"; 1,400 blonde/blue-eyed "Trick" and red-haired/brown-eyed "Treat") .. $175.00 set

Christmas Shoppe

Boy and Girl, Alpine — 8" twins, 1992, in Alpine Christmas outfits, limited to 2,000 sets. $225.00 pr.

Collectors United (C.U.), C. U. Gathering (Georgia)

Yugoslavia — 8", FAD, limited to 625 ....$70.00
Tippi Ballerina — 8", 1988, limited to 800 ....$225.00
Miss Leigh — 8", 1989, limited to 800 ....$75.00
Shea Elf — 8", 1990, limited to 1,000 ....$90.00
Ringmaster — 8", 1991, limited to 800 ....$75.00
Faith — 8", 1992, limited to 800...$125.00
Hope — 8", 1993, blue dress (1910 style), limited to 900 ....$100.00
Love — 8", 1994, gold necklace and pearls on cap, limited to 2,400 ....$70.00
Diane — 8", 1995, Back to the Fifties, limited to 800 ....$75.00
C.U. Varsity Sweater — white sweater, 1995, special event souvenir $40.00
Olympia — 8", 1996, pants costume, with flag, limited to 800 ....$80.00
Olympic Bag — 1996, special Alexander event souvenir...$40.00
C.U. Salutes Broadway — 8", 1997, burgundy theater outfit $100.00
Black Fur Stole — 1997, special Alexander event souvenir..$30.00
Polynesian Princess — 8", 1998, print skirt and top..$125.00
Grass Skirt — 1998, special Alexander event souvenir $30.00
Fortune Teller — 8", 1999, red print costume trimmed in gold...$125.00
Fortune Teller — 21", 1999, red print costume trimmed in gold..$1,050.00
Fortune Teller Accessories — 1999, scarves and bangle bracelets, special event $35.00
Carnival Queen — 16", 1999, pink or blue gown, limited to 24...$300.00
Majestic Midway — 21", 1999, gold costume ....one-of-a-kind
Bonnie Blue Returns to Atlanta — 8", #31485, 2001, blue dress, limited to 500 ....$125.00
Return to Tara — Scarlett, #32105, 2001, with Tara, limited to 100 ....$200.00
Scarlett — 21", #31540, 2001, white dress, green sash $350.00
Greta — 16", #35530, 2002, orange checked dress, white straw bag, limited to 150 ....$175.00
Georgia Peach — 8", 2002, blonde or brunette, peach taffeta dress, straw hat...............$65.00
Coca-Cola Cissy — #35160, 2002, red checked blouse, Coke bottle, straw hat....................$325.00
Coca-Cola Cissy — #35161, 2002, African-American, limited to 40 ....$475.00
Sizzling Cissy — 21", #39195, 2004, limited to 150 ....$350.00
Sizzling Cissy — 21", 2004, African-American $450.00
Candi Corn — 8", #40035, 2004, with kitty and game...$100.00
Treats for Wendy – 8", #39250, 2004, orange dress, tulle skirt $80.00
April — 8", #31705, 2004 (Wendy), white dress, pansy trim, hat.......................................$80.00
Wendy's Tea at the Waldorf — 8", pink dress, limited to 40, 2005 ....$125.00

C.U. Nashville Winter Wonderland

Nashville Skater — 8", 1991, FAD, limited to 200 (Black Forest) $100.00
Nashville Skier — 8", 1992, FAD, limited to 200 (Tommy Tittlemouse) $90.00
First Comes Love — 8", 1993, FAD, limited to 200. ....$225.00
Captain's Cruise — 1994, with trunk and wardrobe, limited to 250..................................$175.00
Nashville Goes Country — 8", 1995, western outfit with guitar $125.00
Nashville Sunny — 8", 1996, yellow raincoat, hat $90.00
Miss Tennessee Waltz — 8", 1997, long ball gown, coat $125.00
C.U. Goes to Camp — 8", 1998 ....$85.00
Irish Cissy — 21", #27460, 2000, green gown, silver cape, limited to 200 ....$500.00
Shannon — 8", #27255, 2000, green costume $75.00
Lindsey — 8", #28920, 2001, print dress, straw hat, limited to 100 ....$75.00
Wendy Learns Nursery Rhymes — 8", #34520, 2002, with cardboard wardrobe and extra clothes.... $125.00
Blue Danube — 21", #30685, 2001, blue gown $250.00

21", African-American, limited to 36...$300.00
8", #28211, blue gown, 2001 ....$85.00
8", African-American, 2001, limited to 100...$125.00
Emily — 8", #38925, 2004, with doll, lavender coat, striped dress $80.00
Coquette N.Y., N.Y. — #40955, pink suit, velvet hat, limited to 60 ....$125.00
City Shopper Wendy — 8", #40970, taffeta dress, straw hat $90.00
Cissy at Harvest Ball — 21", limited to 60 ....$350.00
Autumn Splendor Coquette — 10", 2006, pants, suede jacket..........................$150.00
Autumn Wendy — 8", 2006, pants, velvet jacket $100.00
Demi John — 8", #46795, 2006, sailor outfit $70.00
C.U Cissette's Audition — 10", #41745, 2006 ....$150.00
Daisy — 8", #41740, 2006, Little Women's Meg's daughter...........................$75.00
Wendy Reads Little Women — 8", #41265, 2006, pink dress, limited to 40 ....$125.00
40's Wendy — 8", #47145, 2007, white blouse, pink dotted skirt $85.00
Caroline — 8", #47025, 2007, swimsuit, hat, bag $95.00
Sweetheart Lissy – 12", 2008, red dress $175.00
Sweetheart Wendy – 8", 2008, red dress $75.00
40s Lissy – #47140, 12", 2007, pink long dress $175.00

Sweetheart Lissy, 12", CU centerpiece doll. $175.00.

C.U. Greenville Show
Bride — 8", 1990, FAD, of Tommy Snooks, limited to 250 (Betsy Brooks) $100.00
Witch/Halloween — 8", 1990, FAD, limited to 250 (Little Jumping Joan) $100.00
Oktoberfest — 8", 1992, FAD, limited to 200...$100.00
C.U. Columbia, S.C. Camelot — 8", 1991, FAD (Maid Marian), limited to 400 ...$125.00
C.U. Columbia, S.C., Homecoming Queen — 21", #28205, 2000, white gown, limited to 200....$300.00
C.U. Columbia, S.C., Homecoming Queen — 21", 2000, African-American, limited to 24....$375.00
C.U. Jacksonville — 8" Greta, 1996, black doll, blue sundress......................$125.00

C.U. Doll Shop Exclusives
Cameo Lady — 10", 1991, white dress, black trim, limited to 1,000..................$125.00
Le Petit Boudoir — 10", 1993, FAD, limited to 700 ....$150.00
America's Junior Miss — 8", 1994, white gown, medallion, limited to 1,200 ....$65.00
Fitness — 8", 1995, tennis outfit $60.00
Judge's Interview — 8", 1996, limited to 500..$65.00
Talent — 8", 1996, gold tuxedo jacket, black shorts $65.00
Easter of Yesteryear — 8", 1995, comes with rabbit...................................$75.00
Sailing with Sally — 8", 1998, white dress, wooden boat.............................$100.00
Gary Green — 8", 1998 ....$65.00
Christmas Morn — 8", 1999, #80130, nightgown, teddy bear, limited to 411 pieces..........$70.00
Sterling Light, Sterling Bright — 8", #30721, 2000, silver angel lighted tree topper..........$125.00
Katy — 8", #28925, 2000, printed dress, straw hat, limited to 100 ....$75.00

Colonial Southwest
Tanya — 8", 1999, honors M.A.D.C. former president Tanya McWhorter, limited to 550.....$150.00

Colonial Williamsburg
Charlotte — 10", #26985, 2000, pink taffeta, eighteenth century dress....................$150.00
Colleen — 10", #31535, 2001, vintage cotton dress with panniers........................$150.00
Caroline — 8", #35230, 2002, eighteenth century cape, green costume $175.00
Catherine — 8", #33890, 2003, long satin dress, cape..................................$100.00
Frances — 8", #41835, 2006, white gown, green cape $100.00
Anne (The Spring Season) — 8", #33891, 2004, basket of tulips $100.00
    The Fall Season — 8", #39175, 2004, long green dress $100.00
    The Summer Season — 8", #33892, 2004, white shadow-striped dress $100.00
Diana — 8", #38040, 2006, red taffeta dress $100.00
Sophia — 8", #36415, 2006, blue taffta gown...$90.00
Susanna – 12", #33195, 2007, vintage Williamsburg christening gown $80.00
Hannah – 8", #46075, 2007, lavender silk gown $100.00
Matthew – 8", #47381, 2007, green cape, black hat $100.00
Rachel – 8", #47380, 2007, red cape...$100.00

Tweedledee & Tweedledum, 8",
1994. Disney Showcase of Dolls.
hing outfits with names on collar.
$250.00 pair.

Disney Annual Showcase of Dolls

Cinderella — 10", 1989, #1, blue satin gown, limited to 250 ....$550.00
Snow White — 12", 1990, #2, limited to 750 (Nancy Drew) $150.00
Alice in Wonderland/White Rabbit — 10", 1991, #3, limited to 750 ....$300.00
Queen of Hearts — 10", 1992, #4, limited to 500..$325.00
Alice in Wonderland/Jabberwocky — 11"–12" (Lissy), 1993, #5, limited to 500 ....$300.00
Tweedledee & Tweedledum — 8", 1994, #6, wear beany hats with propellers,
   names on collar, limited to 750 .... $250.00 pr.
Morgan LeFay — 10", #797537, 1995, #7, limited to 500 ....$375.00
Bobby (Bobbie) Soxer — 8", 1990 – 1991 ....$150.00
Mouseketeer — 8", 1991, blue skirt, white top $125.00
Roller Blades — 8", 1992, "Thoroughly Modern Wendy"..$100.00
Round Up Cowgirl — 8", 1992, blue/white outfit..$150.00
Annette (Funicello) — 14" porcelain portrait sculpted by Robert Tonner, 1993, limited to 400....$425.00
Monique — 8", 1993, made for Disney, limited to 250, lavender with lace trim.....................$300.00
Snow White — 10", 1993, Disney crest colors $175.00
Belle — 8" h.p., gold gown, 1994 ....$125.00
Cinderella — 14", 1994, Disney catalog, has two outfits, limited to 900 ....$200.00
   14", 1995, different gown, no extra outfits..$175.00
Wendy's Favorite Pastime — 8", 1994, comes with hula hoop..$75.00
Sleeping Beauty — 14", 1995, waist-length hair, blue gown from movie and two other outfits...$200.00
Blue Fairy Tree Topper — 10", #79545, 1995 catalog exclusive (Cissette) $150.00
Snow White — 14", 1995 ....$125.00
Mary Poppins — 10", 1996, #79403 ....$125.00
Alice — 14", 1996, catalog exclusive, limited to 1,500 ....$150.00
Knave — 8", 1996, #8, wears two of Spades card, limited to 500 ....$150.00
Toto — 8", 1997, #9, comes with wooden basket, limited to 750 ....$125.00
Goldilocks and Baby Bear — 8", 1998, #10, purple print costume with Raikes bear.............$225.00
Mouseketeers — 8", 1999, Alex and Wendy as Mouseketeers, #11..$200.00
My Little Buttercup — 8", 2000, #12, yellow dress/hat, with flowers/ribbons, #30320, ltd to 200...$125.00
Sleeping Beauty — 8", 1999, pink satin gown, limited to 1,000..$125.00
Snow White — 8", 1999, Disney crest colors, limited to 1,000...$125.00
Ariel — 8", 1999, #25085, long red hair, green mermaid costume $100.00
Belle — 8", 1999, #25075, yellow ball gown with gold trim $100.00
Cinderella — 8", 1999, #25080, blue satin gown, limited to 1,000 ....$125.00
Michael and Jane Banks — 8", 1999, #80450, 8" girl, boy limited to 200 ....$150.00
Jasmine — 8", 1999, #25095, lavender chiffon harem outfit..$125.00
Belle Tree Topper — #31770, 2001...$175.00
Wendy's Wardrobe — 8", #31780, 2001, three dresses, cardboard wardrobe, limited to 170 ....$150.00

Disney, Walt

Disney World Auction — 21", one-of-a-kind dolls .... no prices available
   Sleeping Beauty — #1 in Series, 1989, 21", long blonde hair, in pink with rhinestones and pearls
   Christine (Phantom of the Opera) — #2, 1990, blue/white outfit with white mask (Jacqueline)
   Queen Isabella — #3, 1991, green/gold gown, long red hair (Jacqueline)
   It's a Girl — #4, 1992, comes with 8" baby in carriage (Cissy, Baby Genius)
   Emperor and Nightingale — #4, 1992, 8" winged Wendy Ann (23" Emperor bear by Gund)
   Women in the Garden — #5, 1993, four dolls (Cissette) dressed like 1867 Monet painting
   Cissy Bride — 1923 and 8" Flower Girl and Ring Bearer, #5, 1993
   Romeo and Juliet — #6, 21" h.p., 1994, using 1950s bald nude Maggie dolls, rewigged,
   dressed in blue, burgundy, and gold
   Sir Lancelot duLac — #7, 1995, 1950s doll dressed in burgundy and gold
   Queen Guinevere — #7, 1995, 1950s doll dressed in burgundy and gold
   Chess Set — 35 dolls from 8" to 21" on a satin chess board
   Mary Poppins and Children — 1999, 21" Mary Poppins, 14" Jane and Michael

Doll & Teddy Bear Expo

Madame (Alexander) or Shadow of Madame — 8", 1994, in blue, limited to 500 first year...$125.00

Madame with Love — 8", #79536, 1995, has hat with "100" on top, limited to 750 ....$75.00
Maggie's First Doll — 8", 1996, pink cotton dress, carries cloth Alice doll..............................$225.00
Miss Eliza Doolittle — 21", 1996, white lace dress, auction piece ....one-of-a-kind
Josephine Baker — 21", black Cissy, 1996, banana costume, auction piece..................one-of-a-kind
Gingerbread — outfit only, for 8" doll $50.00
Love Is in the Air — 8", Bride, 1999, limited to 100 ....$125.00
Holiday Magic — 8", 1999, limited to 100, red and gold metallic gown...................................$100.00
American as Apple Pie — 8", #27490, 2000, 100 pieces (Maggie)..$100.00
America the Beautiful outfit — 2000, with boots $60.00
Wild, Wild West — 8", #27495, 2000, limited to 100..$200.00
Wendy Visits the World's Fair — 8", #28905, 2002, red checked dress, limited to 100..........$100.00
Happy Birthday — 8", #35885, 2002, purple print party dress...$75.00
Lifetime Achievement — 8", #36360, 2004, pink formal, #36365, African-American $125.00
Acceptance Speech Coquette Cissy — 8", #40150, 2004, Caucasian....................................$125.00
Acceptance Speech Coquette Cissy — 8", #40155, 2004, African-American $125.00
Tea Time Delight Cissy — 21", 2005, centerpiece doll, five panel gown.................................$450.00
Tea Time Delight Coquette Cissy — 10", 2005, limited to 135, silk torso dress.......................$125.00
Sweet Treats Wendy — 8", #41130, 2005, A-line dress, lollipop..$70.00

Doll Reader Collector's Club
All the Way Glam Sienna Evans – 16", #45420, 2007, pink taffeta gown, limited to 80..........$150.00

Doll Finders
Fantasy — 8", 1990, limited to 350 ....$150.00

Dolls and Ducks
Ice Princess — 8", 1999, silver gown and tiara $150.00

Doll Market, The
Jacquetta Coquette, Jacqui — 10", #40105, 2004, blue silk dress $125.00

Dolls 'n Bearland
Pandora — 8", 1991, limited to 3,600 (950 brunettes, 950 redheads, 1,700 blondes).............$150.00

Dolly Dears
Bo Peep — 1987, holds staff, black sheep wears man's hat, white sheep wears woman's hat
    (sheep made exclusively by Dakin) $200.00
Susannah Clogger — 8", 1992, has freckles, limited to 400 (Maggie) $150.00
Jack Be Nimble — 8", 1993, FAD, limited to 288...$90.00
Princess and the Pea — 8", 1993, limited to 1,000 ....$100.00

Dream Dolls and the Doll Peddler
Golden Elegance Coquette Cissy — 10", #41595, 2006, long gold gown $150.00

Elegant Doll Shop
Elegant Easter — 8", 1999, pink checked dress with bunny..$125.00
Heart of Dixie — 8", 1999, red and lace outfit...$75.00

Enchanted Doll House
Rickrack on Pinafore — 8", 1980, limited to 3,000..$225.00
Eyelet Pinafore — 8", 1981, limited to 3,423...$200.00
Blue or Pink Ballerina — 8", 1983 – 1985, FAD, blonde or brunette doll in trunk with extra clothes ...$150.00
Cinderella and Trunk — 14", 1985, has glass slipper...$275.00
25th Anniversary (The Enchanted Doll) — 10", 1988, long gown, limited to 5,000 ....$150.00
Ballerina — 8", 1989, blue tutu, limited to 360 ....$125.00
Vermont Maiden — 8", 1990 – 1992, official Vermont Bicentennial doll, limited to 3,600........$70.00
Farmer's Daughter — 8", 1991, limited to 4,000 (1,000 blondes, 1,500 redheads, 1,500 brunettes) $85.00
Farmer's Daughter — 8", 1992, "Goes To Town" (cape and basket added), limited to 1,600...$75.00

Ethi Dolls
Makeda: Queen of Sheba — 16", 2007, Ethiopian costume, gold jewelery............................$139.00

Fashion Doll Quarterly
Cosmopolitan Coquette Cissy — 10", #40405, 2005, long black coat, with dog $150.00

FAO Schwarz
Pussycat — 18", 1987, pale blue dress and bonnet $100.00
Brooke — 14", 1988, blonde or brunette (Mary Ann), with Steiff bear................................$125.00

Singin' in the Rain, 8", 1996. Gene Kelly, Debbie Reynolds with lamppost, 1952 film. $300.00.

Davy Crockett Boy & Girl, 8". Leather outfits. Made by Rebba Sutherland for souvenirs of 1987 MADC Texas convention. $125.00.

Lilly Pulitzer, 21", 1994 (Cissy). Luncheon centerpiece doll at 1999 Cissy luncheon. Limited to 25. $1,400.00.

The Sky's the Limit Wendy, 8", #49310, 2008 convention souvenir doll. Long blue sparkly dress. $150.00.

David and Diana — 8", 1989, in red, white, and denim, with wooden wagon ....$200.00 set

Samantha — 14", 1989, white with black dots (Mary Ann)..$125.00

Me & My Scassi — 21", 1990, dressed in all red, Arnold Scassi original (Cissy)..................$375.00

Sailor — 8", 1991 ....$125.00

Carnavale Doll — 14", 1991 – 1992 (Samantha) $125.00

Beddy-Bye Brooke — 14", 1991 – 1992 (Mary Ann) $125.00

Beddy-Bye Brenda (Brooke's sister) — 8", 1992, sold only as set with 14" doll ....$225.00 set

Wendy Shops FAO — 8", 1993, red/white outfit, carries FAO Schwarz shopping bag..........$100.00

My Secret Garden — 8", 1994, trunk with wardrobe $250.00

Little Huggums — 12", 1994, red dress, bib and headband, has FAO logo horse $65.00

Little Women — 8", 1994, dressed in outfits from movie, limited to 500 sets.... $125.00 ea., $750.00 set

Princess Trunk Set — 8", #79526, 1995 ....$275.00

Fun with Dick & Jane — 8", #70509, 1995, limited to 1,200 pieces................................$275.00 set

Lucy Ricardo — 8", limited to 1,200..$225.00

I Love Lucy — 8" Fred, Ethel, Lucy, and Ricky, sold as set only, limited to 1,200 ....$600.00 set

Twilight Tango Cissy — 21", #35210, 2003, black and white gown, limited to 100 ....$350.00

Wendy Loves Patrick — 8", #37200, 2003, with dog Patrick $125.00

Chinoiserie Cissy — 21", #33335, 2003, long sheath gown $350.00

The Little Rascals — 8" Alfalfa, Darla, Spanky, Buckwheat, and dog, Petey, 1996,
  limited to 2,000 sets..$550.00 set

Singin' in the Rain — 8" Gene Kelly, Debbie Reynolds, with lamppost, 1996.... $300.00 set

I Dream of Jeannie — 8", harem outfit, military uniform $250.00

Lucy and Ethel — 8", 1997, candy factory episode $165.00

The Honeymooners — 8", 1997, Ralph and Alice Norton and Trixie, limited to 2,000 sets...$450.00

Grease — 1998, 10" Danny and Sandy in leather outfits $175.00

Fay Wray with Steiff King Kong — 1998, 10" doll $500.00

Silver Sensation — 16" Alex fashion doll, limited to 100 ....$200.00

Gallery Opening Alex —16", limited to 500...$250.00

Publisher's Meeting Alex — 16", limited to 200..$150.00

Magnificent Mile Alex — 16", 2000, limited to 40 pieces $550.00

140th Anniversary Wendy — 8", #31660, 2001 ....$125.00

Wendy Loves FAO — 8", #34580, 2003, with FAO bear $150.00

Star Wars — 8" Luke Skywalker, Han Solo, Leia, #35515, 2003, limited to 1,000 ....$400.00

Pinocchio and Blue Fairy — 8", #34035, 2003, limited to 160 ....$175.00

80th Anniversary Wendy Trunk Set — 8", #35215, 2003..$250.00

Lord of the Rings Set — 2004, 8" Frodo in green cape, 10" Coquette Arwen in purple gown,
  limited to 300...$275.00

Dolly Dots Wendy-Kin Wood — 8", #39515, wood jointed doll, red dress.............................$250.00

Cute as a Button Trunk — 8", #39530, 2004, extra clothes, case that looks like a child's blouse ...$300.00

Elegant Attitude Coquette Cissy — 10", #39535, 2004, long black evening dress....................$125.00

Binah — 9", #39525, 2004, cloth doll, with raincoat, umbrella, and mouse $50.00

Going to the Parade Wendy-Kin Wood — 8", #41260, 2005, blue coat, limited to 200..........$275.00

Cissy 50th Anniversary — 21", #41400, 2005, long silver gown $375.00

Pals Forever — 8", #41585, 2005, pink dress, Chaos bear $125.00

Little Mismatched — 14", 2006, cloth doll $45.00

Christmas at FAO — 8", #46715, 2006, red velvet coat, teddy bear...$85.00

Easter Delight with Penelope – 8", #47085, 2007, pink dress, bunny..$85.00

Cinderella Trunk Set – 8", #47405, 2007, extra outfits $250.00

Christmas at FAO 2007 – 8", #47425, red coat, fur collar, bear...$95.00

Rockette Santa – 9", #47910, 2007, velvet body suit, fur..$75.00

First Modern Doll Club (N.Y. Doll Club)

Autumn in N.Y. — 10", 1991, FAD, red skirt, fur-trimmmed cape, hat, muff, and skates,
  limited to 260..$125.00

Gene Convention

Silhouette Cissy — 21", #41570, 2005, limited to 30, centerpiece doll, black satin column dress,
  fuchsia hat $650.00

Soiree Sparkle Cissy — 21", #47051, 2006, limited to 30 ....$650.00

GoCollect.com
Morning Ritual Cissy — 21", 2001, bathrobe, Yardley soap...........................$250.00
Afternoon Out — 16", #30315, 2001, red hair, sheath dress $175.00
Little Wendy Alexander — 8", #31920, 2001, pink gingham dress.....................$80.00

Grand Ol' Doll Club
Wendy Visits the 1940s – 8", #47075, 2007, green check dress..........................$85.00

Grant-a-Wish
Tour D'Jour — 16" Alex fashion doll, #34740, 2002, tweed coat, tan skirt, limited to 350 ....$175.00
Show Stopper Alex — faux fur coat, 16", 2002, red dress ....one-of-a-kind

Home Shopping Network
Blue Angel — 8", 1997, #19972, dark blue and gold dress and halo, resin wings, limited to 3,000.....$150.00

Horchow
Pamela Plays Dress Up — 12", 1993, in trunk with wardrobe, limited to 1,250 (Lissy).........$325.00
Pamela Trousseau — 12", 1994, trunk and trousseau, limited to 265 ....$350.00
14" trunk set, 1995 ....$200.00
Mary Ann Dances for Grandma Trunk Set — 14", 1996 ....$225.00

I. Magnin
Little Huggums (Imaginarium Shop) — 12", 1991, special outfits, bald or wigged $50.00
Little Huggums — 12" with cradle, 1992 ....$100.00
Cheerleader — 8", 1990, FAD, "5" on sweater $70.00
Miss Magnin — 10", 1991 – 1993, limited to 2,500 (Cissette) $150.00
Little Miss Magnin — 8", 1992, with tea set and teddy bear, limited to 3,600 ....$200.00
Bon Voyage Miss Magnin — 10", 1993, navy/white gloves, has steamer trunk, limited to 2,500.....$250.00
Bon Voyage Little Miss Magnin — 8", sailor dress, carries teddy bear and suitcase, 1993,
    limited to 3,500...$225.00
Little Miss Magnin Supports the Arts — 8", 1994, pink painter smock, wears red ribbon
    for AIDS Awareness...$150.00

IDEX
Las Vegas Style Coquette Cissy — 10", 2006, limited to 100, denim pants, jacket $125.00
Las Vegas Style Cissy — 21", 2006, limited to 15, denim pants, jacket $700.00
Hearts for IDEX — 8", #41140, caucasian, #41141, African American, 2006, heart dress.......$95.00
Love Is in the Air Coquette Cissy — 10", #41705, 2006, limited to 130, red dress $125.00
Love Is in the Air Cissy — 21", #41710, 2006, red velvet gown $600.00
Everlasting Reflections Cissette – 10", 2006, magenta silk gown, limited to 85 ....$125.00
Everlasting Reflections Cissette – 10", 2006, African-American, limited to 25 ....$150.00
Everlasting Reflections Cissy – 21", 2006, magenta silk ballgown, limited to 20 ....$700.00

Jacobsons
Wendy Starts Her Collection — 1994, has bear, limited to 2,400................................$150.00
Little Huggums — 1995 ....$60.00

Jean's Doll Shop
Suellen — 12", 1992, FAD $125.00
Wendy Walks Her Dog — 8", #79549, 1995, limited to 500 ....$70.00

Lenox China Company
My Own Bell — 8", #27475, 2000, holiday dress with bell, limited to 1,000 ....$125.00
Halloween — 8", #30715, 2001...$90.00
Christmas Eve — 8', #30710, 2001..$100.00
Little Miss American Pride — 8", #34540, 2003, long white gown.........................$125.00
My Valentine — 8", #33725, 2003, red and white dress $85.00
Snowflake Elegance — 8", #34525, 2003 ....$100.00
Christmas Holly — 8", #34535, 2003 ....$85.00
Faith — 8", #31895, 2001, pink dress, basket $85.00
Easter Lily — 8", #33750, 2003, lavender dress, limited to 1,000 ....$90.00
Lil' Sweetheart — 8", #36420, 2003, with heart ornament $95.00
Little Miss Firecracker — 8", #36425, 2003, long dress, red hair $85.00
Miss Butterfly — 8", #36430, 2003, with Halloween ornament...........................$100.00

The Sky's The Limit Cissette, 10", #49330, 2008 MADC San Diego companion doll. $150.00.

The Sky's the Limit Lissy, 12", #49320, 2008 Convention companion doll. Blue long sparkly gown. Bead bracelet. $175.00.

WWII Wave Lissy, 12", #49200, 2008 Lissy Event souvenir. White uniform and hat with navy tie and shoulder bag. $150.00.

Christmas Candy — 8", #36435, 2003 (Wendy), with ornament $90.00
Winter Rose — 8", #36440, 2003, long rose gown, with ornament $100.00
Cherry Pie — 8", #31710, 2004, red checked dress $85.00
Holiday — 8", #31725, 2004, burgundy dress $80.00
Starlight Witch — 8", #31715, 2004, purple taffeta $100.00
Easter Joy — 8", #38160, 2004, lavender checked dress $100.00
Merrilee — 8", #40965, 2005, lace skirt, green top $85.00
Easter Finery — 8", #39975, 2005, white organza, straw hat $100.00
Easter Egg Hunt — 8", #42855, 2006, white sweater $85.00
Noel Rose — 8", #45645, 2006, green silk dress $95.00
Love Always – 8", #42810, 2007, pink angel, heart $95.00
April – 8", #45650, 2007, silk dress, Lenox bunny $95.00
Holiday Wishes – 8", #47465, 2007, red dress, rocking horse $95.00

Lillian Vernon

Christmas Doll — 8", #79630, 1996, green and gold holly print dress $80.00
Miss Millennium — 8", 1999, #80580, blue ball gown, watch $125.00
Christmas 2000 — 8", #27555, 2000, gown of white net with silver flecks, angel wings,
    silver crown, Christmas 2000 banner $75.00
St. Valentine's Day — 8", #26410, 2000, red and white outfit, limited to 2,000 ......$85.00
Easter — 8", #26150, 2000, white dress, plush bunny $90.00
Halloween Magic — 8", #27750, 2000, black velvet top $80.00
Nutcracker — 8", #27560, 2000, Nutcracker outfit $100.00
1940s Christmas — 8", #31740, 2001, red velvet coat $85.00
St. Patrick's Day — 8', #30325, 2001, ...$90.00
Autumn Fairy — 8", #32040, 2001, bronze and gold outfit $75.00
Halloween — 8", #31465, 2001, black and orange cat costume $75.00
4th of July — 8", #33615, 2003, white dresss $75.00
Peace Angel — 8", #35130, 2003, white gown $125.00
St. Patty's Day — 8", #31695, 2003, green costume $75.00
Trick or Treat Masquerade — 8", #33620, 2003, long black dress $125.00
Valentine's Day — 8", #33620, 2003, red velvet $75.00
Winter Wonderland — 8", #35120, 2003, red velvet, skates $80.00
Angel of Hope — 8", #37155, 2003, velvet costume $125.00
Easter Portrait — 8", #35205, 2003, lavender dress, rabbit $80.00
Happy Holidays to You — 8", #37150, 2003, red checked dress $75.00
He Loves Me — 8", #35145, 2003, valentine outfit $70.00
Irish Eyes — 8", #35150, 2002, red hair, green outfit $75.00
Pumpkins for Sale — 8", #37165, 2003, with pumpkin cart $100.00
Spiderella — 8", #37160, 2003, Halloween outfit $100.00
Bedazzled Lil' Devil — 8", #33735, 2005, red tutu $85.00
American Beauty — 8", #33865, 2005, long white dress trimmed in red...................$80.00
Christmas Caroler — 8", #45655, 2006, plaid dress, green cape $85.00
Christmas Visit – 8", #47620, 2007, red coat, hat, wrapped gifts $85.00

Lord & Taylor

Victoria — 14", 1989 ....$80.00

Madame Alexander Doll Club (M.A.D.C.) Convention Dolls

Fairy Godmother Outfit — 1983, for 8" non-Alexander designed by Judy LaManna $325.00
Ballerina — 8", 1984, FAD, limited to 360 ....$225.00
Happy Birthday — 8", 1985, FAD, limited to 450 ....$225.00
Scarlett — 8", 1986, F.A.D., red instead of green ribbon, limited to 625 ....$250.00
Cowboy — 8", 1987, limited to 720 ....$325.00
Davy Crockett Boy or Girl – 1987, leather outfit, made by Rebba Sutherland..... $125.00
Flapper — 10", 1988, FAD, black outfit instead of red, limited to 720 ....$175.00
Briar Rose — 8", 1989, uses Cissette head, limited to 804 ....$225.00
Riverboat Queen (Lena) — 8", 1990, limited to 925 ....$225.00
Queen Charlotte — 10", 1991, blue/gold outfit, limited to under 900 ....$325.00

WWII Coast Guard Lissy, 12", #49205. Lissy event centerpiece, limited to 45. Navy uniform trimmed in gold. $350.00.

Prom Queen (Memories) — 8", 1992, limited to 1,100 ....$110.00
Drucilla — 14", 1992, limited to 268..$200.00
Diamond Lil (Days Gone By) — 10", 1993, black gown, limited to 876 ....$325.00
Anastasia — 14", 1993, FAD, available at convention, limited to 489 ....$200.00
Navajo Woman — 8", 1994, comes with rug, sheep, and Hopi Kachina, limited to 835 ....$325.00
Flower Girl — 8", companion to 1995 souvenir doll, could be purchased separately............$125.00
Folsom, Frances — 10", 1995 convention doll, #79517 (married Grover Cleveland) $250.00
Showgirl — 10", 1996 convention doll, pink, blue, green, lavender, white feathers $275.00
    10", 1996 convention, black feather, limited to 20 pieces.......................................$500.00
A Little Bit of Country — 8", 1997, #79080, with guitar $200.00
Rose Festival Queen — 8", #79450, 1998, white gown, cape with roses $200.00
Margaret O'Brien — 8", #79590, 1998 Convention Companion doll $150.00
Orange Blossom — 10", 1999, long peach dress and gold straw hat $125.00
Electra — 8", 1999, Convention Companion doll, silver costume.....................................$75.00

Lilly Pulitzer — 21", 1999, Cissy Luncheon centerpiece doll, limited to 25...$1,400.00

Del Spa Cissette, 10", #49250, Cissette 2008 centerpiece. Robe over bikini, straw bag, chair, and turban. $150.00.

Cissy Accessories — 1999, no doll, accessories for 21" doll $60.00
Little Miss Bea — 2000, #26410, 8", honors Madame Bea Alexander, limited to 500.............$175.00
Going to M.A.D.C.C. — 8", #26415, 2000 convention doll, black bodice, ecru tulle, limited to 700...$225.00
Seaside Serenade Gala 2000 — 16" (Alex), long blue gown with rhinestones.........................$325.00
Abigail Adams — 10", #31510, 2001 convention doll, blue and lavender dress (Cissette)......$175.00
Louisa May Alcott — 8", #31511, 2001, limited to 325, vintage blue and white gown............$125.00
Aviatrix — 8", #31512, 2001, leather bomber jacket, khaki pants $125.00
Aviatrix centerpiece — 8", 2001, African-American, limited to 52 ....$175.00
Evening at the Pops Cissy — 21", #31735, 2001, luncheon doll, lavender dress, hat $250.00
Seaside Serenade Gala 2000 Centerpiece — 16", #27510, pink dressing gown (Alex), 2000...$450.00
Charles River Regatta Alex — 16", 2001, navy linen pants, white top, limited to 310 ....$250.00
Alex Regatta Ball — 16", #31650, 2001, limited to 52 ....$475.00
Cissy Gala — 21", 2000 luncheon doll, long blue and silver gown, limited to 300.................$400.00
Cissy Gala 2000 Centerpiece — 21", #27265, 2000, lavender dress, blonde $650.00
Skating Into Your Heart — 8", #26250, 2000, Travel Party...$175.00
Little Miss USA — 8", 2001, short patriotic costume...$85.00
Cissy Diva — #31730, 2001 centerpiece doll, fitted satin gown, faux fur, limited to 45..........$650.00
San Antonio Rose — 8", #34485, 2002, travel doll $175.00
Princess Fairy — 8", #34455, 2002, All in a Row souvenir doll, gold star wand with hearts $125.00
Navajo Boy — 8", #34480, 2002, travel doll centerpiece doll, limited to 45 ....$350.00
Alice in Wonderland — 10", #35415, 2002, Welcome Breakfast centerpiece doll, comes
    with 8" plush bunny, limited to 65...$275.00
Cissy Bridesmaid — 21", #34960, 2002, Cissy Luncheon centerpiece doll, pink lace
    over satin, limited to 40 ....$550.00
Cissy Bride — 21", 2002, Cissy Luncheon doll, white lace over satin, #34955, June Bride ...$350.00
Sketchbook Cissy — 21", #34460, 2002, Banquet centerpiece doll, long pale pink gown, limited to 70 ...$425.00
Sketchbook Cissette — 10", #34445, 2002, Kansas City Convention doll, limited to 450 ....$225.00
Masquerade Alex — 16", #34470, 2002, Alex souvenir, limited to 285, long sleek lavender gown......$150.00
Viva La Paris — 16", #34490, 2002 centerpiece, African-American, lavender feather
    showgirl costume, limited to 40..$250.00
Madame Sketchbook II — 8", #34465, 2002 companion, light pink dress.................................$65.00
White Rabbit — 10", plush, 2002 souvenir, blue dress, limited to 450 ....$20.00

Day at the Del Spa, 10", #49255, 2008 MADC Cissette souvenir. $175.00.

M.A.D.C.C. Flapper — 21", red taffeta with beading, raffle (Cissy) ....one-of-a-kind
Georgia — 10", #37005, 2003 companion, white Victorian dress, lavender sash, limited to 200 ....$175.00
Savannah — 8", #36995, 2003 convention doll, trunk, basket, limited to 525..........................$175.00
Savannah Slumber Party — 8", #32456, gown, blue robe, panties, shoes in black stripe
    hatbox, outfit only...$50.00
Wendy Visits Tybee Island — 8", #37040, 2003, travel doll, shorts, lavender top, pink bag,
    limited to 300..$125.00
Billy Visits Tybee Island — 8", #37245, 2003, travel centerpiece, red top, shorts....................$200.00
Taylor Debutante Alexandra Fairchild Ford — 16", #37765, 2003, Alex centerpiece,

Anchor's Away Lissy, 12", #49235, 2008 20 Plus centerpiece. White pleated dress with blue jacket. $250.00.

Anchor's Away Wendy, 8", #49240, 20 Plus souvenir doll. White pleated dress, blue jacket. Shadow of Lissy centerpiece. $175.00.

white long dress, red curly wig, limited to 35...$275.00

Sweater Set — #32459, 2003, Savannah 20+ souvenir outfit, only for 8", pink knit sweater and hat in black striped box, limited to 60 ....$50.00

Midnight Cissy — 21", #37015, 2003, Cissy event souvenir, black and white suit, hat, olive skintone, limited to 259..$450.00

Mademoiselle Cissy — 21", 37010, 2003, Cissy event centerpiece, suit, hat, limited to 40......$600.00

Southern Belle Cissy — 21", 31105, 2003, banquet centerpiece, blue raw silk and lace antebellum dress, limited to 65...$500.00

Yellow Rose of Texas — 8", #39180, 2004 souvenir doll, yellow and white bustle gown, silver boots and spurs, hat $225.00

Cinco de Mayo Cissette — 10", Cissette, event centerpiece, #34180, red satin dress, limited to 50.....$175.00

Mariachi Cissette — 10", #34220, 2004, souvenir doll, black jacket, skirt $150.00

Quanah Parker — 8", #33930, 2004, breakfast centerpiece, Indian outfit, blanket, long feather headdress $425.00

Blue Bonnet Maiden — 8", #34125, 2004, 20+ Event, Indian outfit, limited to 65 ....$350.00

Lone Star Wendy — 8", #34410, 2004, convention special, black checked shirt $175.00

Billy Bob's Bronco Rider — 8", #33905, 2004, travel doll, red shirt, chaps $125.00

Chisholm Trail Cowgirl — 8", #34156, 2004, All in a Row, blue checked shirt $150.00

Chisholm Trail Cowpoke — 8", #34255, 2004, All in a Row centerpiece, chaps.....................$225.00

Texas Ranger Companion Doll — 8", #33900, 2004, brown suit, long black coat.................$100.00

Western Matinee Lissy Outfit — blue and white cowgirl outfit, blue boots $75.00

1950s Lissy Cowgirl Centerpiece Outfit — red and brown outfit, brown boots.....................$150.00

Dance Hall Cissy — 21", 2004, *77 each of green, red, purple, and turquoise costumes*..........$325.00

Silver Spurs — 21", #33970, 2004, Cissy centerpiece, denim pants, jacket, leather chaps......$650.00

Cattle Baron — 21", #33975, 2004, banquet centerpiece, black suit, hat $600.00

Hall of Fame Alex — 16", 2004, western outfit, suede coat $225.00

Western Debutante — 16", #33990, 2004, striped top, western hat $175.00

Affair to Remember — 10", #37839, 2005 convention souvenir, Coquette, velvet top with white full long skirt..$175.00

Miss California —8", #41035, 2005 companion doll, navy vintage swimsuit, limited to 275.....$85.00

California Poppy —8", #41100, 2005, Thank You doll, gold and green outfit $100.00

Affair to Remember — 16", #41030, 2005, banquet centerpiece, Coco, black velvet top with full skirt...$275.00

Traveling to Disneyland — 8", #41080, 2005, travel souvenir, Maggie, pink cotton dress decorated with Disney characters..$200.00

Traveling with Hannah —10", #37727, 2005, travel party centerpiece, denim pants, jacket, mouse ears hat, small plush Mickey Mouse $70.00

Miss San Jose — 8", #41095, Maggie, 2005, breakfast centerpiece, red vintage bathing suit.....$125.00

Cissy Vixen — 21", #1110, 2005 Souvenir, pink or mauve taffeta dress with rhinestone bar accents, limited to 240 ....$375.00

Cissy Vamp — 21", 2005 Cissy centerpiece, beaded dress $1,100.00

Padre Sierra — 8", #41065, limited to 35, 2005, All in a Row centerpiece, brown hooded robe, cross, and Bible...$110.00

Mission Bride —8", #41070, 2005 AIR souvenir, long white lace dress $100.00

Little Miss California — 5", #37837, 2005, breakfast souvenir doll, vintage bathing suit.........$40.00

League of Her Own —8", #41115, 2005, blue vintage outfit with felt catcher's mitt...............$110.00

Hey Arnold —8", #41120, 2005, white suit, red striped coat and hat, tray of drinks $165.00

Tea with Sarah —8", #41045, 2005, 20+ souvenir, black 1800s costume $200.00

Dance Hall Cissette — 10", #41085, 2005, purple saloon costume with aqua drape $175.00

San Francisco Lady —10", Cissette centerpiece, #41090, long pink checked dress and hat, limited to 45 ....$200.00

Celebration Jadde Lee, 16", #41050, 2005 Alex centerpiece, long red Chinese dress $225.00

Celebration Alexandra Fairchild Ford —16", #41060, black brocade Chinese gown..............$175.00

Martha Jefferson — 8", #41785, 2006 souvenir doll, pink and wine striped ball gown, cameo...$200.00

Thomas Jefferson — 8", #41895, 2006 Companion, green waistcoat, tan pants, black hat $125.00

Patsy Jefferson — 8", #41840, 2006 Travel Doll, blue vintage dress $125.00

Polly Jefferson — 5", 2006 Breakfast Souvenir...$40.00
Mrs. Hopkinson — 10", #41845, 2006 Travel centerpiece, pink print vintage design, straw hat...$225.00
Sally Hemmings — 8", #43025, 2006 Special, African-American, print dress, apron, mop cap.....$300.00
Fife & Drum — 8", #41880, 2006, Companion Event centerpiece, red coat, white pants, drum....$200.00
Happy 20+ Day — 8", #41891, 2006 20+ doll, pink dress, straw hat, baby.............................$150.00
Virginia Dogwood — 8", #41905, 2006 Thank You doll, white petal skirt, wings, green tutu ...$150.00
Kate Greenaway — 8", #45560, 2006 Let's Talk Dolls centerpiece, elaborate pink dress, straw hat....$200.00
Alice in Wonderland — 10", #40508, 2006 Children's Event doll (Hannah Pepper), pig baby ...$95.00
Mame — 10", #41061, 2006 Coquette souvenir, gold dress, black jewel coat $150.00
Rosalind — 10", #40511, 2006 Coquette centerpiece, long red dress, fur trimmed, black gloves....$150.00
Sarah — 8", #41810, 2006 All in a Row souvenir, vintage silk dress, carpet bag....................$150.00
Sophia — 10", #41815, 2006 All in a Row centerpiece, vintage long pleated silk dress, straw hat....$225.00
Camille — 10", #41850, 2006 Cissette Event souvenir, leaf print dress, straw hat, umbrella.....$200.00
Amelie — 10", #41855, 2006 Cissette centerpiece, long white dress with embroidery, umbrella....$250.00
Serving Wench "Lottie" — 10", #41875, 2006 Breakfast centerpiece, red dress, apron, mop cap....$185.00
Princess Royal Lissy — 12", #45360, 2006 Lissy souvenir, blue silk dress, crown $200.00
Royal Reception Lissy — 12", #45365, 2006 Lissy centerpiece, blue rose-trimmed party dress $225.00
Classic Couture Alex — 16", #41805, 2006 centerpiece, pink Chanel type suit.......................$250.00
La Maison De Couture Alexandra — 16", #41800, souvenir, black lace long gown................$225.00
Morgan Le Fay — 21", #41865, 2006 Cissy centerpiece, limited to 60...................................$600.00
Lady of the Lake Cissy — 21", #41865, 2006 Cissy souvenir, blue and white flowing gown..$425.00
Governor's Ball Cissy — 21", #41703, 2006 Banquet centerpiece, limited to 23, purple
    1700s ball gown...$1,200.00
Governor's Ball Cissy — 21", #41702, 2006 Banquet centerpiece,
    blue, green, or pink 1700s ball gown, limited to 23 each ....$900.00 ea.
Wendy, Silver Celebrations — 8", #47240, 2007 companion doll, blue dress.........................$75.00
Little Pierrett — 5", #47320, 2007 breakfast doll, blue dress, white hat................................$35.00
Traveling by Riverboat — 8", #47290, 2007 Travel Event centerpiece, limited to 60, blue stripe pinafore...$100.00
Thank Heaven for Little Girls — 8", #47310, 2007 20 Plus souvenir, purple dress..................$75.00
Butterfly Kisses — 12", #47285, 2007 Lissy Event Centerpiece, limited to 65, lavender check dress....$150.00
Chasing Butterflies — 12", #47280, 2007, Lissy souvenir, limited to 225, print dress, butterfly net...$150.00
Marie Lavoue — 10", #47325, 2007 Convention Special, red and white dress, limited to 125.....$225.00
Jean LaFitte's Lady — 10", #47350, 2007 Cissette Event souvenir, gold ball gown...............$200.00
Jean LaFitte's Privateer Ball — 10", #47345, 2007 Cissette centerpiece, pirate costume $250.00
Missy Pierrett & Missy Harlequin — 8" pair, #47315, 2007 Breakfast centerpiece, limited to 80...$175.00
Steel Magnolia "Past" — 10", #47270, 2007 All in a Row centerpiece, blue long gown, straw hat ...$150.00
Steel Magnolia "Today" — 10", #47275, 2007 All in a Row souvenir, blue suit, straw hat.....$125.00
Louisiana Magnolia — 8", #47255, 2007 Thank You doll, long white dress, limited to 50.....$100.00
Up to the Mississippi in Style — 8", #47295, Travel souvenir, limited to 275, long dress $80.00
Harley Youth Event — 10", #47330, Youth event souvenir, 2007, limited to 50.......................$60.00
Meet Me in the French Quarter — 16", #47305, 2007 Alex centerpiece, limited to 35..........$135.00
A Cotillion Welcome 1810 Coquette — 10", #46335, limited to 40, Coquette centerpiece.....$150.00
King & Queen Mardi Gras — 8" set, limited to 50, 2007 centerpiece at Mardi Gras event...$200.00
MADCC Mardi Gras Queen — 10", #45530, Mardi Gras event souvenir, limited to 200.....$175.00
MADCC Silver Celebration — 10", #47245, 2007 convention doll, limited to 450...............$225.00
Cecelia — 21", #47260, 2007 Cissy Event souvenir, limited to 200, multicolored dress.........$325.00
MADCC Silver Celebration Cissy — 21", #47250, 2007 Banquet centerpiece, limited to 80,
    blue long gown..$500.00
Jazz, Muse of Music Cissy — 21", #47265, 2007 Cissy Event centerpiece, limited to 40......$550.00
The Sky's the Limit Wendy — 8", #49310, 2008 convention doll, blue long sparkly dress...$150.00
The Sky's the Limit Cissette — 10", #49330, 2008 convention companion,
    blue sparkly dress $150.00
The Sky's the Limit Lissy — 12", #49320, 2008 companion doll, blue long sparkly dress....$175.00
WWII Wave Lissy — 12", #49200, 2008 Lissy event souvenir, white uniform, bag ...$150.00
WWII Coast Guard Lissy — 12', #49205, Lissy event center, Navy uniform, ltd. to 45..$350.00
Del Spa Cissette — 10", #49250, Cissette 2008 event center, robe over bikini, bag, chair .$150.00

Madame's First Star, 7", #49270 (Tiny Betty). Scarlett type green print dress and straw hat, parasol. First introduction of new Tiny Betty doll. $175.00.

White Carnation Wendy, 8", #49275, 2008 MADC Thank You Doll, White carnation dress. $175.00.

Quincianta, 10", #49280, 2008 teen souvenir doll. Pink ball gown, silver crown. $150.00.

Stargazing in Hollywood, 8", #49230, 2008 Travel Event Souvenir. Print top, jeans, heart bag, camera, sunglasses, and map. $125.00.

Day at the Del Spa — 10", #49255, 2008 Cissette event souvenir, white top, aqua pants.. $175.00
Anchor's Away Lissy — 12", #49235, 2008 20+ center, white pleated dress, blue jacket.. $250.00
Anchor's Away Wendy — 8", #49240, 20+ souvenir doll, white dress, blue jacket $175.00
Madame's First Star — 7", #49270 (Tiny Betty), Scarlett green print dress, straw hat... $175.00
White Carnation Wendy — 8", #49275, 2008 MADCC Thank You doll,
      white carnation dress $175.00
Quincianta — 10", #49280, 2008 teen souvenir, pink ball gown, silver crown .. $150.00
Stargazing in Hollywood — 8", #49230, 2008 travel event souvenir,
      jeans, heart bag, map, camera $125.00
Sunset Drive Wendy — 8", #49340, AIR souvenir, silk vintage dress, hat $175.00
Off for a Sunset Drive pair — 8", #49335, 2008 AIR center,
      ltd. to 50, vintage outfits, roadster.. $375.00
Cissy in the Garden of Fairies — 21", Cissy event souvenir, 2008, lavender fairy outfit . $300.00
In the Garden Fairy & The Stars Cissy — 21", in long green gown,
      8" Wendy in lavender fairy outfit $475.00
Sunset Cissy, 21", 2008 banquet center, orange long evening gown $475.00
Yachting to the Ball Coquette, 10", 2008 Coquette event, blue top, white pants, straw hat.... $125.00

M.A.D.C. Dolls, Exclusives (available to club members only)

Wendy — 8", 1989, in pink and blue, limited to 4,878, first club doll................... $150.00
Polly Pigtails — 8", 1990 (Maggie Mixup), limited to 4,896................................ $90.00
Miss Liberty — 10", 1991 – 1992, red, white, and blue gown (Cissette)................ $125.00
Little Miss Godey — 8", 1992 – 1993 .... $90.00
Wendy's Best Friend Maggie — 8", 1994.. $65.00
Wendy Loves Being Best Friends — 8", name embroidered on apron, 1994............ $65.00
Wendy Loves the Dionnes — 8", one-of-a-kind set of five dolls, made for 1994 convention ... not available
Ultimate Cissy — 21", one-of-a-kind for 1996 convention .... not available
Wendy Joins M.A.D.C. — 8", #79552, 1995 .... $275.00
Wendy Honors Margaret Winson — 8", 1996 post-mistress outfit, honoring first
      M.A.D.C. president $75.00
From the Madame's Sketchbook — 8", 1997, replica of 1930s Tiny Betty $90.00
Skate with Wendy — 8", 1998, plaid skating outfit, silver key $65.00
M.A.D.C. Boutique — 8", 1998 – 2002, frilly panties, white top $40.00
Electro — 8", 1999 (Maggie), silver space costume, boy $75.00
M.A.D.C. Angel — 8", 2000, pink gown, limited to 800 .... $150.00
M.A.D.C. Ballerina — 8", 2001, blue ballerina $110.00
Springtime Darling — 8", 1999, blue dress, pink trim...................................... $75.00
Summer Blossom — 8", 1999, bikini, skirt, sandals.. $75.00
M.A.D.C. Story Princess — 8", #79550, 2002, rose gown, silver crown................ $175.00
Recipe for Contentment — 8", #37185, 2003, pink outfit.................................. $75.00
Glamour Girl — 8", 2004, #35020, red print dress, club doll............................ $100.00
Signature Wendy — 5", 2005 Renewal Club doll, print dress, straw hat $40.00
Victoria — 8", 2005, pink dress, black hat, club doll (Wendy) $85.00
Blue Danube — 8", 2006 club doll, long blue print gown $88.00
Doll Collector's Day — 8", 2006 special, pink and blue checked dress.................. $88.00
Cotton Candy Lissy — 12", #46146, 2007, club doll, pastel stripe dress $90.00
Cotton Candy Wendy — 8", 2007, club doll, pastel stripe doll $80.00
Tribute to Sisters – 10", 2008 club dolls, brunette, ltd to 150; African-American, limited to 100...... $90.00

M.A.D.C. Symposium/Premiere

Disneyworld — 1984 – 1985 (1984 paper doll) $60.00
Wendy Goes to Disneyworld — #1 Sunshine Symposium, 1986, navy dress with polka
      dots, Mickey Mouse hat, pennant (costume by Dorothy Starling), limited to 100.......... $125.00

M.A.D.C. Snowflake Symposium and Premieres

1st Illinois, 1986, tagged orange taffeta/lace dress, metal pail, and orange, limited to 200........ $80.00
2nd Illinois, 1987, tagged, little girl cotton print dress (costume by Mary Voigt) $80.00
3rd Illinois, 1988, tagged, gold/white print dress, gold bodice (created by Pamela Martenec) $80.00
4th Illinois, 1989, tagged, red velvet ice skating costume (created by Joan Dixon)................. $80.00

5th Illinois, 1990, bride by Linda's Bridal Shop (also Michelau Scarlett could be purchased) $85.00
   Scarlett — 8", 1990, #6, FAD (white medallion – Snowflake Symposium; red medallion –
     Premiere Southern Symposium), limited to 800 ....$150.00
Springtime — 8", 1991, #7, floral dress, scalloped pinafore, straw hat, limited to 1,600 ....$100.00
Wintertime — 8", 1992, #8, all white, fur trim and hat (six locations), limited to 1,650 ....$125.00
Homecoming — 8", 1993, #9 car coat with color trim (eight different colors, one for
   each location), limited to 2,000 ....$125.00
Setting Sail for Summer — 8" 1994, #10 (eight locations), limited to 1,800 ....$125.00
Snowflake — 8", #79404, #11, 1995 (six locations), gold skater, limited to 1,200 ....$125.00
Wendy Starts Her Travels — 8", 1996, #12 (three locations), trunk set, different color
   checked coat each location $175.00
Bobby Takes a Picture — 8", 1996, California companion doll, limited to 215 pieces.............$225.00
Cheshire Cat — 8", 1996, Texas companion doll, limited to 215 pieces...................................$175.00
Wendy Tours the Factory — 8", 1996, New Jersey companion doll...$150.00
Wendy's Tea Party — 8", #13, 1997 (four locations), pink organdy dress, tea set...................$125.00
Boo — 8", 1996, 150 pieces, ghost costume over Mother's Day doll, Illinois event.................$125.00
Diamond Pixie — 8", 1998, #14 (three locations), red Pixie costume $175.00
Starlett Glamour — 10", 1999, #15, black evening gown...$225.00
Millennium Wendy — 8", 2000, #25155, blue dress, straw hat, watch.....................................$150.00
On the Town Alex — 16", 2001, gold dress and coat...$150.00
Evening on the Town Alex — 16", 2001, centerpiece doll, long black gown, stole $350.00
Spring Garden Party — 8", #34495, 2002 (Maggie), yellow dress..$100.00
Spring Garden Party Centerpiece — 10", 2002, #34510 (Cissette), yellow outfit $175.00
M.A.D.C. March Winds, travel party outfit, red striped skirt $50.00
Wendy Turns 50 — 8", #36220, souvenir doll, 2003, lavender satin dress, limited to 400.......$100.00
Wendy Turns 50 Centerpiece — 8", #36621, 2003, mint green satin dress, limited to 45........$150.00
Wendy Turns 50 Travel Outfit — 2003, red straw hat, red dot bathing suit.............................$40.00
Premiere Going Away Wendy — 8", #35801, 2004, white satin dress and hat $125.00
Premiere Bride and Groom Centerpiece — 8", #36595, 2004, limited to 60 ....$250.00
Premiere Bridesmaid Wendy Blue Companion — 8", #34920, 2004, limited to 110 ....$175.00
Premiere Bridesmaid Wendy Violet Companion — 8", #34605, 2004, limited to 110 ....$175.00
Premiere Flower Girl — 5", #34369, 2004, pink satin dress $60.00
Wendy Attends the Ballet — 8", #31830, 2005, travel party, limited to 300.............................$125.00
Evening at the Ballet — 10", 2005, travel party centerpiece, limited to 50 ....$225.00
First Recital Breakfast souvenir — 5", 2005, lion costume..$50.00
First Recital Centerpiece — 8", 2005, lion costume...$225.00
Wendy Loves the Ballet — 8", 2005, banquet centerpiece, limited to 60 ....$175.00
Prima Ballerina — 8", 2005 souvenir doll, black and magenta costume....................................$125.00
Sugar — 8", 2006 souvenir doll, bend knees, pink dress...$95.00
Everything Nice — 5", souvenir, matches Sugar $40.00
Spice Cissette — 10", special doll, red dress $150.00
Cissy Spice — 21", 2006 centerpiece, long red dress $400.00
Puppy Dog Tails — 8", 2006 centerpiece, green outfit, plush dog..$125.00
Wendy's New Jean Jacket — 8", #46895, 2007, pink dress, blue jacket $95.00
Designer Cissette's First Toy Fair — 10", 2008 Premiere souvenir, black dress, red jacket, portfolio $185.00
Grace's Engagement — 21" (Cissy), premiere special, black strapless evening gown, ring $475.00
My Dutch Friend Dana — 12", #48230, 2008 Travel Center Lissy,
   blue stripe Dutch outfit $275.00
Elizabeth's European Vacation — 12", #48240, 2008 Travel souvenir,
   jeans, tweed coat, camera $125.00
Cissette's First Design — 8", #48250 (Wendy), 2008 banquet center,
   ltd. to 65, pink sailor dress, boat $150.00
M.A.D.C. Friendship Luncheon (outfit only)
   Friends Around the Country — 1997, print dress and pinafore outfit $50.00
   Wendy Plays Masquerade — 1998, pink butterfly costume $50.00
   Wendy, Out and About with Friends — 1999, brown felt coat, leopard tam and purse $50.00

Sunset Drive Wendy, 8", #49340, All in a Row souvenir. Silk vintage dress and hat. $175.00.

Off for a Sunset Drive Pair, 8", #49335, 2008 MADC All in a Row centerpiece. Shown is red roadster and luggage. $375.00.

Cissy in the Garden of Fairies, 21", Cissy event souvenir 2008 MADC convention. $300.00.

Sunset Cissy, 21", 2008 MADC Banquet centerpiece. Orange long evening gown. $475.00.

Wendy Emcees Her School Play — 2000, pinafore, print dress, pink tam, standing microphone, limited to 700 ....$50.00
Wendy Starts Holiday Shopping — #31815, 2001, red and black dress and hat $50.00
Thanksgiving at Grandma's — 2002, silk plaid dress $50.00
Thanksgiving at Grandma's Centerpiece — 8", braids, plaid dress (doll included) $125.00
Hugs Wendy — 8", #36230, 2003, souvenir doll, black velvet top, white skirt with x's and o's, limited to 700 ....$75.00
Kisses — luncheon centerpiece, #36231, 2003 (Maggie), pink shirt with x's and o's $100.00
Special Kisses — Helper doll, 8", #36234, 2003 (Maggie), pink skirt, limited to 25 ....$125.00
Special Hugs — Helper doll, #36232, 2003, Wendy, special hairdo, limited to 20 ....$150.00
Hugs African-American — Helper doll, 8", #36233, 2003, white skirt, limited to 30 ....$200.00
Wendy Goes Skating — 8", #38135, 2004, Asian face, limited to 40 ....$150.00
Wendy Goes Skiing — 8", #38570, 2004, pink and blue outfit $75.00
Wendy Goes Sledding — 8", #38795, 2004, centerpiece, limited to 150.................................$125.00
MADC 2005 Special Set — 8" Maggie, 8" African American, #41375, limited to 50, wagon, cat, dog, mini doll $200.00
MADC 2005 Fall Friendship Centerpiece — 8", #41370, dog, cat $125.00
MADC 2005 Fall Friendship Souvenir — 8", #32980, mini doll $75.00
Simonne — 8", #41755, 2006, fuchsia dress $95.00
Juliet — 10", #41760, 2006, auction piece...$175.00
The Captain — 8", #41765, 2006, white jacket $85.00
Going to the Big Game — 8", 2007 Friendship souvenir, jeans, jacket, football $60.00
Marching in the Band — 8", #47225, 2007 centerpiece, uniform, red hat, French horn.. $175.00
Touchdown! Touchdown! — 8" Cheerleader Maggie & 8" Quarterback, auction pair ... $325.00

Madame Alexander Doll Company

Melody & Friends — 25", 1992, limited to 1,000, designed and made by Hildegard Gunzel, 1st anniversary dolls ....$700.00 up, set
Courtney & Friends — 25" and 8" boy and girl, 1993, second anniversary, limited to 1,200, by Gunzel ....$725.00 up, set
Rumpelstiltskin and Miller's Daughter — 8" and 14", #1569, 1992 only, limited to 3,000 ......$275.00
Special Event Doll — 8", 1994, organza and lace in pink with special event banner, ribbon across body, front of hair pulled back in curls $75.00
Wendy Makes It Special — 8", 1998, #31050, pink and white dress, hatbox $85.00
Wendy Salutes the Olympics — 8", #86005, 1996, Olympic medal $85.00
Maggie Mixup — 8", 1998, #31000, Post Office commemorative, blue gingham.....................$50.00
75th Anniversary Wendy — 8", #22420, 1998, pink outfit $80.00
Wendy's Special Cheer — 8", #16510, cheerleader, 1999 ....$70.00
George and Martha Washington — 8", 1999, limited...$200.00 set
Mary McFadden Cissy* — 21", 1999, black and gold gown .... one-of-a-kind
Isaac Mizrahi Cissy* — 21", 1999, gray skirt, red sweater .... one-of-a-kind
Carmen Marc Valvo Cissy* — 21", 1999, long evening gown .... one-of-a-kind
Nicole Miller — 21", 1999, dress and fur coat .... one-of-a-kind
Diane Von Furstenberg Cissy* — 21", 1999, black dress, fur coat .... one-of-a-kind
Yeohlee Cissy* — 21", 1999, black skirt, long black coat .... one-of-a-kind
Betsy Johnson Cissy* — 21", 1999, black short dress trimmed in pink .... one-of-a-kind
Scaasi Cissy* — 21", 1999, white lace gown, red coat with feather $425.00
Jessica McClintock Cissy* † — 21", 1999, #22780, long gold ball gown..................................$475.00
Fernando Sanchez Cissy* † — 21", 1999, #22720, long white gown $400.00
Josie Natori Cissy* † — 21", 1999, #22730 ....$450.00
Anna Sui Cissy* † — 21", 1999, #22590, has braids, brown dress, coat $475.00
Linda Allard for Ellen Tracy Cissy* † — 21", 1999, brown skirt, long black coat $475.00
Dana Buchman Cissy* † — 21", 1999, green dress, coat $475.00
Donna Karan Cissy* † — 21", 1999, long black dress... one-of-a-kind
James Purcell Cissy* † — 21", 1999, long white gown with black circles $375.00
Madame Alexander Celebrates American Design Cissy* † — 21", 1999, #22560.....................$225.00
Badgley Mischka Cissy* † — 21", 1999, #22740, long evening gown $450.00

Marc Bouwer Cissy* † — 21", 1999, #26125, African-American doll, long gown...................$550.00
Carolina Herrera Cissy* † — 21", 1999, #26121, red and white ball gown $475.00
An American Legend book and doll in display box $200.00
Charm and Cheer Lissy — 12", 2006, print dress, pink velvet coat, straw hat .... one-of-a-kind
Silhouette Cissy — 21", #41570, 2006, limited to 30, Gene Convention Special, pink hat,
    blue and black dress...$650.00

Madame Alexander Doll Company Mid-Year Specials
Welcome Home — 8", 1991, black or white, boy or girl, Desert Storm soldier $50.00
Wendy Loves Being Loved — 8", 1992, doll and wardrobe...$100.00
Queen Elizabeth II — 8", 1992, 40th anniversary of coronation $125.00
Christopher Columbus — 8", 1992, #328, burgundy and brown costume $125.00
Queen Isabella — 8", 1992, #329, green velvet and gold gown...$125.00
Santa or Mrs. Claus — 8", 1993...$125.00 ea.
Scarlett O'Hara — 8", 1993, yellow dress, straw hat...$150.00
Wendy Ann — 8", 1995, 100th anniversary, pink coat and hat...$125.00
Sir Lancelot DuLac — 8", 1995, burgundy and gold knight's costume $125.00
Queen Guinevere — 8", 1995, burgundy and gold gown $125.00
Wizard of Oz — 8", 1994, green metallic costume, black hat $125.00
Dorothy — 8", 1994, emerald green checked dress $225.00
Wicked Witch — 8", 1994, green face, black costume...$250.00
Little Miss USA — 8", 2002, red skirt, blue jacket, hat, baton, charity for 9-11 ....$75.00
Tidings of Joy Ballerina — 2006, blonde (#41150), brunette (#41155), red (#41160),
    African-American (#41161), Asian (#41162), red and gold tutu $85.00
The Spirit of New Orleans — 2006, purple Mardi Gras outfit...$100.00

Madame Alexander Heritage Gallery
Perfectly Bewitching — 8", #46740, 2006, Halloween tutu, black cat.......................................$85.00
In the Holiday Spirit — 8", #46735, 2006, #46738 African American, #46736 blonde,
    #46738 redhead $85.00

Marshall Fields
Avril, Jane — 10", 1989, red/black can-can outfit (tribute to T. Lautrec) (Cissette) $125.00
Madame Butterfly — 10", 1990, blue brocade kimono, gold obi $150.00

Matilda Company
Sweet Parfait Blonde — 8", #33590, 2003, silk outfit, #33591, Redhead $90.00
Sweet Parfait African-American — 8", #33592, 2003, silk outfit $90.00
Wendy's Favorite Keepsake — 8", #36780, 2003, ...$85.00
Birthday Wishes — 8", #40207 redhead, #40271 blonde, #40272 brunette, pink dress, 2006...$85.00

Metroplex Doll Club
Spring Break — 8", 1992, two-piece halter/wrap skirt outfit, limited to 400, beach bag.........$150.00
Victorian Tea — 8", #34000, 2002, blue pleated skirt, U.F.D.C. Luncheon $100.00

Meyers 80th Year
8", "Special Event" doll with banner, 1994 ....$75.00

Modern Doll Convention
Modern Romance Alex — 16", 2000, long strapless dress, limited to 200....................................$275.00
Modern Romance Alex centerpiece — 16", 2000, long strapless henna dress, limited to 20...$700.00
Up-to-the-Minute "Mod" Alex — 16", 2002, #35710, black gown, limited to 30.....................$200.00
Up-to-the-Minute "Mod" Cissette — 10", 2002, #35711, centerpiece doll, black gown..........$175.00
1871 Chicago Belle — 10", #36336, 2004, pink taffeta dress..$175.00
Bella — 8", #36560, 2004, blue silk dress, limited to 50..$150.00
Belle of the Ball Alex — 16", centerpiece, limited to 36, 2004 ....$250.00
Fairy Godmother — 10" (Cissette), #40985, 2006, red cape, limited to 40 ....$175.00
Celebration Minnie and Mickey — 8", #40740, Mickey faces, white outfits............................$200.00
Stolling Beneath the Stars Cissette — 10", #41940, 2006, brocade dress.................................$250.00
Strolling Beneath the Stars Cissy — 21", #41915, 2006, brocade dress, limited to 35.............$400.00
Strolling Beneath the Stars Wendy — 8", #41920, 2006, red dress $95.00
Happily Ever After Cinderella — 10", Coquette Jacqui, 10", #40980, 2005, souvenir,
    limited to 300, pink gown $160.00

Victoria, 8", 2005 (Wendy). Second in series of Glamour Girl Club doll. $85.00.

My Dutch Friend Dana, 12", #48230, 2008 Travel Lissy centerpiece. Blue stripe Dutch outfit, lace hat, "wooden" shoes. $275.00.

Elizabeth's European Vacation, 12", #48240, 2008 Travel Doll Souvenir. Print top and hat, tweed jacket and jeans. $125.00.

Indian Princess Cissy – 21", #47580, 2007, Indian outfit................................$550.00
Yellow Rose of San Antonio – 12", #45525, 2007, yellow cowgirl outfit $150.00
Yellow Rose & Indian Princess Companion Set – 10" pair, #47575, 2007
    Indian outfit, cowgirl outfit, limited to 50..................................$250.00

M. Pancner's House of Collectibles
1920s Golden Girl — 10", #17740, 1999, limited to 25...........................$125.00
1950s Sock Hop — 8", #17780, 1999, limited to 50 ....$75.00

My Doll House
Southern Belle — 10", 1989, FAD, all pink gown with parasol and picture hat, limited to 2,300 ....$125.00
Queen Elizabeth I — 10", 1990, limited to 2,400.................................$125.00
Empress Elizabeth of Austria — 10", 1991, white/gold trim, limited to 3,600 (Cissette) $150.00

Neiman-Marcus
Doll with four outfits in trunk — 8", 1990, called "party trunk," limited to 1,044 ....$250.00
Caroline Loves Storyland — 8", 1993, trunk and wardrobe $250.00
Caroline's Adventures — 8", 1994, trunk and costumes for USA, China, Germany, Kenya (Maggie).....$225.00
Anne Series — 8", 1994, trunk set, character from Lucy M. Montgomery books $250.00
ABC Huggums — limited to 650 pieces $65.00
Miss St. John — 21", 1998, limited to 750 ....$500.00
Crayola Sets — 1999, dolls from regular line in ethnic sets $70.00
Holly Day — 8", #28195, #28196, #28197, 2000, red velvet dress...............$100.00
Alex Zenra — 16", #31860, 2001, maroon dress, limited to 250 ....$110.00
Morning Dew Victoria — #28636, 2001, African-American $75.00
Pink Bunny Huggums— #28961, 2001, African-American $65.00
Shopping for Mommy — 8", #40089, 2004, pink dress, shopping bag, limited to 75 ....$150.00
Breakfast at Neiman's — 8", #41725, 2006, pink dress, hat, bag................$85.00
Neiman Marcus Centennial Doll – 10", #47790, 2007, black silk dress, jacket, hat, shopping bag....$185.00

New England Collector Society
Noel — 12", 1989 – 1991, porcelain Christmas doll, limited to 5,000............$200.00
Joy — 12", 1991, porcelain Christmas doll, limited to 5,000 ....$200.00

New York Doll Club
Autumn in New York — 10", FAD, limited to 260...............................$150.00

Nordstrum's
Binah — 12", #39160, 2004, cloth, Nicole, #39446.............................$50.00
Charlotte — 12", #39448, 2004, cloth, Amy, #39444, Grace, #39447 ....$50.00

Oma's Doll Shop
Victorian Seaside Wendy — 8", #35475, 2003, vintage bathing suit, limited to 1,000..............$90.00
Baby Take a Bow — 8", #40960, red dotted cotton dress.......................$85.00
Overlook Hospital Centennial Nurse —10", 2006, blue coat, white uniform $150.00
Wendy's Precious Moments – 8", #45760, 2007, white dress, 3" Precious Moments doll $100.00

Paris Fashion Doll Convention
City Lights Alex —16", 2001, long white gown, limited to 200...................$700.00
City Lights centerpiece — 16", 2001, limited to 20.............................$1,500.00
Festival Paris — 16", 2002, #34545, white dress, black velvet coat, limited to 50 ....$700.00
Festival Alex — 16", 2002, #34550, lavender 20s dress, limited to 50............$700.00
Alex — 16", #37690, 2003, Paris Festival souvenir, blue gown...................$400.00
10th Anniversary Alex — 16", 2004, silk halter dress, limited to 30..............$500.00
Evening in Paris Cissy — 21", #41330, taffeta dress, limited to 20..............$1,200.00
Evening in Paris Coquette — 10", #40035, 2006, taffeta dress, limited to 100......$275.00
Suzette Morgan — 16", 2006, tweed sheath dress, jacket $450.00
Royal Splendor Cissy – 21", 2007, blue ballgown, silver bead trim $750.00

Penney, J.C.
At the Hop — 8", #27860, 2000, skirt with hoops............................$85.00

QVC
Summer Cherry Picking — 8", #79760, 1998 (Wendy), cherry print dress, limited to 500 ....$175.00
Betsy Ross — 8", #79990, 1998 (Wendy), red striped dress, limited to 500........$95.00
Pilgrim Girl — 8", #79980, 1998 (Wendy), long blue dress, limited to 500 ....$90.00

Cissette's First Design, 8", #48250 (Wendy). 2008 Banquet centerpiece. Limited to 65. Pink sailor dress, boat. $150.00.

Home for the Holidays — 10", #79800, 1998 (Cissette), limited to 400 ....$125.00
A Rose for You — 8", 1999 (Wendy), lace-trimmed white dress with rose........................$75.00
Lavender Rose — 10", 1999, lavender ball gown...$100.00
Pollyana — 8", 1999 (Maggie), blue checked dress, straw hat, limited to 500.........................$75.00
Blossom — 8", 1999, pink print dress (Wendy), limited to 500 ....$75.00
Little Bo Peep — 8", 1999, pink gown trimmed in lace, limited to 700.......................$80.00
Investigator Wendy — 8", 1999 (checked coat and hat), limited to 500.......................$80.00
Autumn Breeze — 8", 1999 ....$80.00
Alice — 8", 1999 ....$80.00
Kiss Me, I'm Irish — 8", 1999 (Maggie), green skirt, limited to 500 ....$80.00
Ladybug Garden — 8", 1999..$75.00
Fun at Halloween — 8", 1999, limited to 500 pieces (Maggie), yellow and black costume $80.00
Golden Light Tree Topper — 8", 1999, yellow and black costume, limited to 400 ....$125.00
Spring Flowers — 8", 1999, print dresss, basket of flowers (Maggie) $70.00
Fourth of July — 8", 1999...$75.00
Springtime Bride — 10", 1999, white slender dress, limited to 400 ....$100.00

Reverie Publishing Company
Cissette as Lady Hamilton – 10" $150.00

Robert Moore and Company
Azalea Trail Maid — 8", #34555, 2003, long peach silk gown...................................$150.00
Azalea Trail Green — 8", #35590, Tosca, #33591, brunette $150.00
Pink Azalea Trail Queen — 10", #35095, long pink gown, Brunette, #35096.....................$175.00

Saks Fifth Avenue
Christmas Carol — 8", 1993, tartan plaid taffeta dress with velvet bodice.......................$150.00
Joy of Christmas — 1994, second in series, forest green taffeta dress $100.00
Book Tour Alex with Saks bag — 16", #31207, 2001 ....$125.00

Savannah Doll Club
Georgia State Day — 8", 2002, white dress with black trim, limited to 160 ....$125.00

Sears-Roebuck
Little Women — 1989 – 1990, set of six 12" dolls (Nancy Drew) ....$600.00 set

Shirley's Doll House
Angel Face — 8", 1990 (Maggie Mixup), blue gown, white wings, limited to 3,500................$80.00
Winter Sports — 8", 1991, FAD (Tommy Snooks), skates, tagged hat, limited to 975 ....$70.00
Wendy Visits World's Fair — 1993, 100th anniversary Chicago World's Fair, limited to 3,600 ....$85.00
Winter Angel — 1993, cape with hood, wings, holds golden horn, exclusive, limited to 1,000....$100.00
Maypole Dance — 8", 1994, shop's 20th anniversary doll, pink organdy dress and blue
    pinafore, limited to 3,000 (Wendy Ann)...$75.00
Grandma's Darling — 8", 1996, #79617, yellow dress, white blanket $75.00
Little Collector — 8", 1999, #79820, navy dress, straw hat, basket $80.00
Grandma's Girl — 8", #31545, 2001, brown dress with book, limited to 300.....................$75.00
Once Upon a Time — 8", #31550, 2001, pink dress, crown $80.00

Shriner's First Ladies' Luncheon
8" boy, 1993, wears fez, jeans, shirt, vest with Texas star on back, limited to 1,800 ....$350.00

Smithsonian
Lady in Blue — 10", Cissette, #45750, 2006, limited to 150, blue taffeta evening gown $200.00

South Carolina Chimney Sweep Guild
Lucky Dale — 8", #31975, 2001, top hat, tail, ladder $125.00

Spiegel's
Beth — 10", 1990, 125th anniversary special, 1860s women, pink brocade gown...................$125.00
Christmas Tree Topper (also called Merry Angel) — 8", 1991, gold and red velvet angel costume ... $150.00
Joy Noel — 8", 1992, tree topper angel, white satin/net with gold dots, gold lace, halo and
    skirt, limited to 3,000 ....$100.00
Mardi Gras — 10", 1992, elaborate costume of purple/gold/royal blue, limited to 3,000........$100.00

Toy Shoppe, The
Springtime Silk Wendy-Kin Wood — 8", #40110, 2004, silk dress $275.00
Wendy Ann Felt — 12", #37945, 2004, cloth doll, blue dress $250.00

Marching in the Band, 8", #47225, 2008 Friendship Luncheon centerpiece. $175.00.

Touchdown! Touchdown!, 8" pair, 2007 Friendship Luncheon Auction pair. Maggie cheerleader and quarterback. $325.00.

Yellow Rose of San Antonio, 12", #45525 (Lissy). 2007 Lissy event souvenir. $150.00.

Desert Bird, 8", #41730, 2007 Tuscon Guild Luncheon souvenir. $100.00.

Midnight Elegance Coquette Cissy — 10", #39845, 2005, black satin dress $150.00
Sapphire Symphony Coquette Cissy — 10", #41245, 2005, blue satin dress $150.00
Romance and Roses Coquette Cissy — 10", #41405, 2005, pink taffeta dress $150.00
Wendy Shops at the Toy Shoppe — 8", #41410, 2005, pink jacket, white dress,
    mini Wendy, shopping bag $80.00
Teatime with Teddy — 8", #41420, 2005, blue dress, tiny bear.......................................$80.00
Lilac Swirls — 8", #41930, 2005, limited to 1,000, ballerina...$70.00
Edith the Lonely Doll Felt — 12", #41425, 2005, pink checked dress $250.00
Wendy Loves Rudolph — 8", 2006, red checked dress, deer, doll, limited to 500 ....$90.00
Midnight Elegance — 10", 2007, black outfit...$90.00

Toys 'R Us
Wendy Loves Hello Kitty City – 8", #47475, 2007, yellow and blue outfit, plush kitty.............$95.00

Tuscon Doll Guild Luncheon
Hats Off to Alex — 16", #40935, 2006, blue print sundress, straw hat, limited to 40 ....$135.00
Hats off to Coquette Cissy — 10", #40940, 2006, blue print sundress, straw hat $110.00
Apache Rose – 8", #41731, 2007, red cape $175.00
Desert Bird – 8", #41730, 2007, blue Indian attire $100.00

Two Daydreamers
Whitney — 8", #34106, 2001, ribbon and jewel crown, limited to 120 ....$125.00
Morgan LeFay — 10", #41415, 2006 ....$125.00

U.F.D.C. — United Federation of Doll Clubs
Sailor Boy — 8", 1990, gray gabardine outfit, limited to 260 ....$375.00
Miss Unity — 10", 1991, cotton eyelet dress, limited to 310 ....$325.00
Little Emperor — 8", 1992, elaborate silk and gold costume, limited to 400.........................$325.00
Turn of the Century Bathing Beauty — 10", 1992, U.F.D.C. Region Nine Conference,
    FAD (Gibson Girl), old-fashioned bathing suit, beach bag, umbrella, limited to 300......$225.00
Columbian 1893 Sailor — 12", 1993 (Lissy) $95.00
Gabrielle — 10", 1998 (Cissette), black suit, dressmaker's stand, limited to 400.................$225.00
One Enchanted Evening — 16", 1999, #80260, limited to 310 ....$300.00
Windy City Chic — 16", 2000, pink and black gown, limited to 350............................$125.00
Susan — 8", #27465, 2000, doll, three outfits, case, limited to 400 ....$225.00
Yardley in Lavender — 21", 2001, sheath dress and jacket, with dog, limited to 150.............$275.00
Me & My Shadow Annette — 10", 2001, plum silk dress, limited to 360.........................$175.00
Me & My Shadow Annie — 8", 2001, plum silk dress, limited to 250 ....$150.00
Eloise in Moscow centerpiece — 8", #27735, 2000, yellow coat, black hat.........................$100.00
The Love of Dolls Club Cissette — 10", #31960, 2001, long burgundy gown trimmed in fur......$150.00
Buccaneer Bobby — 8", 2002, Denver luncheon doll, pirate sitting on shoulder, limited to 275....$125.00
Halloween — 8", 2002, centerpiece doll, #31465, black outfit $125.00
King Midas — 8", #33045, limited to 25, gold velvet robe, 2003 centerpiece doll $250.00
Golden Jubilee Wendy — 8", #37130, 2003, limited to 210 ....$125.00
Dolls and Kicks on Route 66 — 8", New Mexico Regional, jeans, 2005 ....$150.00
Belle — 8", #36470, pink striped clown outfit, limited to 90, 2004 centerpiece $150.00
Clara — 8", #39390, blue striped and polka dot clown outfit, limited to 190, 2004.................$100.00
Salon, Salon —10", #40750, 2005, striped dress, 2 wigs...$125.00
Mimi's Salon, Salon — 10", 2005, centerpiece doll, dressing gown, bra, panties, stool $175.00
Charlotte Bronte — 10", #41935, 2006, brown taffeta dress.......................................$175.00
Authors Set — Jane Austen, Lucy Maude Montgomery, Lousia Mae Alcott,
    Agatha Christie, 21", Cissy set...$4,000.00
At the Hop Cissette — 10", #47215, 2007, companion doll, 1950s outfit $85.00
Limited Edition Souvenir UFDC National Convention — 10", 2 extra outfits, wigs,
    jewelry, suede case, etc. $225.00
Charming Melodies Wendy Kin Felt — 9", 2007, UFDC, Alexander Event Souvenir,
    felt doll, painted eyes, metal doll box...$200.00

* Cissy dolls made in limited editions for 1999.

† 1999 designer Cissy dolls were designed to be auctioned for Fashion Targets Breast Cancer.